THE ROARING GIRL

THE ROARING GIRL

Thomas Middleton and Thomas Dekker

a *Broadview Anthology of British Literature* edition

Contributing Editor, *The Roaring Girl*:
Kelly Stage, University of Nebraska-Lincoln

General Editors,
Broadview Anthology of British Literature:
Joseph Black, University of Massachusetts, Amherst
Leonard Conolly, Trent University
Kate Flint, University of Southern California
Isobel Grundy, University of Alberta
Don LePan, Broadview Press
Roy Liuzza, University of Tennessee
Jerome J. McGann, University of Virginia
Anne Lake Prescott, Barnard College
Barry V. Qualls, Rutgers University
Claire Waters, University of California, Davis

broadview press

Broadview Press – www.broadviewpress.com
Peterborough, Ontario, Canada

Founded in 1985, Broadview Press remains a wholly independent publishing house. Broadview's focus is on academic publishing: our titles are accessible to university and college students as well as scholars and general readers. With over 600 titles in print, Broadview has become a leading international publisher in the humanities, with world-wide distribution. Broadview is committed to environmentally responsible publishing and fair business practices.

Library and Archives Canada Cataloguing in Publication

Title: The roaring girl / Thomas Middleton and Thomas Dekker ; contributing editor, The roaring girl: Kelly Stage, University of Nebraska-Lincoln ; general editors, Broadview anthology of British literature: Joseph Black, University of Massachusetts, Amherst, Leonard Conolly, Trent University, Kate Flint, University of Southern California, Isobel Grundy, University of Alberta, Don LePan, Broadview Press, Roy Liuzza, University of Tennessee, Jerome J. McGann, University of Virginia, Anne Lake Prescott, Barnard College, Barry V. Qualls, Rutgers University, Claire Waters, University of California, Davis.
Names: Middleton, Thomas, -1627, author. | Dekker, Thomas, approximately 1572-1632, author. | Stage, Kelly J., 1978- editor.
Series: Broadview anthology of British literature edition.
Description: Series statement: A Broadview anthology of British literature edition
Identifiers: Canadiana 20190067950 | ISBN 9781554812134 (softcover)
Subjects: LCSH: Cutpurse, Moll, 1584?-1659—Drama. | LCSH: Gender identity—Drama. | LCSH: Cross-dressing—Drama.
Classification: LCC PR2714 .R6 2019 | DDC 822/.3—dc23

Broadview Press handles its own distribution in North America:
PO Box 1243, Peterborough, Ontario, K9J 7H5, Canada
555 Riverwalk Parkway, Tonawanda, NY 14150, USA
Tel: (705) 743-8990; Fax: (705) 743-8353
email: customerservice@broadviewpress.com

Distribution is handled by Eurospan Group in the UK, Europe, Central Asia, Middle East, Africa, India, Southeast Asia, Central America, and the Caribbean. Distribution is handled by Footprint Books in Australia and New Zealand.

Broadview Press acknowledges the financial support of the Government of Canada for our publishing activities.

Canada

Developmental Editors: Laura Buzzard and Jennifer McCue
Cover Designer: Lisa Brawn
Typesetter: Alexandria Stuart

PRINTED IN CANADA

Contents

Introduction[1]

In the first half of their respective careers, Thomas Middleton and Thomas Dekker worked together on *The Roaring Girl* (1611) and on about ten other projects. Each also worked independently and with other writers on different projects, and in so doing, they represent typical practitioners of early modern playwriting. They both wrote for several different theater companies, with several different collaborators, and saw great changes in the style and scope of early modern drama during their careers.

Thomas Dekker
c. 1572–1632

The details of Thomas Dekker's birth and parentage are unknown and little documentation exists from his life before he began to write professionally. Comments made in his work suggest that he was born in London and that he stayed there for his adult life. He probably had a typical grammar school education, with knowledge of Latin and likely some German. The document believed to be Dekker's will suggests that he was married, and birth records hint that Dekker may have had three daughters: Dorcas (b. 1594), Elizabeth (b. 1598), and Anne (b. 1602).

Dekker's name began to circulate in London's drama scene in the 1590s, and he is first mentioned in theater impresario Philip Henslowe's account diary in 1598. Henslowe records Dekker's name in relation to dozens of plays, most often as one of several collaborators working for the Admiral's Men, one of the most famous playing companies in London. (The Admiral's Men worked under the patronage of Lord Charles Howard, high lord admiral of England, and had famously been associated with Christopher Marlowe until his death in

---

1   I wish to thank several people who have helped me with this edition, including Mitchell Hobza, Alicia Meyer, Keene Short, Michael Stage, Laura Buzzard, and Thomas Lange.

1593; the group's key competitor was the Lord Chamberlain's Men, the company now best remembered for its writer William Shakespeare.) In the first phase of his career, Dekker also wrote seven plays on his own, most famously *The Shoemaker's Holiday* (1599), which set his reputation as a writer of London comedies. The play—centered on a madcap master shoemaker who becomes London's Lord Mayor—displays a fascination with the urban groups to which Dekker gravitated throughout his career: among them, fashionable young urban elites and gentlemen; master craftsmen, apprentices, and prodigals; urban wives and young ingénues. Another of Dekker's early plays, *Old Fortunatus* (1599/1600), was also successful, and it and *The Shoemaker's Holiday* were played at court, a fine accomplishment for a young writer.

After 1600, Dekker's association with the Admiral's Men became more casual and he wrote for a variety of companies and venues. He became a part of the clash called the "War of the Theaters" (or the *Poetomachia*, a term coined by Dekker himself), in which the playwrights Ben Jonson and John Marston—and later, Dekker and other allies—exchanged thinly veiled insults incorporated into their plays. In *Poetaster* (1601), Jonson presents Dekker (with whom he had previously collaborated) in the character of Demetrius Fannius, a "dresser of plays" who is made to wear the costume of a fool; Dekker's response, *Satiromastix* (1601), lampoons Jonson as a self-inflated elitist. Eventually, the conflict cooled, although Jonson never came to consider Dekker a respectable writer. Nonetheless, the two writers worked together again, collaborating with Middleton and Stephen Harrison to produce King James I's coronation procession; Dekker also published a prose account of the procession, *The Magnificent Entertainment* (1604).

An important development in Dekker's career occurred in 1603, when plague broke out in London and the threat of infection shut down the theaters. Unable to make money as a playwright, Dekker began publishing pamphlets. His *The Wonderful Year* (1603) documented Queen Elizabeth's death and the plague's arrival, and Dekker collaborated with Middleton on a 1604 pamphlet, *News from Gravesend*, which was also a plague account. Middleton and Dekker carried their collaboration into the theater, and their comedy *The Honest Whore, Pt. 1* premiered after the theaters reopened in 1604. (Dekker wrote *Pt. 2* on his own the following year.)

Although Dekker returned to playwriting, he continued to write topical prose pamphlets for his London audience as an additional source of income—and as a main source of income when plague returned at the end of the decade. His popular pamphlets include *The Bellman of London* (1608) and its follow-up, *Lantern and Candlelight* (1608), both of which expose the so-called "villainies" of city life. These texts reflect Dekker's fascination with London's urban underbelly, showcasing the kinds of criminals that we meet in plays such as *The Roaring Girl* and featuring the secret cant language of London thieves that appears in that play. Another of Dekker's well-known pamphlets from this period, *The Gull's Hornbook* (1609), reveals the frivolity of fashionable young men in London and skewers the materialist obsessions of the age.

Despite his high productivity, Dekker was rarely comfortable financially. Debt dogged him throughout his life, and it is sadly fitting that a 1598/9 promissory note, in which Dekker promises to pay Henslowe for a three pound loan, serves as an early artifact of Dekker's complete signature. In 1598 and 1599, Dekker spent time in debtor's prison. A little over a decade later—despite writing a number of successful plays, including *Match Me in London* (1611) and *The Roaring Girl*, and being commissioned to write the Lord Mayor's show *Troia-Nova Triumphans* (1612)—Dekker found himself broke once again. He was arrested for debt for an unpaid bill in 1613 and spent most of the next seven years in the King's Bench Prison. He may have revised *Lantern and Candlelight* for a 1616 reprinting to reflect the horror of his experience.

When Dekker returned to dramatic writing, he had a reinvigorated final decade in the theater; plays such as *The Witch of Edmonton* (1621, a tragicomedy written with William Rowley and John Ford) and *The Noble Spanish Soldier* (1622) re-asserted Dekker's place in London's drama community. However, after yet another plague year, which Dekker memorialized in the pamphlet *A Rod for Runaways* (1625), his career stagnated. He wrote a few Lord Mayor's Shows after 1625, but traces of his productivity disappear in 1632 and scholars assume that he is the "Thomas Decker" buried in Clerkenwell in that year. Because that man's widow renounced his estate's administration, Dekker is thought to have died as he lived: in debt.

Thomas Middleton
1580–1627

Thomas Middleton was a Londoner like Dekker, but his early life is less mysterious. He was born in 1580, in the Old Jewry, a street in central, commercial London and close to two important guild halls: the Mercer's Hall and Founder's Hall. (It had been so named because it had been a Jewish enclave hundreds of years earlier; Jews were expelled from England in 1290.) William Middleton, Thomas's father, was a gentleman, but he was also a bricklayer and citizen of the City of London. Unfortunately for Thomas, William Middleton died when his son was just a young boy, and Thomas's mother, Anne, remarried soon after in 1586. Almost immediately following the marriage, Middleton's stepfather, the youthful grocer Thomas Harvey, began to chip away at the inheritance marked for Thomas and his sister, Avis. Lawsuits thus dominated the Middleton home life. As a result, although Thomas matriculated at Oxford in 1598, he was frequently called back to London for legal dealings. When he lost his fellowship, young Middleton began selling pieces of his inheritance to continue at school. By the time he left Oxford in 1601, all of the land he had once been promised had been sold or taken by Harvey. He came back to London and claimed the £25 earmarked for him and held in trust by the City Corporation since his father's death, and that money was likely the entirety of the young man's wealth. Given Middleton's early life experiences, it is unsurprising that his plays often feature bad marriages, zealous lawyers, endless paperwork, and indolent men.

Middleton had already begun his public literary career while at Oxford, though one of his earliest works, *Microcynion: Six Snarling Satires* (1599), was doomed almost as soon as it was printed. The so-called Bishops' Ban (1599), a decree issued by the archbishop of Canterbury and bishop of London, called for the prohibition of satires (and some other works) and the destruction of several texts already published. Middleton's *Microcynion* was on the list, and existing copies were publicly burned. When Middleton returned to London from Oxford, he shifted his focus from satires and poetry to profitable opportunities in the theater. He started writing with the Admiral's Men in 1602, and began to work with Dekker and other playwrights. In 1603, Middleton married Mary (Magdalen) Marbeck, and their son Edward was born in the winter of 1603/04. By then, Middleton had branched out from the Admiral's Men, and his first solo play, *The Phoenix*, premiered with the Children of Paul's playing company (or Paul's Boys) in 1603. This inaugurated a fruitful partnership with that company, for which Middleton wrote five plays. In addition to his collaborations with Dekker in this period, Middleton offered up a string of successful urban comedies, including *A Trick to Catch the Old One* (1605), *A Mad World, My Masters* (1606), and *Michaelmas Term* (1604–06) for Paul's Boys. He also wrote tragedies, including *The Revenger's Tragedy* (1606), a darkly violent work that is seen by many modern critics as a masterful near-parody of the revenge tragedy genre. Like Dekker, Middleton had to adapt when the theaters were closed from 1608 to 1610 because of plague, and he also turned to pamphlet-writing to support himself and his family. After the theaters reopened, Middleton and Dekker's *The Roaring Girl* was part of another fruitful period for Middleton, which included two other women-focused plays: *No Wit, No Help Like a Woman's* and *The Second Maiden's Tragedy* (both 1611).

While Dekker was in the King's Bench Prison, Middleton's career accelerated. He began a pageant-writing career with *The Triumphs of Truth* (1613) for Lord Mayor Thomas Myddelton and later became the chief writer of city works from 1616–1626, composing many more Lord Mayor's shows and pageants, including the *Triumphs of Honor and Industry* (1617). He parleyed these successes into a stable position as Chronologer of the City, the keeper of the official *Annals of London*. Although Ben Jonson was more commonly favored by King James as a writer of entertainments, Middleton did write masques for royals, including *The Masque of Cupids* (1613) and *The World Tossed at Tennis* (with William Rowley, 1620).

In the commercial playwriting world, Middleton's success continued, and his work changed with the times. After *A Chaste Maid in Cheapside* (1613), he began experimenting with different forms and drifted away from the London comedies he had been writing for nearly a decade. *The Witch* (c. 1613–16) marks an experiment in theatrical spectacle—and, perhaps, an evocation of a contemporary

political scandal surrounding the murder of the poet Thomas Overbury and the ensuing trial. Middleton also began collaborating frequently with William Rowley in this period, eventually producing
tragicomedies with diverse settings. However, their first play, *Wit at
Several Weapons* (c. 1613), was still in the mode of city comedy, following the stories of characters typical of the form, such as the rich
old city businessman and knight "Sir Perfidious Oldcraft" and the
impoverished, and sometimes crossed-dressed, "Lady Ruinous Gentry." *A Fair Quarrel* (with Rowley, c. 1615–16), the experimental *The
Old Law* (1618, with Rowley and Thomas Heywood), and the Span-
ish-focused play *The Changeling* (1622, with Rowley) mark Middleton and Rowley's move to tragicomedy. Middleton also continued to
write plays on his own, including the tragedy *Women Beware Women*
(1620) and his most scandalous and arguably most famous play, *A
Game at Chess* (1624).

   A Game at Chess commented on contemporary English and Euro-
pean politics—especially James I's attempt to build an alliance with
Catholic Spain—through a complex metaphor of a chess match, and
its premiere created an immediate sensation. After more than a week
of consecutive performances—an oddity in early modern repertory
practice attesting to the play's popularity—the play was shut down
by order of the Privy Council. A warrant was issued for Middleton's
arrest, which he initially ducked; however, after his son was arrested
and examined, Middleton was himself jailed. He was released, but the
incident placed his career on hold, and another outbreak of plague
in 1625 further disrupted his return to theater. His final theatrical
project was the unsuccessful Lord Mayor's show of 1626. Middleton
died in 1627, leaving no financial support for his widow, whose own
death followed within the year.

The Roaring Girl

Dekker and Middleton's collaboration *The Roaring Girl*, which
premiered with Prince Henry's Men at the Fortune Theater in
1611, features a complex plot and a wide array of characters, but at

the center of the play is the fascinating figure of Moll Cutpurse, a cross-dressing, wise-cracking, head-breaking, viol de gamba-playing, smoke-'em-if-you-got-'em, single woman. Moll Cutpurse was not just a larger-than-life persona; she was a real person, Mary Frith, a Londoner with a reputation for cross-dressing, lewd speaking, selling stolen goods, and showing up at theaters. Dekker and Middleton must have been most fascinated by her remarkable story to take the unusual step of writing a new play about a living woman who was not a noble.

In 1611, Frith was sufficiently well known and apparently enough of a curiosity that her exploits could form the backbone of a popular play, and fifty years later her fame was still relevant enough to warrant the anonymously penned 1662 biography *The life and death of Mrs. Mary Frith commonly called Mal Cutpurse exactly collected and now published for the delight and recreation of all merry disposed persons*. The biography is likely highly fabricated; yet, its existence and its mostly positive portrayal of Moll marks out her continued notoriety and the growth of her legend. According to her biographer, Moll used her boisterousness, criminality, and transvestitism as assets, and charmed her way in life through "heroic impudence."

Such "heroic impudence" could carry legal repercussions, as court records made during Frith's lifetime attest. In 1612, Frith was examined by the Bishop of London in the Consistory Court for an offense registered on Christmas Day, 1611: Frith had walked through St. Paul's with her petticoat tucked up and wearing a man's cloak, an offense for which the Lord Bishop remanded her to Bridewell Prison while he considered what other action to take. The court record also indicates that Mary had already served time in Bridewell earlier that year, and it includes a list of her former transgressive behaviors, including visiting taverns, alehouses, and playhouses while in the "habit of a man"; public drunkenness; immodest and lascivious speech; swearing; and associating with ruffians, cutpurses, and drunks.

Perhaps of most note for drama critics, the record also states that in the spring of 1611, she attended a play at the Fortune Theater wearing boots and "a sword by her side." She had, the reference continues, "sat there upon the stage in the public view of all the people there present in man's apparel & played upon her lute & sang a song." The reference has caused critics to speculate that Mary Frith could have appeared at a performance of *The Roaring Girl* during its initial run, which would give added meaning to the claim made in Dekker and Middleton's epilogue that "The Roaring Girl herself, some few days hence, / Shall on this stage, give larger recompense" (Ep. 35–36). Regardless of whether the play and Mary's appearance at the Fortune did coincide, the document attests that she was no stranger to theaters and taverns—or to flouting gender expectations. While the play would have already been published by the time of the Christmas offense and later hearing, the record confirms that Frith had been in and out of court and in the public eye earlier in 1611.

Plenty of early modern English people wore excessive or idiosyncratic clothing—at least if we believe the interest in fashionable behavior that we see in city comedies and in texts such as Dekker's *The Gull's Hornbook*—but Moll's unusual clothing choices are of a sort that were considered punishable, as her time in Bridewell shows. Elizabethan sumptuary laws—which had regulated the proper kinds of clothing that could be worn, as well as types of fabric, colors, and accessories permitted to one's gender and status—meant that women could be punished for cross-dressing. Those arrested for clothing transgressions were often accused of prostitution or general moral looseness at the same time. Under James I, the sumptuary proclamations were repealed, but similar associations between immorality and deviant dress persisted, and women offenders were brought through the church courts, as in Mary Frith's case. Clothing that flouted prescribed gender roles was the subject of substantial cultural anxiety during this period. In 1620, crossdressing was addressed in the tract *Hic Mulier; or The Man-Woman*, in which the anonymous author laments that "since the days of Adam women were never so masculine" not only in their clothing but also "in mood, from bold speech to impudent action." The tract was quickly followed by a retort, *Haec Vir; or the Womanish Man*, also in 1620. Around the same time, King James ordered London priests to sermonize against women dressing as men. The court records, sermonizing, and pamphlet dispute together suggest that in the early seventeenth century cross-dressing may have happened more than we might otherwise assume. In their dramatization of Moll Cutpurse's gender transgressions, Dekker and Middleton were clearly taking on a fraught subject in early modern English culture.

Cross-dressing was very much a part of early modern theater, and cross-dressing young women appear frequently in early modern plays—a trope complicated by the fact that all stage performance in the period, including that of women characters, was done by men. Moll Cutpurse is nonetheless an unusual figure in early modern drama. Unlike Shakespeare's cross-dressing heroines, such as Rosalind from *As You Like It* (c. 1599) and Viola from *Twelfth Night* (c. 1601), Moll does not disguise herself as a man in order to hide her identity. Moll wears men's clothing because she wants to do so; her choices are a part of her identity. In more typical female cross-dressing scenarios on stage, characters such as Viola and Rosalind are eventually revealed to be women and returned to happy and heterosexual lives at the end of their respective plays (setting aside the issues of all-male performance during this period). There is no such conclusion for Moll, given that she is not masquerading as someone else and does not need to be revealed as such. Her disdain for a typical life, and for marriage in particular, remains intact at the end of the play, and she remains able to support herself without a husband. Her example stands as an extreme given the dangers and challenges that single women—especially poor ones—faced in early modern London.

Moll may desire to remain on the margins and disconnected from normative roles, but this stance positions her as a clear-eyed observer of Londoners' follies, able to engage with and size up Londoners from a remarkable range of classes and positions. In Dekker and Middleton's time, London's population was expanding with remarkable speed, more than doubling between 1550 and 1615. The City proved alluring to the desperately poor, who came seeking employment but instead often found themselves swelling the ranks of the urban unemployed; on the other end of the spectrum, the City also attracted gentry interested in the opportunities the urban landscape could afford. London's status as a commercial center also supported substantial classes of professionals, tradespeople, and craftspeople. Many of London's artisans and shopkeepers were also "citizens," a specific title awarded to men who had achieved membership in their guild and been granted the "freedom" of the City of London—the right to earn wages, to produce wares, and to sell them within the bounds of the City.

In the course of the play, Moll participates in a number of plot-lines—most of them typical of London comedies of the early seventeenth century—incorporating different components of the City's population. The highest-status characters are featured in the play's main story, a romance plot in which the lovers Sebastian Wengrave and Mary Fitzallard attempt to trick Sebastian's father, Sir Alexander, into consenting to their marriage. This plotline, with its frustrated lovers and clever machinations, reflects the influence that ancient Greek and Roman "new comedy" exerted on early modern English plays. A subplot about the prodigal Davy Dapper, incompetent lawmen, and the rogues of London becomes a remarkable comment on those in high and low places and a celebration of cant language. Through this subplot, Moll is established as a streetwise figure whose experience as a former criminal gives her the ability to act as a liaison to every kind of Londoner.

Meanwhile, a tangle of citizen intrigues—involving wives, husbands, and gallants mutually attempting to cheat, blackmail, and ruin each other—threads through *The Roaring Girl*'s main plot. Like many other city comedies of the period, *The Roaring Girl* portrays the lives of London's middle classes with an eye to the manipulation of class, money, and reputation—and to matters of sex and marriage in the urban marketplace. This plot incorporates not only citizens but also citizens' wives, Mistress Gallipot, Mistress Openwork, and Mistress Tiltyard, who are shown taking care of their husbands' businesses and participating in the everyday buying and selling that make the city run. The upper-class gallants—Laxton, Goshawk, Greenwit, and the hapless Jack Dapper—circulate in the marketplace and among the city wives, and in so doing, they illustrate the uncomfortable but expected overlap between the sale of commodities and of sex. While the buyers in the market flaunt their gentle status and their fashionable qualities, they conspicuously lack money—whether, as in Laxton's case, because they have sold their lands and source of income, or because they are, like Dapper, prodigals in debt. Their lives of leisure thus contrast dramatically with the commerce-driven lives of the citizens and their wives.

Present-day critics have often noted that the sheer density of *The Roaring Girl*'s activity may overwhelm audiences; as *The Guardian*'s drama critic Michael Billington put it in a 2014 review, many feel the play has "too many subplots." But the play's title character—our guide who brings these threads of plot together and leads us through London's expansive social world—remains a continuous source of fascination for scholars and general audiences. After centuries of relative obscurity, *The Roaring Girl* rose to prominence in the early 1980s with scholars such as Mary Beth Rose and Jean E. Howard bringing new feminist criticism to bear on the play. Rose and Howard's arguments cast Moll as a representative of transgressive femininity, but also emphasize the ways that the play attempts to contain or sanitize some of her gender power. Much debate has followed since these critical interventions. To what extent is *The Roaring Girl* a radical attack on early modern gender norms? To what extent does it leave those norms undisturbed, or even reinforce them? Questions such as these keep Dekker and Middleton's play in the spotlight in the twenty-first century.

Note on the Text

This text of *The Roaring Girl*, which has been regularized and modernized for this edition, is based upon the original 1611 publication issued in London by Nikolas Okes for Thomas Archer. See the "Further Reading" materials at the end of this volume for a list of works the editor consulted in the preparation of this edition.

The Roaring Girle.

OR
Moll Cut-Purse.

As it hath lately beene Acted on the Fortune-stage by the Prince his Players.

Written by *T. Middleton* and *T. Dekkar.*

My case is alter'd, I must worke for my liuing.

Printed at *London* for *Thomas Archer*, and are to be sold at his shop in Popes head-pallace, neere the Royall Exchange. 1611.

First Edition.

THE ROARING GIRL

OR

MOLL CUTPURSE

[Epistle]

To the Comic Play-Readers: Venery and Laughter.[1]

The fashion of playmaking I can properly compare to nothing so naturally as the alteration in apparel.[2] For in the time of the great-crop doublet,[3] your huge bombasted plays, quilted[4] with mighty words to lean purpose was only then in fashion. And, as the doublet fell, neater inventions[5] began to set up. Now in the time of spruceness,[6] our plays follow the niceness[7] of our garments: single plots, quaint conceits, lecherous jests, dressed up in hanging sleeves;[8] and those are fit for the times, and the termers.[9] Such a kind of light-colour summer stuff,[10] mingled with diverse colours, you shall find this published comedy—good to keep you in an afternoon from dice, at home in your chambers; and for venery you shall find enough, for sixpence, but well couched and you mark it.[11] For Venus,[12] being a woman, passes through the play in doublet and breeches[13]—a brave

---

1 *Venery and Laughter*   Enjoyment, especially of sexually charged or dirty material.
2 *alteration in apparel*   Changes in clothes fashion.
3 *great-crop doublet*   Short, close fitting outer garment, with or without sleeves, for the upper body, often with a padded stomach.
4 *bombasted*   Padded and stuffed, with a pun on "bombast"'s additional meaning of "inflated rhetoric"; *quilted*   Padded or layered and stitched together.
5 *fell*   Went out of style;   *neater inventions*   Here, sleek and clean subjects and plots.
6 *spruceness*   Trim, neat, sharp, well-appointed appearance.
7 *niceness*   Fineness, elegance.
8 *hanging sleeves*   Sleeves that hang from the shoulder on a women's gown, open in the front.
9 *termers*   Lawmen and gallant gentlemen who came to London during the law terms, when the courts were in session.
10 *stuff*   Fabric.
11 *well couched*   Concealed, hidden in the words;   *and you mark it*   If you pay attention.
12 *Venus*   Roman goddess of love and beauty, associated with sexual desire.
13 *breeches*   Men's legged garment covering the lower midsection, thigh, and rump, extending to the knees.

disguise[1] and a safe one, if the statute untie not her codpiece point.[2] The book I make no question but is fit for many of your companies, as well as the person itself, and may be allowed both gallery room at the playhouse and chamber-room at your lodging.[3] Worse things, I must needs confess, the world has taxed her for than has been written of her;[4] but 'tis the excellency of a writer[5] to leave things better than he finds 'em. Though some obscene fellow—that cares not what he writes against others, yet keeps a mystical bawdy-house[6] himself, and entertains drunkards to make use of their pockets, and vent his private bottle-ale[7] at midnight—though such a one would have ript up[8] the most nasty vice that ever hell belcht forth and presented it to a modest assembly,[9] yet we rather wish in such discoveries, where reputation lies bleeding, a slackness of truth, than fullness of slander.[10]

THOMAS MIDDLETON

---

1 *brave disguise* Splendid, with an additional suggestion of the bravado entailed in wearing such clothes.

2 *statute* Statutes of Apparel, which regulated proper dress according to gender and social status, had been in effect during Elizabethan times, but they were voided by King James I in 1604. Still, other laws remained that regulated morality, and so cross dressing, considered indecent, could be prosecuted in ecclesiastical courts, as the real Mary Frith's story shows; *codpiece point* A codpiece is a bag or purse attached to the front of breeches over the male genitals.

3 *book ... lodging* Middleton assures his audience that the play is fit for all or to be read at home.

4 *Worse things ... her* Worse things have been said about Moll than the play records.

5 *excellency of a writer* Speciality of a writer, or in this case, poetic license.

6 *mystical bawdy-house* Secret brothel.

7 *vent* Sell; *private bottle-ale* Secretly made illegal beer.

8 *ript up* Laid bare, exposed.

9 *modest assembly* Gathering of respectable company.

10 *Though some ... slander* Middleton writes against those who, not being of sound character themselves, are only too happy to wound someone's reputation, and argues that a loose grip on the truth is preferable to overzealous slander.

DRAMATIS PERSONAE

Sir Alexander Wengrave, and Neatfoot,[1] his man
Sir Adam Appleton[2]
Sir Davy Dapper
Sir Beauteous Ganymede[3]
Lord Noland
Sir Thomas Long[4]
Young [Sebastian] Wengrave
Jack Dapper, and Gull[5] his page
Goshawk[6]
Greenwit[7]
Laxton[8]

Cives[9]
[Master] Tiltyard[10]
[Master] Openwork[11]
[Master Hippocrates] Gallipot[12]

Uxores[13]
[Mistress Tiltyard
Mistress Rosamond Openwork
Mistress Prudence Gallipot]

---

1   *Neatfoot*   Neat's foot, a cow or ox heel used for food.
2   *Adam Appleton*   Allusion to the first man and his fall, possibly as well to a physical characteristic of a large Adam's apple.
3   *Ganymede*   Name of Jupiter's cupbearer, who was chosen for his beauty.
4   *Thomas Long*   Tom Long is a nickname for someone who takes too long getting somewhere or finishing a story.
5   *Jack Dapper*   Reference to a dapper-jack, one who is excessively fashionable;   *Gull*   Fool, simpleton.
6   *Goshawk*   Large hawk with short wings.
7   *Greenwit*   Inexperienced youth, or one whose intellect has not yet matured.
8   *Laxton*   The pun in this name suggests that Laxton "lacks stones," meaning he lacks land, and, with "stones" a slang term for testicles, that he also lacks his manhood.
9   *Cives*   Latin: Citizens.
10 *Tiltyard*   Enclosed yard for jousting. Combatants in the tiltyard often wore decorative plumage, and Tiltyard sells feathers.
11 *Openwork*   Needlework with decorative openings; Openwork is a tailor.
12 *Hippocrates*   Ancient Greek physician, founding figure in the development of medicine;   *Gallipot*   Vessel, usually pottery, for mixing and grinding herbs to make drugs.
13 *Uxores*   Latin: Wives. N.B. The 1611 quarto lists only "*Cives et Vxores*" to indicate that the men are citizens and that their wives appear. I have given the women their own billing.

Moll [Cutpurse], the Roaring Girl[1]
[Ralph] Trapdoor
[Tearcat][2]

Sir Guy Fitzallard
Mary Fitzallard, his daughter
Curtalax, a sergeant[3]
Hanger, his yeoman[4]
Ministri[5]
[Gentlemen
Fellow with a Long Rapier
Porter
Tailor
Coachman
Cutpurses]

PROLOGUE

[*Enter Prologue.*]

[PROLOGUE.]   A play—expected long—makes the audience look
For wonders: that each scene should be a book,
Composed to all perfection. Each one° comes   *playgoer*
And brings a play in's° head with him: up he sums,   *in his*
5   What he would of a roaring girl have writ;
If that he finds not here, he mews[6] at it.
Only we entreat you think our scene

---

1   *Moll*   Nickname for Mary that is also a common name for prostitutes;   *Cutpurse*   One who surreptitiously snatches purses by snipping them from unsuspecting victims' belts;   *Roaring Girl*   "Roaring Boys" were riotous young men who engaged in loud, boisterous behavior, fighting or whoring, and had a reputation for drinking; in this case, unusually, "Roaring" is used in reference to a girl.
2   *Tearcat*   Bombastic swaggerer, a bully.
3   *Curtalax*   Corruption of cutlass, a short broad sword;   *sergeant*   Arresting and summoning officer.
4   *Hanger*   Short sword, or the belt from which one was hung;   *yeoman*   In this case, an assistant to an official.
5   *Ministri*   Latin: Servants.
6   *mews*   Derides with a whine or whimper.

Cannot speak high, the subject being but mean.[1]
A roaring girl, whose notes till now never were,[2]
Shall fill with laughter our vast theatre;   10
That's all which I dare promise: tragic passion,
And such grave stuff, is this day out of fashion.
I see attention sets wide ope her gates
Of hearing, and with covetous list'ning waits,
To know what girl this roaring girl should be,   15
For of that tribe are many.[3] One is she
That roars at midnight in deep tavern bowls,[4]
That beats the watch,[5] and constables controls;
Another roars i'th'daytime, swears, stabs, gives braves,[6]
Yet sells her soul[7] to the lust of fools and slaves.   20
Both these are suburb-roarers.[8] Then there's besides
A civil city-roaring girl, whose pride,
Feasting, and riding, shakes her husband's state,[9]
And leaves him roaring through an iron grate.[10]
None of these roaring girls is ours: she flies   25
With wings more lofty. Thus her character lies—
Yet what need characters,[11] when to give a guess,
Is better than the person to express?[12]
But would you know who 'tis? Would you hear her name?
She is called mad° Moll; her life, our acts proclaim.   *wild, exuberant*   30

---

1   *entreat ... mean*   Ask you to consider that our rhetoric should not be too lofty because the subject matter is low or ordinary.

2   *whose ... were*   Whose story was never heard till now.

3   *of that tribe are many*   There are many different kinds of roaring girls.

4   *roars ... bowls*   Stays out all night drinking at taverns;   *bowls*   Wide drinking vessels associated with conviviality.

5   *beats the watch*   Gets away from or beats upon members of the night watch.

6   *gives braves*   Makes threats or challenges.

7   *sells her soul*   I.e., engages in prostitution.

8   *suburb-roarers*   Roarer in the areas just beyond the city wall, popularly considered poor, dangerous, crowded, and filthy areas.

9   *whose ... state*   Who spends her husband's money to support her ostentatious display, consumption, and going out (possibly for sex), all of which undermines the husband's position.

10   *leaves him ... grate*   Her excess leads the husband to debtor's prison, where he will yell through a grate, begging for money.

11   *characters*   Sketches of character types, like the general descriptions of a roaring girl above.

12   *Is ... express*   Expresses someone better than a vague example (a character sketch) can.

ACT 1, SCENE 1

(Enter Mary Fitzallard disguised like a sempster with a case for
bands,[1] and Neatfoot, a servingman with her, with a napkin on his
shoulder and a trencher[2] in his hand as from table.)

NEATFOOT. The young gentleman, our young master, Sir
Alexander's son—is it into his ears, sweet damsel, emblem of
fragility, you desire to have a message transported, or to be
transcendent?[3]

5   MARY. A private word or two, sir, nothing else.

NEATFOOT. You shall fructify in that which you come for; your
pleasure shall be satisfied to your full contentation.[4] I will, fairest
tree of generation, watch when our young master is erected[5]—
that is to say up—and deliver him to this your most white

10   hand.

MARY. Thanks, sir.

NEATFOOT. And withal certify him that I have culled out for him,
now his belly is replenished, a daintier bit or modicum than any
lay upon his trencher at dinner. Hath he notion of your name, I

15   beseech your chastity?[6]

MARY. One, sir, of whom he bespake falling-bands.[7]

NEATFOOT. Falling-bands: it shall so be given him.—If you please
to venture your modesty in the hall, amongst a curl-pated[8]
company of rude servingmen, and take such as they can set before

20   you, you shall be most seriously, and ingeniously, welcome.

MARY. I have dined indeed already sir.

---

1   *bands* Collars or ruffs. Often ornate and decorative, bands were separate garments tied to
the neckline of one's shirt.

2   *trencher* Wooden, metal, or clay plate or platter; sometimes trenchers could be hardened
slices of bread.

3   *to be transcendent* To rise up or to ascend, but in this case, to deliver the message.

4   *contentation* Contentment or satisfaction.

5   *erected* Awake, with a sexual pun. Neatfoot's speech is frequently littered with double
meanings.

6   *beseech ... chastity* Neatfoot sarcastically implies that the visitor is a prostitute.

7   *of ... bespake* From whom he requested; *falling-bands* Fashionable collars that spread
over the shoulders and back.

8   *curl-pated* Curly-haired.

NEATFOOT. Or will you vouchsafe to kiss the lip of a cup of rich
    Orleans in the buttery[1] amongst our waiting women?
MARY. Not now, in truth sir.
NEATFOOT. Our young Master shall then have a feeling of your   25
    being here presently. It shall so be given him.

(*Exit Neatfoot.*)

MARY. I humbly thank you sir, but that my bosom
    Is full of bitter sorrows, I could smile
    To see this formal ape play antic° tricks;   *fantastical, strange*
    But in my breast a poisoned arrow sticks,   30
    And smiles cannot become me. Love woven slightly,°   *loosely*
    Such as thy false heart makes, wears out as lightly,
    But love being truly bred i'th the soul, like mine,
    Bleeds even to death, at the least wound it takes,
    The more we quench this, the less it slakes.   35
    Oh, me!

(*Enter Sebastian Wengrave with Neatfoot.*)

SEBASTIAN. A sempster speak with me, say'st thou?
NEATFOOT. Yes, sir, she's there, *viva voce*, to deliver her auricular[2]
    confession.
SEBASTIAN. [*To Mary.*] With me, sweetheart? What is't?   40
MARY. I have brought home your bands, sir.
SEBASTIAN. Bands?—Neatfoot!
NEATFOOT. Sir.
SEBASTIAN. Prithee look in,[3] for all the gentlemen are upon rising.
NEATFOOT. Yes, sir, a most methodical attendance shall be given.   45
SEBASTIAN. And dost hear, if my father call for me, say I am busy
    with a sempster.

---

1 *Orleans* Wine made in Orléans, France;   *buttery* Pantry or closet for provisions, often
   including butter, bread, wine, and other foodstuffs.
2 *viva voce* Latin: in the living voice, meaning that Mary is present;   *auricular* Audible.
3 *look in* Sebastian directs Neatfoot to check on Sir Alexander and his guests in the other
   room.

NEATFOOT. Yes, sir. He shall know it that you are busied with a
   needlewoman.[1]
50 SEBASTIAN. In's ear,[2] good Neatfoot.
NEATFOOT. It shall be so given him.

(*Exit Neatfoot.*)

SEBASTIAN. Bands? You're mistaken sweetheart, I bespake none.
   When? Where? I prithee, what bands? Let me see them.
MARY. Yes, sir, a bond[3] fast sealed with solemn oaths,
55   Subscribed unto—as I thought—with your soul,
   Delivered as your deed in sight of heaven.
   Is this bond cancelled? Have you forgot me?[4]
SEBASTIAN. Ha! Life of my life: Sir Guy Fitzallard's daughter,
   What has transformed my love to this strange shape?
60   Stay: make all sure. [*He checks the doors.*] So: now speak and be
      brief,
   Because the wolf's at door[5] that lies in wait,
   To prey upon us both. Albeit mine eyes
   Are blest by thine, yet this so strange disguise
   Holds me with fear and wonder.
MARY.   Mine's a loathed sight,
65   Why from it are you banisht else so long?
SEBASTIAN. I must cut short my speech. In broken language,
   Thus much, sweet Moll:[6] I must thy company shun;
   I court another Moll. My thoughts must run
   As a horse runs that's blind: round in a mill,

---

1   *needlewoman*   Woman who does needlework; with sexual overtones.
2   *In's ear*   Whisper it in his ear.
3   *bond*   Contract—here, a marriage contract—with a pun on "bands" and "bonds."
4   *cancelled*   Refers to ending a bond or obligation between two people, especially as in a
   marriage or mortgage;   *Have ... me?*   Mary asks if Sebastian cannot recognize her in her
   disguise—but also if he has forsaken her for another.
5   *wolf's at door*   Reference to Sir Alexander, who is on the other side of a door in the house.
   The proverb "Keep the wolf from the door" means to keep the wolf from eating your sheep;
   i.e., to avert poverty.
6   *Moll*   Here, Sebastian uses "Moll" as a nickname for Mary; in the following line, he uses
   the same name to refer to Moll Cutpurse.

Out every step, yet keeping one path still.[1] 70
MARY. Um! must you shun my company? In one knot
  Have both our hands by th'hands of heaven been tied,
  Now to be broke? I thought me once your bride—
  Our fathers did agree on the time when—
  And must another bedfellow fill my room? 75
SEBASTIAN. Sweet maid, let's lose no time. 'Tis in heaven's book
  Set down that I must have thee; an oath we took
  To keep our vows, but when the knight, your father,
  Was from mine parted, storms began to sit
  Upon my covetous father's brow, which fell 80
  From them on me. He reckoned up what gold
  This marriage would draw from him, at which he swore
  To lose so much blood could not grieve him more.[2]
  He then dissuades me from thee, called thee not fair,
  And askt "What is she, but a beggar's heir?" 85
  He scorned thy dowry of five thousand marks.[3]
  If such a sum of money could be found,
  And I would match with that, he'd not undo it,
  Provided his bags might add nothing to it,
  But vowed, if I took thee—nay more, did swear it— 90
  Save birth from him I nothing should inherit.[4]
MARY. What follows then, my shipwreck?
SEBASTIAN.   Dearest no.

---

1 *As ... still* Sebastian refers to a workhorse powering a mill. The horse is harnessed to the arm of the mill shaft, so even if blind and off-balance at every step, the horse has no choice but to keep going around in circles. Sebastian insists to Mary that he too must stick to one path and that even if his various steps seem misdirected, they will together lead to the ultimate goal, their marriage.

2 *He ... more* Alexander realized how much the marriage would cost him, and then swore that he could lose an equal amount of his own blood and be less pained than he would be spending the money.

3 *five thousand marks* A mark was two-thirds of a pound. In 1611, a worker might expect to make between two pounds (as a servant) and twenty-five pounds (as an artisan) yearly in London. Five thousand marks is a very respectable, if not huge, dowry for minor aristocracy.

4 *If ... inherit* Sir Alexander has said he would not prevent Sebastian marrying someone with five thousand marks, but refuses to add any additional support. He furthermore threatens Sebastian with disinheritance if he were to marry Mary.

Though wildly in a labyrinth[1] I go,
My end is to meet thee. With a side wind[2]
95 Must I now sail, else I no haven can find,
But both must sink forever. There's a wench
Called Moll, Mad Moll, or Merry Moll, a creature
So strange in quality, a whole city takes
Note of her name and person. All that affection
100 I owe to thee, on her, in counterfeit passion,°   *feigned desire*
I spend to mad° my father. He believes   *make mad*
I dote upon this roaring girl, and grieves
As it becomes a father for a son,
That could be so bewitcht: yet, I'll go on
105 This crooked way, sigh still for her, feign dreams,
In which I'll talk only of her. These streams
Shall, I hope, force my father to consent
That here° I anchor rather then be rent°   *with Mary / broken*
Upon a rock so dangerous. Art thou pleased,
110 Because thou seest we are waylaid,° that I take   *blocked*
A path that's safe, though it be far about?
MARY. My prayers with heaven guide thee!
SEBASTIAN.   Then I will on.
My father is at hand; kiss and be gone.
Hours shall be watcht for meetings.[3] I must now,
115 As men for fear, to a strange idol bow.[4]
MARY. Farewell.
SEBASTIAN. I'll guide thee forth. When next we meet,
A story of Moll shall make our mirth more sweet.

(*Exeunt.*)

---

1   *labyrinth*   Maze, with an implied comparison of Sebastian to the mythical Greek hero
    Theseus, who, with the help of the princess Ariadne, navigated a labyrinth and killed the
    minotaur imprisoned inside. Ariadne and Theseus were then married.
2   *side wind*   Indirect means.
3   *Hours ... meetings*   We will vigilantly await an opportunity for another meeting.
4   *to a strange ... bow*   Sebastian compares obeying his father to engaging in profane and
    foreign idolatry.

[ACT I, SCENE 2]

(*Enter Sir Alexander Wengrave, Sir Davy Dapper, Sir Adam Appleton,*
Goshawk, Laxton, and Gentlemen.)

OMNES.[1]   Thanks, good Sir Alexander, for our bounteous cheer.
SIR ALEXANDER.   Fie, fie! In giving thanks you pay too dear![2]
SIR DAVY.   When bounty spreads the table, faith, 'twere sin,
   At going off, if thanks should not step in.
SIR ALEXANDER.   No more of thanks, no more. Ay, merry sir,   5
   Th'inner room was too close,[3] how do you like
   This parlour[4] gentlemen?
OMNES.   Oh, passing° well.   *very*
SIR ADAM.   What a sweet breath the air casts here; so cool.
GOSHAWK.   I like the prospect° best.   *view*
LAXTON.   See how 'tis furnisht.
SIR DAVY.   A very fair, sweet room.   10
SIR ALEXANDER.   Sir Davy Dapper,
   The furniture that doth adorn this room,
   Cost many a fair gray groat[5] 'ere it came here;
   But good things are most cheap, when they're most dear.[6]
   Nay, when you look into my galleries,[7]
   How bravely they are trimmed up,[8] you all shall swear   15
   You're highly pleased to see what's set down there:
   Stories of men and women, mixt together,
   Fair ones with foul, like sunshine in wet weather.

---

1   OMNES   Latin: All (except, here, Alexander). The following line is probably given as an
    example of the kind of comments which all the gentlemen on stage offer. "Omnes" does not
    indicate a chorus or in-unison speech.
2   *pay too dear*   Pay too much.
3   *close*   Crowded, stuffy.
4   *parlour*   Room for gathering inside a private house, a sitting room or place for conver-
    sation.
5   *groat*   Four pence coin; proverbially, a small amount.
6   *good ... dear*   Things that are the most valuable are always the best deal, no matter the
    actual cost.
7   *galleries*   His galleries for art. In the following extended metaphor, Sir Alexander indicates
    theater galleries, the tiered levels of seating above a theater's ground floor, and he compares
    the audience's faces to painted portraits on display.
8   *How bravely ... up*   How splendidly decorated they are.

Within one square a thousand heads are laid
20   So close that all of heads the room seems made;
As many faces there, filled with blithe looks,
Show like the promising titles of new books
Writ merrily, the readers being their own eyes,
Which seem to move and to give plaudities.[1]
25   And here and there, whilst with obsequious ears
Thronged heaps° do listen, a cutpurse thrusts and leers   *crowds*
With hawk's eyes for his prey. I need not show him;
By a hanging villainous look, yourselves may know him,
The face is drawn so rarely.[2] Then sir below,
30   The very floor,[3] as't'were, waves to and fro,
And, like a floating island, seems to move
Upon a sea bound in with shores above.[4]

(*Enter Sebastian and Mr. Greenwit.*)

OMNES. These sights are excellent.
SIR ALEXANDER.   I'll show you all;
Since we are met, make our parting comical.[5]
35   SEBASTIAN. This gentleman, my friend, will take his leave, sir.
SIR ALEXANDER. Ha? Take his leave, Sebastian? Who?
SEBASTIAN.   This gentleman.
SIR ALEXANDER. [*To Greenwit.*] Your love sir, has already given me
    some time,
And if you please to trust my age with more,
It shall pay double interest. Good sir, stay.
40   GREENWIT. I have been too bold.
SIR ALEXANDER.   Not so, sir. A merry day
'Mongst friends being spent, is better than gold saved.—
Some wine, some wine! Where be these knaves I keep?

---

1 *plaudities* Applause.
2 *rarely* Exceptionally, extremely well.
3 *floor* The "floor" is the stage, and faces crowded around the stage are figured as waves
   lapping against the shore.
4 *sea ... above* The "sea" of people in the theater's pit is "bound in" by the theater's lower
   galleries.
5 *comical* Like a comedy ending—a happy ending.

(*Enter three or four Servingmen, and Neatfoot.*)

NEATFOOT. At your worshipful° elbow, sir.   *honorable*

SIR ALEXANDER.   You are

Kissing my maids, drinking, or fast asleep.

NEATFOOT. Your Worship has given it us° right.   *described us*   45

SIR ALEXANDER.   You varlets° stir!   *servants*

Chairs, stools, and cushions.

[*Servants fetch the requested items.*]

                              Prithee,[1] Sir Davy Dapper,

Make that chair thine.

SIR DAVY.   'Tis but an easy gift,

And yet I thank you for it, sir; I'll take it.

SIR ALEXANDER. [*To Neatfoot.*] A chair for old sir Adam Appleton.

NEATFOOT. [*To Sir Adam, with chair.*] A backfriend[2] to Your   50

Worship.

SIR ADAM.   Marry, good Neatfoot,

I thank thee for it: backfriends sometimes are good.

SIR ALEXANDER. Pray make that stool your perch, good Master

Goshawk.

GOSHAWK. I stoop to your lure[3] sir.

SIR ALEXANDER.   Son Sebastian,

Take Master Greenwit to you.

SEBASTIAN.   Sit, dear friend.

SIR ALEXANDER. Nay, Master Laxton. [*To Servant.*] Furnish Master   55

Laxton

With what he wants: a stone.[4]—A stool I would say, a stool.

---

1 *Prithee* I pray thee.

2 *backfriend* The chair is literally a friend to the back, though Neatfoot puns on "back-friend" as someone who is a false friend. As Adam suggests in his next line, "backfriend" can also indicate that a supportive friend is a "backer."

3 *perch ... lure* Goshawk and Alexander trade hawking terms—"perch" and "lure"—in this exchange.

4 *wants: a stone* Lacks: a testicle. Sir Alexander puns on Laxton's name to imply that Laxton is unmanly or impotent, and then tries to pass off his wording as a slip.

LAXTON. I had rather stand,[1] sir.
SIR ALEXANDER. I know you had, good Mr. Laxton. So, so—

(*Exeunt [Neatfoot and] Servants.*)

Now here's a mess° of friends, and, gentlemen,   *big group*
60   Because time's glass shall not be running long,
I'll quicken it with a pretty tale.
SIR DAVY.   Good tales do well,
In these bad days, where vice does so excel.
SIR ADAM. Begin, Sir Alexander.
SIR ALEXANDER.   Last day I met
An aged man upon whose head was scored
65   A debt of just so many years as these
Which I owe to my grave.[2] The man you all know.
OMNES. His name, I pray you, sir.
SIR ALEXANDER.   Nay you shall pardon me.
But when he saw me, with a sigh that break,
Or seemed to break, his heart-strings, thus he spake:
70   "Oh my good knight," says he—and then his eyes
Were richer even by that which made them poor,
They had spent so many tears they had no more—
"Oh sir," says he, "you know it, for you ha' seen
Blessings to rain upon mine house and me;
75   Fortune, who slaves men, was my slave; her wheel
Hath spun me golden threads, for I thank heaven,
I ne'er had but one cause to curse my stars."
I ask't him then what that one cause might be.
OMNES.   So, Sir.
SIR ALEXANDER. He paused, and as we often see
80   A sea so much becalmed there can be found
No wrinkle on his brow, his waves being drowned
In their own rage; but when th'imperious winds
Use strange invisible tyranny to shake

---

1   *stand* Instead of sitting, but Laxton's wording is also a bawdy pun to counter Sir Alexander's implications.
2   *An aged ... grave* A man the same age as Sir Alexander; *scored* Etched, with a pun on "score" meaning twenty.

Both heaven's and earth's foundation at their noise,
The seas, swelling with wrath to part that fray   85
Rise up, and are more wild, more mad, than they.
Even so this good old man was by my question
Stirred up to roughness. You might see his gall[1]
Flow even in's eyes; then grew he fantastical.[2]

SIR DAVY. Fantastical? Ha, ha!   90
SIR ALEXANDER.   Yes, and talked oddly.
SIR ADAM. Pray sir, proceed. How did this old man end?
SIR ALEXANDER. Marry, sir, thus:
  He left his wild fit to read o'er his cards,[3]
  Yet then, though age cast snow on all his hairs,[4]
  He joyed because, says he, "the god of gold   95
  Has been to me no niggard; that disease
  Of which all old men sicken, avarice,
  Never infected me—"
LAXTON. [*Aside.*] He means not himself, I'm sure.
SIR ALEXANDER.   "For like a lamp,
  Fed with continual oil, I spend and throw   100
  My light to all that need it, yet have still
  Enough to serve myself. Oh, but," quoth he,
  "Though heaven's dew fall thus on this aged tree,
  I have a son that's like a wedge doth cleave[5]
  My very heart-root."[6]   105
SIR DAVY.   Had he such a son?
SEBASTIAN. [*Aside.*] Now I do smell a fox strongly.
SIR ALEXANDER. Let's see: no, Master Greenwit is not yet
  So mellow in years as he. But as like Sebastian,
  Just like my son Sebastian—such another.[7]

---

1 *gall* One of the four humors, substances in the body whose balance or imbalance was
    thought to govern human health and temperament. Gall, also called yellow bile, was asso-
    ciated with the choleric disposition—fiery and quick to anger—and with bitterness.
2 *fantastical* Strange; absorbed in his imagination.
3 *read ... cards* Contemplate the hand he was dealt (figurative).
4 *age ... hairs* He had white hair.
5 *doth cleave* That does split.
6 *heart-root* Source of deepest emotions; the bottom of one's heart.
7 *Just ... another* Alexander says that his son, Sebastian, is just like the son in the old man's
    story.

110 SEBASTIAN. [*Aside.*] How finely like a fencer my father fetches his
    by-blows[1] to hit me! But if I beat you not at your own weapon of
    subtlety—
    SIR ALEXANDER. "This son," sayeth he, "that should be
    The column and main arch unto my house,
115   The crutch unto my age, becomes a whirlwind
    Shaking the firm foundation."
    SIR ADAM.   'Tis some prodigal.[2]
    SEBASTIAN. [*Aside.*] Well shot, old Adam Bell![3]
    SIR ALEXANDER. No city monster[4] neither, no prodigal,
    But sparing, wary, civil, and—though wifeless—
120   An excellent husband,[5] and such a traveller,
    He has more tongues° in his head than some have teeth.   *languages*
    SIR DAVY. I have but two in mine.
    GOSHAWK.   So sparing and so wary,
    What then could vex his father so?
    SIR ALEXANDER.   Oh, a woman.
    SEBASTIAN. [*Aside.*] A flesh-fly,[6] that can vex any man.
125 SIR ALEXANDER. A scurvy woman,
    On whom the passionate° old man swore he doted.[7]   *angry, emotional*
    "A creature," sayeth he, "nature hath brought forth
    To mock the sex of woman." It is a thing
    One knows not how to name; her birth began
130   Ere she was all made.[8] 'Tis woman more than man,
    Man more than woman, and—which to none can hap°—   *happen*

---

1 *by-blows* Strokes or blows from the side; alternatively, strokes that miss.

2 *prodigal* One who is reckless or wayward in handling money, with an allusion to the
biblical parable of the prodigal son (Luke 15.11–32), who returns to his father after squan-
dering his inheritance.

3 *Adam Bell* Outlaw hero of the English ballad tradition. He is renowned for his skill in
archery, and in the popular ballad *Adam Bell, Clim of the Clough, and William of Cloudesly*
(c. fifteenth-century composition, printed in the late sixteenth century) he shoots an apple
that has been placed on his young son's head.

4 *city* City of London; *monster* Something extraordinary or prodigious (in addition to
the more typical definitions of unnatural or malformed).

5 *husband* Keeper or head of a household.

6 *flesh-fly* Fly that deposits its eggs in dead flesh.

7 *On ... doted* The son doted, according to the old father, on the scurvy woman.

8 *Ere ... made* Before she was fully formed. Sir Alexander implies that Moll was born before
her sex had been finally determined and that she may be an intersex person.

The sun gives her two shadows to one shape.
Nay, more, let this strange thing, walk, stand, or sit,
No blazing star° draws more eyes after it.   *shooting star*
SIR DAVY. A monster. 'Tis some monster.   135
SIR ALEXANDER.   She's a varlet.¹
SEBASTIAN. [*Aside.*] Now is my cue to bristle.²
SIR ALEXANDER. A naughty pack.³
SEBASTIAN. [*To Alexander.*]   'Tis false!
SIR ALEXANDER.   Ha, boy?
SEBASTIAN.   'Tis false!
SIR ALEXANDER. What's false? I say she's naught.°   *wicked, worthless*
SEBASTIAN.   I say that tongue
That dares speak so—but yours—sticks in the throat
Of a rank villain.⁴ Set yourself aside.—   140
SIR ALEXANDER. So, sir, what then?
SEBASTIAN.   Any here else had lied.⁵
    (*Aside.*) I think I shall fit⁶ you.
SIR ALEXANDER. Lie?
SEBASTIAN.   Yes.
SIR DAVY.   Doth this concern him?
SIR ALEXANDER.   Ah, sirrah boy, ⁷
Is your blood heated? Boils it?⁸ Are you stung?
I'll pierce you deeper yet.—Oh, my dear friends,   145
I am that wretched father, this that son
That sees his ruin, yet headlong on doth run.
SIR ADAM. [*To Sebastian.*] Will you love such a poison?
SIR DAVY.   Fie, fie!
SEBASTIAN.   You're all mad.

---

1 *varlet* Rogue or low person.
2 *cue to bristle* Sebastian notes that his father is expecting a reaction from him at this point, and that he will begin to play along. Rather than speak aside, he will now interact as though this is his "cue" to act in a drama.
3 *naughty pack* Promiscuous woman, prostitute, and generally immoral person.
4 *I ... villain* Except for you, I'd call anyone who says such things a foul villain.
5 *Any ... lied* If anyone else here had lied, I'd have called him a liar.
6 *fit* Punish, answer.
7 *sirrah boy* Insult expressing contempt that is used to show authority and status over the subject.
8 *Boils it?* Does it boil?

SIR ALEXANDER. Thou'rt sick at heart, yet feelst it not. Of all these,
150 What gentleman—but thou—knowing his disease
     Mortal,° would shun the cure?—Oh, Master Greenwit,   *deadly*
     Would you to such an idol¹ bow?
GREENWIT.   Not I, sir.
SIR ALEXANDER. Here's Master Laxton. Has he mind to² a woman
     As thou hast?
LAXTON.   No, not, I sir.
SIR ALEXANDER.   Sir, I know it.
155 LAXTON. Their good parts are so rare, their bad so common,
     I will have naught to do with³ any woman.
SIR DAVY. 'Tis well done, Master Laxton.
SIR ALEXANDER.   Oh, thou cruel boy,
     Thou wouldst with lust an old man's life destroy,
     Because thou see'st I'm halfway in my grave,
160 Thou shovel'st dust upon me.⁴ Would thou mightest have
     Thy wish,⁵ most wicked, most unnatural!
SIR DAVY. Why, sir, 'tis thought Sir Guy Fitzallard's daughter
     Shall wed your son Sebastian.
SIR ALEXANDER.   Sir Davy Dapper,
     I have upon my knees wooed this fond boy
165 To take that virtuous maiden.
SEBASTIAN.   Hark you a word,⁶ sir.
     [*To Sir Alexander, apart.*] You, on your knees, have curst that
        virtuous maiden,
     And me for loving her; yet do you now
     Thus baffle⁷ me to my face? Wear° not your knees   *wear out*
     In such entreats!° Give me Fitzallard's daughter!   *supplications*
170 SIR ALEXANDER. I'll give thee ratsbane° rather!   *rat poison*
SEBASTIAN.   Well then, you know

---

1 *idol* False idol; in this case, Moll.
2 *mind to* Care for, desire for.
3 *have naught to do with* Literally, "have nothing to do with." Figuratively, Laxton says the
   opposite: "to do naught" means "to have sex."
4 *Because ... me* Because you perceive me as old and near death, you prematurely try to bury
   me; that is, you do not care about my desires and are willing to destroy my life.
5 *Would ... wish* I wish that you would get your wish.
6 *Hark ... word* Listen to what I'm saying.
7 *baffle* Frustrate or confound.

What dish I mean to feed upon.[1]

SIR ALEXANDER. [*To all.*]   Hark, gentlemen,
He swears to have this cutpurse drab° to spite my gall.   *slut, whore*
OMNES.   Master Sebastian!
SEBASTIAN.   I am deaf to you all.
I'm so bewitcht, so bound to my desires,
Tears, prayers, threats, nothing can quench out those fires   175
That burn within me.

(*Exit Sebastian.*)

SIR ALEXANDER. [*Aside.*]   Her blood shall quench it, then.
[*To others.*] Lose him not.[2] Oh dissuade, him gentlemen!
SIR DAVY.   He shall be weaned, I warrant you.
SIR ALEXANDER.   Before his eyes
Lay down his shame, my grief, his miseries.
OMNES.   No more, no more! Away!   180

(*Exeunt all but Sir Alexander.*)

SIR ALEXANDER.   I wash a negro,[3]
Losing both pains and cost. But take thy flight;
I'll be most near thee, when I'm least in sight.
Wild buck, I'll hunt thee breathless; thou shalt run on,
But I will turn[4] thee when I'm not thought upon.

(*Enter Ralph Trapdoor.*)

Now sirrah, what are you? Leave your ape's tricks[5] and speak.   185

---

1   *you ... upon*   You know who (Moll Cutpurse) I intend to pursue.
2   *Lose him not*   Don't let him go.
3   *I wash a negro*   Play on the proverbial phrase "to wash the Ethiop white," referring to
    something impossible.
4   *turn*   Literally, cause one's prey to reverse course, forcing it to run toward the hunter with-
    out realizing it.
5   *Leave ... tricks*   When Trapdoor enters, he does "ape's tricks" by miming servile postures or
    gestures.

TRAPDOOR. A letter from my captain[1] to your worship.

SIR ALEXANDER. Oh, oh, now I remember, 'tis to prefer thee into
my service.

TRAPDOOR. To be a shifter under your worship's nose of a clean
190 trencher, when there's a good bit upon't.[2]

SIR ALEXANDER. Troth honest fellow—humh—ha—let me see,
[*Reads letter.*]
[*Aside.*] This knave shall be the axe to hew that down
At which I stumble.[3] H'as° a face that promiseth   *he has*
Much of a villain. I will grind his wit,
195 And if the edge prove fine, make use of it.[4]—
Come hither sirrah. Canst thou be secret, ha?

TRAPDOOR. As two crafty attorneys plotting the undoing of their
clients.

SIR ALEXANDER. Did'st never, as thou hast walked about this town,
200 Hear of a wench called Moll, Mad, Merry Moll?

TRAPDOOR. Moll Cutpurse, sir?

SIR ALEXANDER. The same; dost thou know her, then?

TRAPDOOR. As well as I know 'twill rain upon Simon and Jude's
day[5] next. I will sift all the taverns i'th'city, and drink half-pots
205 with all the watermen o'th'Bankside,[6] but, if you will, sir, I'll find
her out.

---

1 *my captain* Trapdoor claims that he is a displaced soldier, something he reinforces by
bringing Sir Alexander a supposed letter of reference. While there were many former and
wounded soldiers on the streets of Elizabethan and Jacobean London, plays and popular
literature often feature rogues and vagabonds merely pretending to be such victims.

2 *To ... upon't* To be the one who shifts a plate away from under Alexander's nose and provides
a clean one when there's still food to be eaten. In other words, to be a trickster in the open.

3 *This knave ... stumble* Trapdoor will be the solution to Alexander's problem—that is, the
means to spoil Sebastian's plan.

4 *if ... it* Extension of Alexander's axe metaphor: he will grind Trapdoor's wit and use it if he
becomes sharp enough.

5 *Simon and Jude's day* October 28, reputed to be always rainy on the basis of a story in
Holinshed's *Chronicles*, in which a battle between King Henry VIII and Yorkshire rebels on
St. Simon and St. Jude's Day, 1536, was averted on account of rain.

6 *half-pots* Half-tankards of ale; *watermen o'th'Bankside* People who ferried customers
back and forth on the Thames in small boats. The Bankside was directly south from the
heart of the city of London, on the Southwark side of the river, and it was the home of
theaters such as the Globe and the Rose as well as bear-baiting and bull-baiting rings.

SIR ALEXANDER. That task is easy; do't then.—Hold thy hand up.
[*Looking over the hand.*] What's this, is't burnt?[1]
TRAPDOOR. No, sir, no: a little singed with making fireworks.
SIR ALEXANDER. [*Giving Trapdoor money.*] There's money; spend it.   210
That being spent, fetch more.
TRAPDOOR. Oh, sir, that all the poor soldiers in *England* had such a
leader! For fetching, no water spaniel is like me.[2]
SIR ALEXANDER. This wench we speak of strays so from her kind,
Nature repents she made her. 'Tis a mermaid[3]   215
Has tolled° my son to shipwreck.   *allured*
TRAPDOOR. I'll cut her comb[4] for you.
SIR ALEXANDER. I'll tell out gold for thee then; hunt her forth,
Cast out a line hung full of silver hooks[5]
To catch her to thy company. Deep spendings   220
May draw her that's most chaste to a man's bosom.[6]
TRAPDOOR. The jingling of golden bells, and a good fool with a
hobbyhorse, will draw all the whores i'th' town to dance in a
morris.[7]
SIR ALEXANDER. Or rather—for that's best—they say sometimes   225
She goes in breeches: follow her as her man.[8]
TRAPDOOR. And when her breeches are off, she shall follow me.
SIR ALEXANDER. Beat all thy brains to serve her.
TRAPDOOR. Zounds sir, as country wenches beat cream 'till butter
comes.[9]   230

---

1   *is't burnt?*   Criminals were commonly branded on the hand for felonies. Alexander checks
    to see if Trapdoor has been marked.
2   *For ... me*   A boast; Trapdoor declares he can beat the best hunting dog at fetching
    (stealing).
3   *mermaid*   In sixteenth- and seventeenth-century England, the term could refer not only
    to a half-woman, half-fish creature, but also to a siren, a mythical creature who was part
    woman, part bird and whose enchanted singing could lure sailors to their deaths.
4   *cut her comb*   Take her down; tame her—with an added sense of emasculating her, as in
    cutting a cock's comb.
5   *silver hooks*   Money to lure Moll.
6   *May ... bosom*   May draw even the most chaste woman to the embrace of a man.
7   *morris*   Morris dance, a holiday dance, often for May Day celebrations, that involved a
    group of revelers coming together, wearing bells and ribbons, and usually with a lead dancer
    dressed as a fool.
8   *as her man*   Become her manservant.
9   *Zounds*   By God's wounds;   *'till butter comes*   With bawdy implications, as have many of
    Trapdoor's innuendo-laden comments.

SIR ALEXANDER. Play thou the subtle spider; weave fine nets
    To ensnare her very life.
TRAPDOOR.   Her life?
SIR ALEXANDER.   Yes, suck
    Her heart-blood° if thou canst. Twist thou but cords   *lifeblood*
    To catch her, I'll find law to hang her up.[1]
235 TRAPDOOR. Spoke like a worshipful bencher.[2]
SIR ALEXANDER. Trace all her steps; at this she-fox's den
    Watch what lambs enter. Let me play the shepherd
    To save their throats from bleeding, and cut hers.
TRAPDOOR. This is the goll° shall do't.   *hand*
SIR ALEXANDER.   Be firm, and gain me
240 Ever thine own.[3] This done I entertain thee.
    How is thy name?
TRAPDOOR. My name, sir, is Ralph[4] Trapdoor, honest Ralph.
SIR ALEXANDER. Trapdoor, be like thy name: a dangerous step
    For her to venture on, but unto me—
245 TRAPDOOR. As fast as your sole to your boot or shoe, sir.
SIR ALEXANDER. Hence then, be little seen here as thou canst.
    I'll still be at thine elbow.
TRAPDOOR.   The trapdoor's set.
    Moll, if you budge, you're gone. This me shall crown:
    A roaring boy the Roaring Girl puts down.
250 SIR ALEXANDER. God-a-mercy,[5] lose no time.

(*Exeunt.*)

---

1 *Twist ... up* Make ties to bind her, but do not act further. I'll find a way to get Moll convicted of a crime that will send her to the gallows.
2 *bencher* Judge or high-ranking magistrate.
3 *gain me ... thine own* You will acquire me as your permanent friend.
4 *Ralph* Pronounced "Rafe."
5 *God-a-mercy* God have mercy; thanks.

[ACT 2, SCENE I]

(*The three shops open in a rank: the first a pothecary's shop, the next a
feather shop, the third a sempster's shop.*[1] *Mistress Gallipot in the first,
Mistress Tiltyard in the next, Master Openwork and his wife in the
third. To them enters Laxton, Goshawk, and Greenwit.*)

MISTRESS OPENWORK. Gentlemen, what is't you lack?[2] What is't
you buy? See fine bands and ruffs, fine lawns, fine cambrics.[3]
What is't you lack, gentlemen, what is't you buy?
LAXTON. Yonder's the shop.
GOSHAWK. Is that she?   5
LAXTON. Peace!
GREENWIT. She that minces tobacco?
LAXTON. Ay. She's a gentlewoman born I can tell you, though it be
her hard fortune now to shred Indian pot-herbs.[4]
GOSHAWK. Oh, sir, 'tis many a good woman's fortune, when her   10
husband turns bankrupt, to begin with pipes and set up again.[5]
LAXTON. And indeed the raising of the woman is the lifting up
of the man's head at all times: if one flourish, t'other will bud as
fast,[6] I warrant ye.
GOSHAWK. Come, thou'rt familiarly acquainted there, I grope[7] that.   15

---

1 *pothecary's shop* Druggists's shop; *feather shop* Shop selling feathers, a fashionable
   accessory at the time; *sempster's shop* Shop for selling and mending garments; *sempster* Person who sews and mends.
2 *what is't you lack?* Common cry of shopkeepers and peddlers for advertising wares.
3 *ruffs* Detachable frills—generally pleated or fluted, and of various sizes, fabrics, and
   shapes—worn by men and women around the neck; *lawns* Very fine fabrics, generally
   linens; *cambrics* High quality white linens, originally produced in Cambray, Flanders.
4 *Indian pot-herbs* In this case, tobacco, but a pot-herb may be any herb or leaf vegetable
   that is consumed cooked.
5 *pipes* Tobacco pipes, or penises; *set up again* Start over, or, provide another erection.
6 *raising of the woman* Bettering of the woman; *lifting ... head* Brings up the man's fortune; *if one flourish ... bud as fast* When husband or wife do well, the other's fortunes follow. The whole statement continues the previous sexual innuendo, indicating that mutual
   arousal leads to mutual completion.
7 *familiarly acquainted* Known intimately; *grope* Grasp or understand, with an added
   sexual connotation.

LAXTON. And you grope no better i'th'dark, you may chance lie
i'th'ditch when you're drunk.[1]

GOSHAWK. Go, thou'rt a mystical lecher.

LAXTON. I will not deny but my credit may take up an ounce of
20   pure smoke.

GOSHAWK. May take up an ell of pure smock![2] Away, go. [*Aside.*]
'Tis the closest striker.[3] '*Life*,[4] I think he commits venery forty
foot deep; no man's aware on't.[5] I, like a palpable smockster, go
to work so openly with the tricks of art that I'm as apparently
25   seen as a naked boy in a vial;[6] & were it not for a gift of treachery
that I have in me to betray my friend[7] when he puts most trust in
me—mass yonder he is too—and by his injury to make good my
access to her,[8] I should appear as defective in courting as a farmer's
son the first day of his feather, that doth nothing at court but woo
30   the hangings and glass windows for a month together and some
broken waiting woman forever after.[9] I find those imperfections
in my venery that, were't not for flattery and falsehood, I should
want discourse and impudence;[10] and he that wants impudence
among women, is worthy to be kickt out at bed's feet.—He[11] shall
35   not see me yet.

---

1 *And ... drunk* If you don't grope better in the dark, you'll end up in a ditch when you're
  drunk. The sentence carries a possible innuendo with "lie i'th'ditch" as slang meaning "have
  sex."

2 *ell ... smock* Yard (roughly; an ell was a little longer) of a shift or chemise—a woman's
  undergarment. With his pun on *smock* for "smoke," Goshawk jokes that Laxton really looks
  to lift up Mistress Gallipot's skirts.

3 *striker* Fornicator; seducer.

4 '*Life* God's life (an oath).

5 *venery ... deep* Pursues sexual pleasure as though in a hole dug forty feet underground
  (because it is so secret);   *no ... on't* Nobody knows about it.

6 *palpable smockster* Tangible, clearly visible bawd or seducer; *I'm ... vial* It's as easy to see
  what I'm doing as it would be to see a naked, infant specimen stored in a glass jar.

7 *friend* Master Openwork.

8 *mass* By the mass (an exclamation or oath); *by his ... to her* By injuring (slandering)
  Openwork behind his back, Goshawk gains opportunity to seduce Mistress Openwork.

9 *I ... feather* I would seem as useless as a farm boy on the first day of his arrival at court,
  wearing a fancy feathered cap; *doth ... after* Who stares at pictures and windows to practice his technique and only ever manages to woo a servant woman past her prime.

10 *were't ... impudence* Without using flattery and telling lies to women, I would struggle to
  make conversation and not have the audacity to maintain it.

11 *He* Openwork.

[At the tobacco shop.]

GREENWIT. Troth, this is finely shred.

LAXTON. Oh, women are the best mincers.[1]

MISTRESS GALLIPOT. 'T had been a good phrase for a cook's wife, sir.

LAXTON. But 'twill serve generally, like the front of a new almanac, as thus: calculated for the meridian of cooks' wives, but generally   40
for all Englishwomen.[2]

MISTRESS GALLIPOT. Nay, you shall ha't, sir, I have filled it for you.

(She puts [his pipe] to the fire.)

LAXTON. The pipe's in a good hand, and I wish mine always so.[3]

GREENWIT. But not to be used i'that fashion![4]

LAXTON. Oh, pardon me, sir, I understand no French.[5] I pray be   45
covered.[6] Jack, a pipe of rich smoke?

GOSHAWK. Rich smoke; that's sixpence a pipe is't?[7]

GREENWIT. To me, sweet lady.[8]

[They smoke.]

---

1 *mincers* Multiple meanings are possible: shredders of herbs, cutting speakers, or pretentious people.

2 *almanac* Annual publication of tables, including calendars for astronomical and meteorological information with the motions of the sun, moon, and other predictable happenings like tides. Almanacs may have included information such as religious holidays and expectations about how much rain a given month might see; *meridian ... Englishwomen* Like an almanac that is specifically crafted for a particular place but more widely applicable, Laxton claims his phrase is applicable to cook's wives as the specific "meridian" (location) but that women more generally are also aptly described by it.

3 *pipe* Double entrendre, with pipe also meaning penis; *good hand* Mistress Gallipot's hand; *wish ... so* Wish always for a woman to be handling my penis.

4 *used ... fashion* Put to the fire and smoked, continuing Laxton's double entendre. "Being burnt" was also slang for catching a venereal disease, especially syphilis.

5 *French* Continuing the sexual word play, Laxton denies any syphilis threat by claiming ignorance of French because syphilis was considered the "French pox."

6 *be covered* Put on your hat.

7 *Rich ... is't?* Goshawk seems to be implying that this tobacco is quite expensive and questioning the price.

8 *To ... lady* Give a pipe to me, please, sweet Mistress Gallipot.

MISTRESS GALLIPOT. [*Aside to Laxton.*] Be not forgetful; respect my
50   credit; seem strange;[1] art and wit makes a fool of suspicion; pray,
be wary.
LAXTON. [*Aside to Mistress Gallipot.*] Pish, I warrant you.[2] [*Aloud, to
Goshawk and Greenwit.*] Come, how is't gallants?
GREENWIT. Pure and excellent.
55   LAXTON. I thought 'twas good, you were grown so silent. You are
like those that love not to talk at victuals,[3] though they make
a worse noise i'the nose than a common fiddler's prentice, and
discourse a whole supper with snuffling. [*To Mistress Gallipot.*]
I must speak a word with you anon.[4]
60   MISTRESS GALLIPOT. [*Aside to Laxton.*] Make your way wisely then.

[*Mistress Gallipot and Laxton stand aside to talk.*]

GOSHAWK. Oh, what else, sir? He's perfection itself: full of manners,
but not an acre of ground belonging to 'em.[5]
GREENWIT. Ay, and full of form; h'as ne'er a good stool[6] in's
chamber.
65   GOSHAWK. But above all religious: He prayeth daily upon elder
brothers.[7]
GREENWIT. And valiant above measure: h'as run three streets from a
sergeant.[8]

([*Laxton*] *blows tobacco in* [*Goshawk and Greenwit's*] *faces.*)

LAXTON. Pooh, pooh.

---

1   *Be ... credit* Mistress Gallipot asks Laxton not to abuse or expose their familiar-
ity; *credit* Reputation; *seem strange* Act like a stranger.
2   *I warrant you* I guarantee you I will.
3   *victuals* Meals.
4   *anon* Right away.
5   *perfection* Moral, virtuous; *manners* Morals and courtesy, but also "manors" or
land; *not ... to 'em* He has no land to back up his status. Also a play on the proverb "One
acre of possession is worth a whole land of promise." Goshawk says that Laxton presents
himself as being stuffed full of all good things and intentions, but he has no real possessions.
6   *form* Formality, but also bench; *stool* Furniture for one, or property in general, playing
off "form."
7   *prayeth ... brothers* Prays with the Puritans; punning on "pray" and "prey," Goshawk
accuses Laxton of attempting to exploit elder sons who have land and money.
8   *run ... sergeant* Runs three streets to escape an officer who arrests debtors.

GREENWIT AND GOSHAWK. Oh, pooh, ho, ho!   70

[*All coughing. Laxton moves away and continues speaking apart with Mistress Gallipot.*]

LAXTON. So, so.
MISTRESS GALLIPOT. What's the matter now, sir?
LAXTON. I protest I'm in extreme want of money. If you can supply me now with any means, you do me the greatest pleasure—next to the bounty of your love—as ever poor gentleman tasted.   75
MISTRESS GALLIPOT. What's the sum would pleasure ye, sir?[1] Though you deserve nothing less at my hands.
LAXTON. Why 'tis but for want of opportunity, thou know'st.
  [*Aside.*] I put her off with opportunity still. By this light I hate her, but for means to keep me in fashion with gallants;[2] for   80
  what I take from her, I spend upon other wenches, bear her in hand still.[3] She has wit enough to rob her husband, and I ways enough to consume the money. [*Goshawk and Greenwit begin coughing, Laxton addresses them.*] Why, how now? What, the chin-cough?[4]   85
GOSHAWK. Thou hast the cowardliest trick to come before a man's face and strangle him ere he be aware. I could find in my heart to make a quarrel in earnest.
LAXTON. Pox and thou dost, thou know'st I never use to fight with my friends, thou'll but lose thy labor in't.[5]   90

(*Enter [Jack] Dapper and his man Gull.*)

Jack Dapper!

---

1 *What's ... sir?* How much money do you want?
2 *By this light* Mistress Gallipot is ugly to me in the light of day; *but ... gallants* But I need her money to keep up appearances and compete with gallants.
3 *bear ... still* I keep her in my grip.
4 *chin-cough* Violent and explosive cough or whooping cough.
5 *I never ... friends* I don't engage in fighting with friends; *thou'll ... in't* Laxton would not fight if challenged, so challenging him would be a waste of Greenwit's energy.

GREENWIT. Monsieur Dapper, I dive down to your ankles.[1]

JACK DAPPER. Save ye gentlemen, all three, in a peculiar[2] salute.

GOSHAWK. He were ill to make a lawyer: he dispatches three at
95 once![3]

LAXTON. So, well said. [*Receiving what appears to be a bag of tobacco, actually a purse of money.*] But is this of the same tobacco, Mistress Gallipot?

MISTRESS GALLIPOT. The same you had at first, sir.

100 LAXTON. I wish it no better. This will serve to drink[4] at my chamber.

GOSHAWK. Shall we taste a pipe on't?

LAXTON. Not of this, by my troth gentlemen; I have sworn before you.

105 GOSHAWK. What, not Jack Dapper?[5]

LAXTON. Pardon me, sweet Jack, I'm sorry I made such a rash oath, but foolish oaths must stand. [*Dapper starts to move toward the feather shop.*] Where art going, Jack?

JACK DAPPER. 'Faith, to buy one feather.

110 LAXTON. One feather? [*Aside.*] The fool's peculiar still.

JACK DAPPER. Gull.

GULL. Master.

JACK DAPPER. Here's three halfpence for your ordinary,[6] boy. Meet me an hour hence in Paul's.

115 GULL. [*Aside.*] How, three single halfpence? 'Life, this will scarce serve a man in sauce, a ha'porth of mustard, a ha'porth of oil, and a ha'porth of vinegar; what's left then for the pickle herring?[7] This

---

1   *dive ... ankles* I bow deeply in greeting. A dive-dapper is, literally, a small diving waterfowl, but the term is applied to people who appear ridiculous.

2   *Save ye* Typical greeting, an abbreviation of "God save ye"; *peculiar* Singular; strange. Dapper offers one salute for all three of them, which is made even more bizarre by whatever histrionics are required to greet three in one salute.

3   *He were ... once* Dapper would make a poor lawyer because he takes care of three claims together rather than dealing individually and drawing out the process, which would result in higher fees for a lawyer.

4   *drink* To draw in, or inhale, tobacco.

5   *What ... Dapper?* What, no tobacco for Jack Dapper?

6   *ordinary* Fixed price meal at a tavern or inn—the meal or the tavern could be called an ordinary.

7   *ha'porth* Halfpenny worth; *pickle herring* Main dish; Gull's small allowance will pay for sauces but not for actual food.

shows like small beer i'th morning after a great surfeit of wine oe'r
night.[1] He could spend his three pound last night in a supper
amongst girls and brave bawdy-house boys—I thought his pockets   120
cackled not for nothing: these are the eggs of three pound.[2] I'll go
sup'em up presently.

(*Exit Gull.*)

LAXTON.   Eight, nine, ten angels.[3] Good wench, i'faith, and one
that loves darkness well. She puts out a candle with the best tricks
of any drugster's wife in England. But that which mads her: I rail   125
upon opportunity still,[4] and take no notice on't. The other night
she would needs lead me into a room with a candle in her hand to
show me a naked picture, where no sooner entered but the candle
was sent of an errand.[5] Now I—not intending to understand her,
but like a puny at the Inns of venery[6]—called for another light   130
innocently. Thus reward I all her cunning with simple mistaking. I
know she cozens her husband to keep me,[7] and I'll keep her honest, as long as I can, to make the poor man some part of amends.[8]
An honest mind of a whoremaster![9]

---

1   *small beer i'th morning ... o'er night*   Weak or watered-down, inferior beer consumed in the
    morning after a long night of drinking wine and carousing. The former night's excess gives
    way to a meager maintenance.
2   *brave bawdy-house boys*   Showy, resplendent young men of the brothel;   *his pockets
    cackled*   Money jingled in his pockets, making a sound like hens cackling, the noise asso-
    ciated with hens laying eggs. Gull's comment suggests that the noise of Dapper's pockets
    did indicate something left of his original three pounds, but that all that is left from the
    allowance are just a few pence;   *eggs of three pound*   The proverb "As dear as two eggs a
    penny," would indicate that three halfpennies were equal to three eggs, and all that Dapper's
    pockets' cackling may produce for Gull are the three halfpennies.
3   *angels*   Ten-shilling coins. Five pounds (ten angels, or 100 shillings) is a generous sum.
4   *I ... still*   I still claim that there is no opportunity for the two of us to have sex.
5   *no sooner ... an errand*   She put out the candle as soon as she lured Laxton in to the room
    (supposedly to look at a picture of a naked person).
6   *puny ... venery*   New pupil in the college of sexual pursuit, playing on the term "puny,"
    which refers to a new pupil at the Inns of Court, London's law schools.
7   *she ... me*   She cheats her husband to support me.
8   *I'll ... amends*   I'll put off Mistress Gallipot's advances for as long as possible to make
    amends to Master Gallipot for taking his money.
9   *honest ... whoremaster*   Virtuous intentions from a lecher like me!

135 [*To Goshawk et al.*] How think you amongst you? What a fresh
pipe? Draw in a third man.
GOSHAWK. No, you're a hoarder; you engross[1] by th'ounces.

(*At the feather shop now.*)

JACK DAPPER. Pooh, I like it not.
MISTRESS TILTYARD.   What feather is't you'd have, sir?
These are most worn and most in fashion
140 Amongst the beaver gallants, the stone riders,
The private stage's audience, the twelvepenny-stool gentlemen[2]
I can inform you, 'tis the general feather.[3]
JACK DAPPER. And therefore, I mislike it. Tell me of general!
Now a continual Simon and Jude's rain
145 Beat all your feathers as flat down as pancakes![4]
Show me—a—spangled° feather.   *speckled*
MISTRESS TILTYARD.   Oh, to go a-feasting with.
You'd have it for a henchboy;[5] you shall.

(*At the sempster's shop now.*)

OPENWORK. Mass, I had quite forgot.
His honor's footman was here last night, wife.
150 Ha' you done with my lord's shirt?[6]
MISTRESS OPENWORK.   What's that to you, sir?
I was this morning at his honor's lodging,
'Ere such a snail as you crept out of your shell.

---

1 *engross* Use it all; monopolize.
2 *beaver gallants* Fashionable beaver-hat-wearing gentlemen; *stone riders* Stallion riders;
private stage's audience Those attending the smaller, indoor theaters; *twelvepenny-stool
gentlemen* Ostentatious playgoers who paid exorbitantly to see a play and sit on a stool
onstage, thus displaying themselves while watching the show.
3 *general feather* Favored feather, fashionable choice.
4 *Tell me ... pancakes* Dapper curses Mistress Tiltyard for not showing him an eccentric
enough feather.
5 *henchboy* Page.
6 *His honor* Respectful way to refer to a nobleman; *my lord's shirt* Nobleman's under-
shirt, often made of linen and worn next to the skin.

OPENWORK. Oh, 'twas well done, good wife.

MISTRESS OPENWORK.   I hold it better, sir,
   Than if you had done't yourself.

OPENWORK.   Nay, so say I.
   But is the Countess's smock almost done, mouse?[1]   155

MISTRESS OPENWORK. Here lies the cambric, sir, but wants,[2] I fear
   me.

OPENWORK. I'll resolve you of that presently.[3]

MISTRESS OPENWORK. Heyday! Oh, audacious groom!
   Dare you presume to noble women's linen?[4]
   Keep you your yard to measure shepherds' holland.[5]   160
   I must confine you, I see that.

(*At the tobacco shop now.*)

GOSHAWK. What say you to this gear?[6]

LAXTON. I dare the arrantest critic[7] in tobacco to lay one fault
   upon't.

(*Enter Moll in a frieze jerkin and a black safeguard.*[8])

GOSHAWK. 'Life. Yonder's Moll.   165

LAXTON. Moll? Which Moll?

GOSHAWK. Honest Moll.

LAXTON. Prithee, let's call her.—Moll!

---

1   *mouse*   Pet name.
2   *but wants*   The piece is lacking; perhaps it is unfinished or perhaps the cambric is not fine
    enough.
3   *I'll ... presently*   I'll take care of the smock now.
4   *groom*   Serving man or attendant;   *presume ... linen*   Do you think you are good enough
    to work on a noblewoman's underclothes?
5   *yard*   Yardstick, with a pun on "yard" as penis;   *shepherds' holland*   Linen cloth, not as
    fine in quality as good cambric. Mistress Openwork decries her husband's social status while
    also suggesting he has lascivious motives in offering to work on the noblewoman's garment.
6   *gear*   Goods, things—here, the tobacco.
7   *arrantest critic*   Most rascally, unmitigated critic.
8   *frieze jerkin*   Men's short, collared jacket made from coarse, woolen cloth, jerkins
    were sometimes sleeveless and designed to be worn over a doublet or take the place of
    one;   *safeguard*   Thickly gathered skirt worn with a short jacket; sometimes made from
    rich materials and highly decorated, they were intended to protect women's clothing
    during riding.

OMNES. Moll, Moll, psst, Moll!

170 MOLL. How now, what's the matter?

GOSHAWK. A pipe of good tobacco, Moll?

MOLL. I cannot stay.

GOSHAWK. Nay, Moll, pooh! Prithee hark, but one word, i'faith.

MOLL. Well, what is't?

175 GREENWIT. Prithee come hither, sirrah.[1]

LAXTON. [*Aside.*] Heart,[2] I would give but too much money to be
nibbling with that wench. 'Life, sh'has the spirit of four great
parishes and a voice that will drown all the City. Methinks a
brave captain might get all his soldiers upon her, and ne'er be

180 beholding to a company of Mile End milksops,[3] if he could
come on and come off[4] quick enough. Such a Moll were a
marrowbone before an Italian; he would cry "*bona roba*"[5] till
his ribs were nothing but bone. I'll lay hard siege to her. Money
is that *aqua fortis*[6] that eats into many a maidenhead. Where the

185 walls are flesh & blood, I'll ever pierce through with a golden
auger.[7]

GOSHAWK. [*Offers tobacco to Moll.*] Now thy judgment, Moll: is't
not good?

MOLL. Yes, faith, 'tis very good tobacco. How do you sell an

190 ounce?[8] Farewell. God b'y you Mistress Gallipot. [*Moll starts to
move on.*]

GOSHAWK. Why Moll, Moll!

---

1 *sirrah*   When applied to women, as here, a term of friendly greeting. For men, it was a
term of abnegation intended to demonstrate the speaker's authority because the title was
otherwise reserved for boys.

2 *Heart*   By God's heart.

3 *get ... upon her*   Conceive all his soldiers with her;   *Mile End milksops*   Ordinary citizens
turned soldier for militia practice at Mile End, an area of common fields one mile beyond
Aldgate, the easternmost gate allowing entry into the City of London. In other words, a
smart captain would use Moll to mother an army and avoid ever having to pick through city
stock for soldiers.

4 *come on and come off*   Advance and retreat; have sex.

5 *marrowbone*   Food popularly considered an aphrodisiac;   *Italian*   Italians were considered especially lecherous;   *bona roba*   Italian: good stuff.

6 *aqua fortis*   Solvent, nitric acid.

7 *auger*   Tool for making holes.

8 *faith*   In faith;   *How ... ounce*   How much per ounce?

MOLL. I cannot stay now i'faith. I am going to buy a shag ruff.[1] The
shop will be shut in presently. [*Moll moves on.*]

GOSHAWK. 'Tis the maddest, fantasticalest girl! I never knew so   195
much flesh and so much nimbleness put together.

LAXTON. She slips from one company to another like a fat eel
between a Dutchman's fingers. [*Aside.*] I'll watch my time for
her.

MISTRESS GALLIPOT. Some will not stick[2] to say she's a man, and   200
some, both man and woman.

LAXTON. That were excellent; she might first cuckold the husband
and then make him do as much for the wife.[3]

(*The feather shop again.*)

MOLL. [*To Mistress Tiltyard, as Moll approaches her.*] Save you.[4] How
does Mistress Tiltyard?   205

JACK DAPPER. Moll!

MOLL. Jack Dapper!

JACK DAPPER. How dost, Moll?

MOLL. I'll tell thee by and by; I go but to th'next shop.

JACK DAPPER. Thou shalt find me here this hour about a feather.   210

MOLL. Nay, an[5] a feather hold you in play a whole hour, a goose
will last you all the days of your life. ([*Moll moves on to*] *the sempster's shop.*) Let me see a good shag ruff.

OPENWORK. Mistress Mary, that shalt thou i'faith, and the best in
the shop.   215

MISTRESS OPENWORK. How now, greetings? Love terms, with a
pox,[6] between you? Have I found out one of your haunts?[7] I
send you for hollands, and you're i'th the low countries with a

---

1   *shag ruff*   Ruff made of a thickly piled worsted or silk with a double warp, creating a velvet
    texture.
2   *stick*   Hesitate.
3   *she ... wife*   First, she can sleep with the wife and cuckold the husband, and then, she can
    sleep with the husband and return the punishment of adultery to the wife.
4   *Save you*   God save you.
5   *an*   If.
6   *pox*   Sexually transmitted disease, usually syphilis.
7   *Have ... haunts?*   Have I discovered one of your mistresses?

mischief?[1] I'm served with good ware by th'shift, that makes it lie
220 dead so long upon my hands, I were as good shut up shop, for
when I open it, I take nothing.[2]
OPENWORK. Nay, an you fall a-ringing once, the devil cannot stop
you. I'll out of the belfry[3] as fast as I can.—Moll!
MISTRESS OPENWORK. (*[To] Moll.*) Get you from my shop.
225 MOLL. I come to buy.
MISTRESS OPENWORK. I'll sell ye nothing. I warn[4] ye my house and
shop!
MOLL. You goody Openwork, you that prick out a poor living
And sews many a bawdy skin-coat together,[5]
230 Thou private pandress between shirt and smock,
I wish thee for a minute but a man;
Thou should'st never use more shapes. But as th'art,
I pity my revenge.[6] Now my spleen's up.°   *I'm angry*
I would not mock it willingly.[7]

(*Enter a fellow with a long rapier by his side.*)

235 Ha! Be thankful.
Now, I forgive thee.
MISTRESS OPENWORK. Marry, hang thee! I never askt forgiveness in
my life!

---

1 *send ... mischief* Extended sexual metaphor, playing on "hollands," which is linen from the
Netherlands or low countries. Mistress Openwork suggests that when Master Openwork
goes off to get linen he is actually visiting the "nether-lands" of his mistress.
2 *I'm ... nothing* Mistress Openwork protests that Master Openwork serves her good
ware—or male genitals—"by th'shift," in a makeshift way, and when he does, they are no
longer ready for action. She in turn might as well close her doors—that is, become sexually
unavailable—because when she is ready to receive, she gets nothing.
3 *you fall a-ringing* Openwork compares his wife's scolding to a ringing a bell: once she gets
started, she does not stop; *belfry* Bell tower.
4 *warn* Refuse.
5 *goody* Goodwife, title for a married woman without high status and here probably
intended as an insult; *prick* Sew with a needle, with a sexual innuendo; *sews ...
together* Reference to the idea that poor seamstresses end up working as prostitutes.
6 *Thou ... revenge* You will never appear other than as you are, a woman, and so, I take pity
on you and abandon my revenge. Moll switches to the informal "thou/thee" form in this
speech to insult Mistress Openwork.
7 *I would ... willingly* I wouldn't scorn it on purpose, if I were you.

MOLL. [*To fellow.*] You, goodman[1] swine's face.

FELLOW. What, will you murder me?[2]   240

MOLL. You remember slave, how you abused me t'other night in a
tavern?

FELLOW. Not I, by this light.

MOLL. No, but by candlelight you did. You have tricks to save your
oaths—reservations have you? And I have reserved somewhat for   245
you.[3] [*She hits him.*] As you like that,[4] call for more. You know the
sign again.

FELLOW. Pox on't. Had I brought any company along with me to
have born witness on't, 'twould ne'er have grieved me; but to be
struck and nobody by, 'tis my ill fortune still.[5] Why, tread upon   250
a worm, they say 'twill turn tail, but indeed a gentleman should
have more manners.[6]

(*Exit fellow.*)

LAXTON. Gallantly performed, i'faith, Moll, and manfully. I
love thee forever for't. Base rogue! Had he offered but the least
counterbuff, by this hand, I was prepared for him.[7]   255

MOLL. You prepared for him? Why should you be prepared for
him? Was he any more than a man?

---

1   *goodman*   Similar to goody or goodwoman, again used by Moll to insult.

2   *murder me?*   The fellow's question suggests that Moll has done something threatening, like
draw a sword. However, there is no indication in the existing stage directions that Moll is
wearing a sword, and the fellow may be merely taunting her for daring to insult him.

3   *reservations have ... for you*   Moll mocks the fellow's equivocation: his response, "by this
light," allows him to quibble over the circumstance of Moll's accusation by expressing a
"reservation" or qualification regarding the charge against him. Moll then uses "reserved" to
mean held back, in reserve, when she refers to the stroke she intends to give him.

4   *that*   Her stroke.

5   *Had ... still*   The fellow wishes he had a companion who would be able to testify that Moll
hit him first; without this, he claims he must not retaliate.

6   *Why ... manners*   Even a worm would turn against his attackers, but a gentleman should
have manners (and not do so). This alludes to the proverbial expression "Tread on a worm
and it will turn." Contrary to the idea of turning tail and running, the caution here is that
even a despised, low creature will turn and defend itself when provoked; however, the fellow
insists his gentlemanly status prevents him from striking back.

7   *Had ... him*   If the fellow had tried to retaliate in the slightest way, I was prepared to fight
(for Moll).

LAXTON. No, nor so much by a yard and a handful, London measure.[1]

260 MOLL. Why do you speak this then? Do you think I cannot ride a stone horse unless one lead him by th'snaffle?[2]

LAXTON. Yes, and sit him bravely, I know thou canst Moll. 'Twas but an honest mistake through love, and I'll make amends for't any way. Prithee, sweet plump Moll, when shall thou and I go out

265 o'town together?

MOLL. Whither? To Tyburn,[3] prithee?

LAXTON. Mass, that's out o'town indeed. Thou hang'st so many jests upon thy friends still. I mean honestly to Brentford, Staines, or Ware.[4]

270 MOLL. What to do there?

LAXTON. Nothing but be merry and lie together. I'll hire a coach with four horses.

MOLL. I thought 'twould be a beastly journey. You may leave out one well; three horses will serve, if I play the jade[5] myself.

275 LAXTON. Nay, pish thou'rt such another kicking wench. Prithee be kind and let's meet.

MOLL. 'Tis hard, but we shall meet,[6] sir.

LAXTON. Nay, but appoint the place then. [*He offers money.*] There's ten angels in fair gold Moll; you see I do not trifle with you.

280 Do but say thou wilt meet me, and I'll have a coach ready for thee.

MOLL. Why, here's my hand; I'll meet you, sir.

LAXTON. [*Aside.*] Oh, good gold!—The place, sweet Moll?

MOLL. It shall be your appointment.[7]

---

1 *London measure* London drapers supposedly counted their yard as a little more than a standard yard, which would be the extra handful that Laxton references. Laxton implies that the fellow does not "measure up" to standards of manliness.

2 *Do ... th'snaffle* Do you not think I can ride a stallion (fight a man) unless someone leads it (him) by the bridle?

3 *Tyburn* Location of a gallows for hanging criminals, to the west of the city.

4 *Brentford ... Ware* Marketing towns outside of London that were known as destinations for assignations.

5 *jade* Overworked horse, but also a slang term for "hussy."

6 *'Tis ... meet* It's tricky, but we will surely meet.

7 *your appointment* Your appointed choice.

LAXTON. Somewhat near Holborn,[1] Moll.   285
MOLL. In Gray's Inn Fields[2] then.
LAXTON. A match![3]
MOLL. I'll meet you there.
LAXTON. The hour.
MOLL. Three.   290
LAXTON. That will be time enough to sup at Brentford.

(*Fall from them to the other.*[4])

OPENWORK. [*To Goshawk.*] I am of such a nature, sir, I cannot
endure the house when she scolds. Sh'has a tongue will be heard
further in a still morning than Saint Antholin's[5] bell. She rails
upon me for foreign wenching, that I being a freeman[6] must   295
needs keep a whore i'th suburbs, and seek to impoverish the
liberties.[7] When we fall out, I trouble you still to make all whole
with my wife.[8]
GOSHAWK. No trouble at all. 'Tis a pleasure to me to join things
together.[9]   300

---

1 *Holborn*   West-end neighborhood defined by High Holborn, a main street near the law
   schools (the Inns of Court).
2 *Gray's Inn Fields*   Large green space that was part of Gray's Inn, one of the four Inns of
   Court.
3 *A match!*   It's a date.
4 *Fall ... other*   The focus of the scene shifts to other groups of shopkeepers and Gallants,
   whom Moll and Laxton rejoin.
5 *Saint Antholin's*   Parish church in central London that was notorious because its bell began
   ringing at five in the morning.
6 *foreign wenching*   Carrying on with "foreign" women—those not of the City of London;   *freeman*   Man possessing the freedom of the city as granted by the Corporation of
   London, a master of his trade and invested with the right to practice his craft within the city.
7 *suburbs*   Highly populated areas lying just beyond the city wall, often regarded as where
   the working poor, criminals, prostitutes, and vagrants resided;   *liberties*   Areas of license
   within London and its jurisdictional boundaries that were exempt from city regulations
   and well known for their brothels. Mistress Openwork accuses her husband of seeking out
   whores in the suburbs for his extramarital action, and questions why he does not spend his
   money locally—that is to say, on her.
8 *When ... wife*   When my wife and I quarrel, I ask you to smooth things out between us.
9 *'Tis ... together*   To help patch things up, with a bawdy secondary meaning, as Goshawk
   intends to seduce Mistress Openwork and "join things" for himself.

OPENWORK. Go thy ways. [*Aside.*] I do this but to try[1] thy honesty, Goshawk.

(*The feather shop.*)

JACK DAPPER. How lik'st thou this, Moll?

MOLL. Oh, singularly! You're fitted now for a bunch. [*Aside.*] He
305   looks for all the world with those spangled feathers like a nobleman's bedpost.[2] The purity of your wench would I fain[3] try. She
seems like Kent unconquered,[4] and I believe as many wiles are in
her. Oh, the gallants of these times are shallow lechers: they put
not their courtship home enough[5] to a wench. 'Tis impossible to
310   know what woman is thoroughly honest, because she's ne'er thoroughly tried. I am of that certain belief there are more queans[6]
in this town of their own making than of any man's provoking.
Where lies the slackness then? Many a poor soul would down,[7]
and there's nobody will push 'em.
315   Women are courted, but ne'er soundly tried.
As many walk in spurs that never ride.[8]

(*The sempster's shop.*)

MISTRESS OPENWORK. Oh, abominable.

GOSHAWK. Nay, more: I tell you in private, he keeps a whore
i'th'suburbs.
320   MISTRESS OPENWORK. Oh, spittle dealing! I came to him a gentlewoman born. I'll show you mine arms[9] when you please, sir.

---

1   *try*   Test.
2   *He ... bedpost*   Feathers were frequently used as decoration in Jacobean bedrooms, especially on four-poster beds.
3   *would I fain*   I would gladly.
4   *Kent unconquered*   According to legend, Kent was the only part of England unconquered
following the Norman invasion.
5   *put not ... enough*   Don't push their courtship hard enough to finish the job.
6   *queans*   Hussies.
7   *would down*   Would like to lower themselves to immorality.
8   *As many ... ride*   Just as many men wear spurs (as fashionable accessories) but do not ride
horses, men approach women but never really test their chastity.
9   *spittle*   Sick house, a form of hospital, where one might go if sick with venereal disease or
leprosy;   *arms*   Coat of arms.

GOSHAWK. [*Aside.*] I had rather see your legs, and begin that way.

MISTRESS OPENWORK. 'Tis well known he took me from a lady's service, where I was well-beloved of the steward.[1] I had my Latin tongue, and a spice of the French before I came to him, and now 325 doth he keep a suburbian[2] whore under my nostrils.

GOSHAWK. There's ways enough to cry quit with him.[3] Hark, in thine ear. [*Whispers.*]

MISTRESS OPENWORK. There's a friend worth a million.

MOLL. [*Aside.*] I'll try one spear against your chastity, Mistress 330 Tiltyard, though it prove too short by the burr.[4]

(*Enter Ralph Trapdoor.*)

TRAPDOOR. [*Aside.*] Mass, here she is. I'm bound already to serve her, though it be but a sluttish[5] trick. [*To Moll.*] Bless my hopeful young Mistress with long life and great limbs! Send her the upper-hand of all bailiffs and their hungry adherents! 335

MOLL. How now, what art thou?

TRAPDOOR. A poor ebbing gentleman that would gladly wait for the young flood of your service.[6]

MOLL. My service! What should move you to offer your service to me, sir? 340

TRAPDOOR. The love I bear to your heroic spirit and masculine womanhood.

MOLL. So, sir, put case we should retain you to us: what parts are there in you for a gentlewoman's service?

---

1   *steward*   Person in charge of the household affairs, including the domestic budget and staff.

2   *had ... tongue*   Knew my Latin; *spice of the French*   Some French language, although the phrase carries another meaning of having caught syphilis, the "French pox"; *suburbian*   Suburban.

3   *cry quit with him*   Retaliate to get even with him.

4   *too ... burr*   Inadequate. Burrs were iron rings behind the handgrip on tilting spears.

5   *sluttish*   Dirty.

6   *ebbing ... service*   Gentleman whose estate is falling, or whose value rushes away like the tide, and who looks for fortune by entering Moll's service.

345 TRAPDOOR. Of two kinds right worshipful: moveable and immoveable—moveable to run of errands, and immoveable to stand when
you have occasion to use me.[1]

MOLL. What strength have you?

TRAPDOOR. Strength, Mistress Moll? I have gone up into a steeple
350 and stayed the great bell as't has been ringing; stopt a windmill
going.

MOLL. And never struck down yourself?

TRAPDOOR. Stood as upright as I do at this present.

(*Moll trips up his heels. He falls.*)

MOLL. Come, I pardon you for this. It shall be no disgrace to you;
355 I have struck up the heels of the high German's[2] size ere now.—
What, not stand?

TRAPDOOR. I am of that nature where I love. I'll be at my mistress's
foot to do her service.

MOLL. Why, well said. But say your mistress should receive injury:
360 have you the spirit of fighting in you? Durst you second her?[3]

TRAPDOOR. Life, I have kept a bridge myself, and drove seven at a
time before me.[4]

MOLL. Ay?

TRAPDOOR. (*Aside.*) But they were all Lincolnshire bullocks, by my
365 troth.

MOLL. Well, meet me in Gray's Inn Fields between three and four
this afternoon, and upon better consideration, we'll retain you.

TRAPDOOR. I humbly thank your good mistress-ship. [*Aside.*] I'll
crack your neck for this kindness.

---

1   *moveable and immoveable*   Moveable property is personal property and immoveable property signifies permanent or real property, such as land;   *stand*   Wait on you or have an
erection;   *use me*   Have use for me, have sex with me.

2   *high German*   Reference to a tall German fighter who was popular in London at the time.
His name has been lost, but Middleton also mentions him in *The Owl's Almanac* (1618):
"the German Fencer cudgeled most of our English fencers, now about a month past."

3   *Durst ... her?*   Do you dare to stand with your mistress and fight with her?

4   *I ... me*   Trapdoor says he was an officer in control of a bridge, initially implying that he
had to drive away seven people. In the following aside, he admits that he actually drove
seven bull calves over the bridge.

(*Exit Trapdoor. Moll meets Laxton.*)

LAXTON. Remember three.   370
MOLL. Nay, if I fail, you hang me.
LAXTON. Good wench, i'faith.

(*Then Openwork [joins them, in disguise].*)

MOLL. Who's this?
OPENWORK. 'Tis I, Moll.
MOLL. Prithee, tend thy shop and prevent bastards.¹   375
OPENWORK. We'll have a pint of the same wine² i'faith, Moll.

(*The bell rings.³*)

GOSHAWK. Hark, the bell rings. Come gentlemen. Where shall's all
munch?
JACK DAPPER. I am for Parker's ordinary.
LAXTON. [*Aside to the gallants.*] He's a good guest to'm; he deserves   380
his board. He draws all the gentlemen in a term time⁴ thither.
[*To Jack.*] We'll be your followers Jack, lead the way. [*Aside.*] Look
you, by my faith, the fool has feathered⁵ his nest well.

(*Exeunt gallants.*)

(*Enter Master Gallipot, Master Tiltyard, and servants with water
spaniels and a duck.*)

---

1 *prevent bastards* Keep away from brothels, or, keep an eye on your wife.
2 *same wine* A sweet Spanish wine called "bastard."
3 *The bell rings* City marketing times were regulated, and the bell indicates the close of the
   marketing day or at least a break. Some markets closed in the morning and reopened in the
   afternoon.
4 *he ... board* Dapper deserves to have his board complimentary because he brings Parker's
   so much business; *term time* Times of the year when the law courts were in session.
   During the year's four terms, lawyers, law students, judges, and country gentlemen flooded
   London.
5 *feathered* Jack is apparently decked out in his new spangled feathers.

TILTYARD. Come shut up your shops. Where's Master Openwork?
385 MISTRESS OPENWORK. Nay, ask not me Master Tiltyard.
GALLIPOT. Where's his water dog? Pooh—psst—hur—hur—psst![1]

[*Dog comes.*]

TILTYARD. Come, wenches come. We're going all to Hogsden.[2]
MISTRESS GALLIPOT. To Hogsden, husband?
GALLIPOT. Ay, to Hogsden, pigsney.[3]
390 MISTRESS TILTYARD. I'm not ready husband.
TILTYARD. 'Faith that's well. (*Spits in the dog's mouth.*[4])
Hum—psst—psst.
GALLIPOT. Come Mistress Openwork, you are so long.[5]
MISTRESS OPENWORK. I have no joy of my life, Master Gallipot.
395 GALLIPOT. Pish, let your boy lead his water spaniel along, and we'll
show you the bravest sport at Parlous Pond.[6] Hey Trug,[7] hey Trug,
hey Trug! Here's the best duck in England, except my wife![8] Hey,
hey, hey, fetch, fetch, fetch!
Come, let's away.
400 Of all the year, this is the sportful'st day!

[*Exeunt.*]

---

1 *Pooh ... psst* Noises made to call the dog.
2 *Hogsden* Hoxton, a village north of London.
3 *pigsney* Sweetheart, with a pun on "Hogsden."
4 *Spits ... mouth* This action was thought to obtain a dog's loyalty. Consider the contemporary proverbial saying, "Spit in his mouth and make him a mastiff (as men do with dogs)."
5 *long* Long in the face.
6 *bravest* Best; *Parlous Pond* Pond on the way to Hogsden, north of the city; "perilous" because, according to John Stow, "diverse youths swimming therein have been drowned" (1.16).
7 *Trug* Dog's name.
8 *except ... wife* "Duck" was a common term of endearment at the time, so Gallipot's reference to his wife here is an affectionate one.

[ACT 2, SCENE 2]

(*Enter Sebastian solus.*[1])

SEBASTIAN. If a man have a free will, where should the use
More perfect shine than in his will to love?
All creatures have their liberty in that;

(*Enter Sir Alexander [unseen] and [he] listens to [Sebastian].*)

Though else kept under servile yoke and fear,
The very bondslave has his freedom there.   5
Amongst a world of creatures voiced and silent,
Must my desires wear fetters? [*Aside, seeing Sir Alexander.*] Yea,
     are you
So near? Then I must break with my heart's truth;
Meet grief at a back way. [*Aloud.*] Well: why suppose
The two-leaved[2] tongues of slander or of truth   10
Pronounce Moll loathsome; if before my love[3]
She appear fair, what injury have I?
I have the thing I like. In all things else
Mine own eye guides me, and I find 'em prosper;[4]
Life, what should ail it° now? I know that man   *Sebastian's eye* 15
Ne'er truly loves—if he gainsay't,° he lies—   *denies it*
That winks and marries with his father's eyes.[5]
I'll keep mine own wide open.

(*Enter Moll and a porter with a viol*[6] *[on] his back.*)

SIR ALEXANDER. [*Aside.*]   Here's brave willfulness.
A made match:[7] here she comes; they met o'purpose.

---

1 *solus* Alone.
2 *two-leaved* Made of two parts, hinged or forked.
3 *before my love* In my loving gaze.
4 *I find ... prosper* I find success.
5 *I know ... eyes* If a man closes his eyes—"winks"—and chooses his bride according to
     what his father sees rather than what he sees, he will never truly find love. Anyone who says
     otherwise is lying.
6 *viol* Viol de gamba, a large, stringed instrument similar to a cello.
7 *made match* Arranged encounter.

20 PORTER. Must I carry this great fiddle to your chamber, Mistress
      Mary?
    MOLL. Fiddle, goodman hog-rubber?¹ [*Aside.*] Some of these
      porters bear so much for others they have no time to carry wit for
      themselves.
25 PORTER. To your own chamber, Mistress Mary?
    MOLL. [*Aside.*] Who'll hear an ass speak? [*To Porter.*] —Whither
      else, goodman pageant-bearer?² [*Aside.*] —They're³ people of the
      worst memories.

    (*Exit Porter.*)

    SEBASTIAN. Why 'twere too great a burden, love, to have them carry
30   things in their minds and o'their backs together.
    MOLL. Pardon me sir; I thought not you so near.
    SIR ALEXANDER. [*Aside.*] So, so, so.
    SEBASTIAN. I would be nearer to thee, and in that fashion that
      makes the best part of all creatures honest.⁴ No otherwise I wish
35   it.
    MOLL. Sir, I am so poor to requite you, you must look for nothing
      but thanks of me. I have no humor to marry. I love to lie a'both
      sides o'th'bed myself; and again, o'th'other side,⁵ a wife, you know,
      ought to be obedient, but I fear me I am too headstrong to obey,
40   therefore I'll ne'er go about it. I love you so well, sir, for your
      good will, I'd be loath you should repent your bargain after, and
      therefore we'll ne'er come together at first. I have the head now
      of myself, and am man enough for a woman.⁶ Marriage is but a
      chopping and changing, where a maiden loses one head and has a
45   worse i'th place.⁷

---

1   *hog-rubber* Yokel.
2   *pageant-bearer* One who carries or moves the equipment, carts, or props for municipal
    pageants, as for Lord Mayor's pageants or royal processions.
3   *They're* Porters are.
4   *in that ... honest* I.e., nearer to her by marriage.
5   *again ... side* On the other hand.
6   *I have ... woman* Men were typically seen as the head of the household and also of the wife;
    Moll claims she is head of herself and is enough of a man to control the woman in her.
7   *maiden ... place* When she marries, a maid loses her maidenhead and gains her husband's
    head as he becomes head of the household.

SIR ALEXANDER. [*Aside*.] The most comfortablest[1] answer from a
roaring girl that ever mine ears drunk in.

SEBASTIAN. This were enough now to affright a fool forever from
thee, when 'tis the music that I love thee for.

SIR ALEXANDER. [*Aside*.] There's a boy spoils all again.   50

MOLL. Believe it, sir, I am not of that disdainful temper, but I could
love you faithfully.[2]

SIR ALEXANDER. [*Aside*.] A pox on you for that word. I like you not
now. You're a cunning roarer; I see that already.

MOLL. But sleep upon this once more, sir. You may chance shift a   55
mind[3] tomorrow; be not too hasty to wrong yourself. Never
while you live, sir, take a wife running;[4] many have run out at
heels[5] that have done't. You see, sir, I speak against myself, and
if every woman would deal with their suitor so honestly, poor
younger brothers would not be so often gulled with old cozening   60
widows that turn o'er all their wealth in trust to some kinsman
and make the poor gentleman work hard for a pension.[6] Fare you
well, sir. [*Moll begins to leave.*]

SEBASTIAN. Nay, prithee one word more!

SIR ALEXANDER. [*Aside*.] How do I wrong this girl; she puts him off   65
still.

MOLL. Think upon this in cold blood, sir; you make as much haste
as if you were a-going upon a sturgeon voyage.[7] Take deliberation,
sir; never choose a wife as if you were going to Virginia.[8]

---

1   *comfortablest*   Most relief-inducing, most comforting.

2   *I am ... faithfully*   I am not such a shrew that I could not love a man—you—faithfully.

3   *shift a mind*   Change your mind.

4   *running*   Hastily, with superficial consideration.

5   *run out at heels*   Proverbial: fallen out of fortune; literally, worn through one's socks.

6   *poor ... pension*   Second sons without inherited land would not be tricked by wealthy
    widows who entice them into bad marriages, in which the widows keep their fortunes by
    signing them over to a relative and make their new husbands subordinate. Moll implies that
    such young men "work hard" paying their sexual debts to the cozening widows in order to
    get an allowance.

7   *sturgeon voyage*   Likely a long trip to Russia, where sturgeon were commonly fished.

8   *never choose ... Virginia*   Never choose a wife quickly out of the assumption that there will
    be a shortage of women, as there would be in Virginia. Moll's examples oppose each other:
    one must be careful not to choose a wife thinking one can simply leave her behind (the
    sturgeon voyage), nor to grab whatever is available because of an assumed necessity (the
    Virginia trip).

[*Moll moves away.*]

70 SEBASTIAN. [*Demonstratively.*] And so we parted, my too cursèd fate.

[*Sebastian stands apart.*]

SIR ALEXANDER. [*Aside.*] She is but cunning, gives him longer time in't.

(*Enter a Tailor.*)

TAILOR. Mistress Moll, Mistress Moll! Soho ho, soho![1]
MOLL. There, boy, there, boy. What, dost thou go a-hawking after
75 me with a red clout[2] on thy finger?
TAILOR. I forgot to take measure on you for your new breeches.
SIR ALEXANDER. [*Aside.*] Heyday, breeches! What will he marry a
monster with two trinkets?[3] What age is this? If the wife go in
breeches, the man must wear long coats[4] like a fool.
80 MOLL. What fiddlings here, would not the old pattern[5] have served
your turn?
TAILOR. You change the fashion. You say you'll have the great Dutch
slop,[6] Mistress Mary.
MOLL. Why, sir, I say so still.
85 TAILOR. Your breeches then will take up a yard more.

---

1   *soho!* Exclamation of discovery, used in falconry and in hunting rabbits.
2   *red clout* Hawking lures were often red cloth, though Moll here may be playfully refer-
    ring to the tailor's measuring tape or pincushion, which he uses later in the scene.
3   *monster* Malformed or deformed human, considered unnatural or unhuman, ascribed to
    hermaphrodites; *two trinkets* Two testicles, or, possibly two sets—male and female—of
    genitals.
4   *long coats* Petticoats, long-skirted garments worn by women or by young children of either
    sex.
5   *fiddlings* Fine or fussy adjustments or alterations; with a bawdy innuendo; *old pat-
    tern* The previous pattern for sewing her clothes. Moll objects to requiring a new fitting
    and the tailor re-measuring.
6   *You change the fashion* You've asked for a different style; *Dutch slop* Slops were breeches
    that were knee length or shorter and very baggy. The Dutch slop was especially loose and
    took a great deal of fabric.

MOLL. Well, pray look it be put in,[1] then.

TAILOR. It shall stand round and full,[2] I warrant you.

MOLL. Pray make 'em easy enough.

TAILOR. I know my fault now; t'other was somewhat stiff between
the legs, I'll make these open enough,[3] I warrant you.   90

SIR ALEXANDER. [*Aside.*] Here's good gear[4] towards! I have brought
up my son to marry a Dutch slop and a French doublet: a codpiece daughter.

TAILOR. So, I have gone as far as I can go.[5]

MOLL. Why then, farewell.   95

TAILOR. If you go presently to your chamber, Mistress Mary, pray
send me the measure of your thigh, by some honest body.[6]

MOLL. Well, sir, I'll send it by a porter presently.

(*Exit Moll.*)

TAILOR. So you had need; it is a lusty one. Both of them[7] would
make any porter's back ache in England.   100

(*Exit Tailor.*)

SEBASTIAN. [*To himself.*] I have examined the best part of man—
Reason and judgment—and in love, they tell me,
They leave me uncontrolled.[8] He that is swayed
By an unfeeling blood, past heat of love,

---

1 *yard* Measure of fabric, but here also jokingly references the word's connotation of
   "penis"; *look it be put in* Continuation of the bawdy implications of yard.

2 *stand ... full* Reference to the wide, round leg of the slop, but also an innuendo for a male
   erection, continuing the sexual wordplay.

3 *stiff ... legs* Extension of the bawdy play on erection; *open enough* Reference both to the
   female body and to the fit of the breeches.

4 *Here's good gear* Expression of satisfaction, here meant sarcastically, with an additional pun
   on "gear" as apparel and genitals.

5 *as ... go* Implying first that it would be indecent for him to take any more measurements,
   as of the thigh discussed later, and second that he has no more sexual plays to make.

6 *by ... body* By someone honest.

7 *them* Moll's thighs.

8 *in love ... uncontrolled* Reason and judgment do not control me when I am in love.

105   His springtime must needs err:[1] his watch ne'er goes right
       That sets his dial by a rusty clock.
       SIR ALEXANDER. [*Comes forward.*] So, and which is that rusty clock,
         sir, you?
       SEBASTIAN. The clock at Ludgate,[2] sir, it ne'er goes true.
       SIR ALEXANDER. But thou goest falser. Not thy father's cares
110   Can keep thee right, when that insensible work[3]
       Obeys the workman's art, lets off the hour,
       And stops again when time is satisfied;
       But thou runst on, and judgment, thy main wheel,
       Beats by all stops as if the work would break,
115   Begun with long pains for a minute's ruin,[4]
       Much like a suffering man brought up with care,
       At last bequeathed to shame and a short prayer.
       SEBASTIAN. I taste you bitterer than I can deserve, sir.
       SIR ALEXANDER. Who has bewitched, thee son? What devil or drug
120   Hath wrought upon the weakness of thy blood°   *passion*
       And betrayed all her hopes[5] to ruinous folly?
       Oh, wake from drowsy and enchanted shame,
       Wherein thy soul sits with a golden dream
       Flattered and poisoned! I am old my son,
125   Oh, let me prevail quickly,
       For I have weightier business of mine own[6]
       Than to chide thee. I must not to my grave,
       As a drunkard to his bed, whereon he lies
       Only to sleep, and never cares to rise.
130   Let me dispatch in time:[7] come no more near her.

---

1 *unfeeling blood* Blood no longer led by passion and vigor; *past heat of love* Old; *spring-time* Time for the passion of love in youth; *err* Go astray or fail. Sebastian says that one ruled by someone who has a dampened sense of passion will never enjoy his own.

2 *Ludgate* One of the city gates, where there was a large clock.

3 *that insensible work* I.e., the clock at Ludgate.

4 *But ... ruin* Alexander compares Sebastian to a clock that is out of control: the wheel of the clock does not stop at the hour as it should, but continues running, threatening to destroy itself; *minute's ruin* Reference to the suddenness of Sebastian's dalliance with Moll and the short-term satisfaction that is the cause of his destruction in Alexander's eyes.

5 *her hopes* The hopes of his blood, i.e., his lineage.

6 *weightier ... mine own* The business of his own approaching death.

7 *dispatch in time* Go away, or, do my business quickly (rather than have to deal with this supposed love affair).

SEBASTIAN. Not honestly? Not in the way of marriage?
SIR ALEXANDER. What say'st thou, "marriage"? In what place, the
    sessions house?[1]
And who shall give the bride, prithee? An indictment?
SEBASTIAN. Sir, now ye take part with the world to wrong her.
SIR ALEXANDER. Why, wouldst thou fain marry to be pointed at?   135
Alas, the number's great; do not o'erburden't.[2]
Why, as good marry a beacon on a hill,
Which all the country fix their eyes upon,
As her thy folly dotes on.[3] If thou long'st
To have the story of thy infamous fortunes   140
Serve for discourse in ordinaries and taverns,
Thou'rt in the way;[4] or to confound thy name,
Keep on, thou canst not miss it;[5] or to strike
Thy wretched father to untimely coldness,
Keep the left hand still, it will bring thee to't.[6]   145
Yet if no tears wrung from thy father's eyes,
Nor sighs that fly in sparkles[7] from his sorrows,
Had power to alter what is willful in thee,
Methinks her very name should fright thee from her,
And never trouble me.   150
SEBASTIAN. Why is the name of Moll so fatal, sir?
SIR ALEXANDER. Many one, sir, where suspect is entered,
Forseek° all London from one end to t'other   *search thoroughly*
More whores of that name, than of any ten other.[8]
SEBASTIAN. What's that to her? Let those blush for themselves.   155
Can any guilt in others condemn her?
I've vowed to love her. Let all storms oppose me

---

1   *sessions house*   Courthouse.
2   *Alas ... o'erburden't*   A great number of people make foolish choices in marriage; don't add
    to the total.
3   *Why ... on*   It would be as good to marry a bright light on a hill that draws everyone's eyes
    as to marry Moll, whom you foolishly dote upon.
4   *Thou'rt ... way*   You're on your way.
5   *thou canst ... it*   You can't fail to do it.
6   *untimely coldness*   Early death;   *Keep ... to't*   Keep on the path (left) you have chosen, and
    it will hasten that death.
7   *in sparkles*   Like sparks.
8   *Many ... other*   Many constables (i.e., those who enter the names of suspects into a log)
    search London for whores and find ten times as many prostitutes named Moll as any other.

That ever beat against the breast of man;
Nothing but death's black tempest shall divide us.
160 SIR ALEXANDER. Oh, folly, that can dote on nought but shame!
SEBASTIAN. Put case[1] a wanton itch runs through one name
More than another: is that name the worse
Where honesty sits possessed in't? It should rather
Appear more excellent and deserve more praise
165 When through foul mists a brightness it can raise.
Why, there are of the devil's,[2] honest gentlemen,
And well descended, keep° an open house;[3]   who keep
And some o'th'good man's° that are errant knaves.   Christ's name
He hates unworthily that by rote contemns,
170 For the name neither saves, nor yet condemns.[4]
And for her honesty, I have made such proof on't[5]
In several forms, so nearly° watched her ways,   closely
I will maintain that strict against an army,
Excepting you, my father. Here's her worst:°   worst quality
175 Sh'has a bold spirit that mingles with mankind,°   manliness
But nothing else comes near it,[6] and oftentimes
Through° her apparel somewhat shames her birth,[7]   because of
But she is loose in nothing but in mirth.
Would all Molls were no worse!
180 SIR ALEXANDER. [Aside.] This way I toil in vain and give but aim[8]
To infamy and ruin. He will fall;
My blessing cannot stay him. All my joys
Stand at the brink of a devouring flood
And will be willfully swallowed, willfully!
185 But why so vain let all these tears be lost?
I'll pursue her to shame, and so all's crossed.°   thwarted

---

1 *Put case* Suppose.
2 *of the devil's* Of the devil's name; even those who share the nickname of the devil—like "Old Nick" or "Old Ned"—can be honest.
3 *open house* Hospitable home.
4 *He ... condemns* He who scorns ("contemns") in a mechanical way ("by rote"), does so unfairly; a name neither saves nor damns ("condemns").
5 *honesty ... on't* I have proven her honesty so well to myself.
6 *But ... near it* None of her other parts come near men.
7 *oftentimes ... birth* Through her manly clothing choices, Moll brings shame upon herself—her birth status—or her female sex.
8 *give but aim* Only give Sebastian a target.

(*Exit Sir Alexander.*)

SEBASTIAN. He is gone with some strange purpose, whose effect
Will hurt me little if he shoot so wide
To think I love so blindly. I but feed
His heart to this match to draw on th'other,[1]   190
Wherein my joy sits with a full wish crowned—
Only his mood excepted,[2] which must change
By opposite policies, courses indirect;[3]
Plain dealing in this world takes no effect.
This mad girl I'll acquaint with my intent,   195
Get her assistance, make my fortunes° known;   *circumstances*
'Twixt lovers' hearts, she's a fit instrument,
And has the art to help them to their own.
By her advice, for in that craft she's wise,
My love and I may meet, spite of all spies.   200

(*Exit Sebastian.*)

[ACT 3, SCENE I]

(*Enter Laxton in Gray's Inn Fields with the Coachman.*)

LAXTON. Coachman!
COACHMAN. Here, sir.
LAXTON. There's a tester[4] more; prithee drive thy coach to the hither
    end of Marybone Park,[5] a fit place for Moll to get in.
COACHMAN. Marybone Park, sir?   5
LAXTON. Ay, it's in our way, thou know'st.

---

1   *I but feed ... th'other*   I only encourage my father to believe I pursue Moll to get my
    preferred match (Mary Fitzallard).
2   *Only ... excepted*   Unless Alexander does not approve of her.
3   *By opposite ... indirect*   By opposing strategies and indirect means.
4   *tester*   Sixpence.
5   *Marybone Park*   Marylebone Park, which is today Regent's Park, was to the west and north
    of Gray's Inn Fields. It was a Royal Hunting Park until the English Civil War. Laxton plans
    to have the coach meet them at the end of the park and then drive them to Brentford.
    Laxton may also reference "marrowbones" when he calls it *Marybone*, a name the Coachman
    confirms in the next line.

COACHMAN. It shall be done, sir.

LAXTON. Coachman!

COACHMAN. Anon, sir.

10 LAXTON. Are we fitted with good frampold jades?[1]

COACHMAN. The best in Smithfield,[2] I warrant you, sir.

LAXTON. May we safely take the upper hand of any coached velvet cap or tuftaffety[3] jacket? For they keep a wild swaggering in coaches nowadays; the highways are stopt with them.

15 COACHMAN. My life for yours, and baffle 'em,[4] too, sir.—Why, they are the same jades, believe it, sir, that have drawn all your famous whores to Ware!

LAXTON. Nay, then they know their business; they need no more instructions.

20 COACHMAN. They're so used to such journeys, sir, I never use whip to 'em; for if they catch but the scent of a wench once, they run like devils.

(*Exit Coachman with his whip.*)

LAXTON. Fine Cerberus![5] That rogue will have the start of a thousand ones, for whilst others trot afoot, he'll ride prancing to hell
25 upon a coach-horse.[6]—Stay, 'tis now about the hours of her appointment, but yet I see her not.

(*The clock strikes three.*)

---

1 *frampold jades* Fiery, spirited horses. Jades were draught horses or cart horses rather than fine riding horses.

2 *Smithfield* Large cattle and meat market in east London, close to Gray's Inn.

3 *velvet cap* Student or doctor, who wears a distinctive velvet cap; *tuftaffety* Luxurious fabric—taffeta with tufts of velvet nap—which would have been worn by the fashionable wealthy, or those attempting to appear as such. Laxton asks the coachman if they can outpace or get around other coaches full of finely dressed swaggerers, or insolent quarrelers, who clog the roadways.

4 *My life for yours* I'd bet my life on it; *baffle 'em* Humiliate and confound them.

5 *Cerberus* Three-headed hound who guards the gate to hell in Greek and Roman mythology.

6 *the start of* A head-start on; *whilst ... coach-horse* Others follow the coachman to hell by foot while he rides his horse.

Hark, what's this? One, two, three: three by the clock at Savoy.[1]
This is the hour, and Gray's Inn Fields the place, she swore she'd
meet me. Ha, yonder's two Inns o'Court men[2] with one wench,
but that's not she: they walk toward Islington[3] out of my way.   30
I see none yet drest like her. I must look for a shag ruff, a frieze
jerkin, a short sword, and a safeguard, or I get none: why, Moll,
prithee make haste, or the coachman will curse us anon.

(*Enter Moll like a man.*[4])

MOLL. [*Aside.*] Oh, here's my gentleman. If they would keep their
days as well with their mercers as their hours with their harlots,   35
no bankrupt would give seven score pound for a sergeant's place.[5]
For, would you know a catchpole rightly derived: the corruption
of a Citizen is the generation of a sergeant.[6] How his eye hawks
for venery![7] [*To Laxton.*] Come are you ready, sir?
LAXTON. Ready? For what, sir?   40
MOLL. Do you ask that now, sir? Why was this meeting 'pointed?[8]
LAXTON. I thought you mistook me, sir.
You seem to be some young barrister;
I have no suit in law—all my land's sold,
I praise heaven for't, 't has rid me of much trouble.   45
MOLL. Then I must wake you, sir. Where stands the coach?
LAXTON. Who's this? Moll? Honest Moll?
MOLL. So young and purblind?[9] You're an old wanton in your eyes,
I see that.

---

1 *Savoy* Former medieval palace near the Inns of Court.
2 *Inns ... men* Students of law or benchers residing at the Inns of Court. Inns men were
   reputed as playboys.
3 *Islington* Village just north of London.
4 *like a man* In a new outfit fully comprised of men's clothing.
5 *If they ... place* If gallants would keep their appointments with those to whom they owe
   money as well as they do with their harlots, then they wouldn't be paying one hundred and
   forty pounds to become sergeants (thereby obtaining an income to save themselves from
   debtors' prison, while helping to send others there); *mercers* Textile dealers.
6 *For ... sergeant* Moll deduces the origins of a "catchpole" (a sergeant): a tradesman becomes
   a sergeant to avoid prison for his debts.
7 *his eye ... venery* Laxton has a sharp eye for sexual conquests.
8 *'pointed* Appointed.
9 *purblind* Partly blind.

50 LAXTON. Thou'rt admirably suited for the Three Pigeons[1] at Brentford. I'll swear, I knew thee not.

MOLL. I'll swear you did not: but you shall know me now.

[*Moll starts to remove her cloak.*]

LAXTON. No, not here! We shall be spied, i'faith! The coach is
better, come.

[*Laxton begins to leave.*]

55 MOLL. Stay!

LAXTON. What, wilt thou untruss a point,[2] Moll?

(*She puts off her cloak and draws [a sword].*)

MOLL. Yes, here's the point that I untruss; 't has but one tag.[3] 'Twill
serve, though, to tie up a rogue's tongue.

LAXTON. How?

60 MOLL. [*Shows money to Laxton.*] There's the gold
With which you hired your hackney,[4] here's her pace.
She racks hard, and perhaps your bones will feel it.
Ten angels of mine own, I've put to thine;
Win 'em, & wear 'em.[5]

LAXTON.   Hold, Moll! Mistress Mary—

65 MOLL. Draw or I'll serve an execution on thee
Shall lay thee up 'till doomsday.[6]

LAXTON. Draw upon a woman? Why, what dost mean Moll?

MOLL. To teach thy base thoughts manners. Thou'rt one of those
That thinks each woman thy fond flexible[7] whore.

---

1 *Three Pigeons* Popular Brentford tavern and a destination for Londoners.

2 *untruss a point* Undo one of the laces that fastens Moll's hose to her doublet.

3 *point* Sword; *tag* Lace or ribbon for trussing.

4 *hackney* Literally, a horse for hire; figuratively, a prostitute.

5 *Win ... 'em* Moll challenges Laxton to fight her and win the money.

6 *I'll ... doomsday* I'll hit you so hard you'll be laid up until the day of judgment; *serve an
   execution* Legal action meaning to seize someone's goods; Moll indicates the literal beating
   she is ready to administer.

7 *fond flexible* Silly, easy to manipulate.

THOMAS MIDDLETON AND THOMAS DEKKER

If she but cast a liberal eye upon thee,   70
Turn back her head, she's thine;[1] or amongst company,
By chance drink first to thee,[2] then she's quite gone,
There's no means° to help her; nay for a need,[3]   *way*
Wilt swear unto thy credulous fellow lechers
That thou'rt more in favour with a lady   75
At first sight than her monkey all her lifetime.[4]
How many of our sex by such as thou
Have their good thoughts paid with a blasted name°   *reputation*
That never deserved loosely or did trip
In path of whoredom beyond cup and lip?[5]   80
But for the stain of conscience and of soul,
Better had women fall into the hands
Of an act silent than a bragging nothing;[6]
There's no mercy in't. What durst move you, sir,
To think me whorish? A name which I'd tear out   85
From the high German's throat, if it lay ledger° there   *was resident*
To dispatch privy slanders against me!
In thee I defy all men, their worst hates
And their best flatteries, all their golden witchcrafts
With which they entangle the poor spirits of fools:°   *innocents* 90
Distressed° needlewomen and trade-fall'n° wives—   *poor / bankrupt*
Fish that must needs bite or themselves be bitten—
Such hungry things as these may soon be took
With a worm fast'ned on a golden hook.
Those are the lecher's food, his prey. He watches   95

---

1   *If... thine*   If any woman looks at you with a kind eye or turns her head to look at you, you
    think she wants to have sex with you.
2   *drink ... thee*   Is the first to toast him.
3   *for a need*   By necessity.
4   *Wilt ... lifetime*   You'll swear to your friends that a lady will love you more at first sight
    than she loves the monkey that she's had her whole life. Monkeys were pets considered a
    substitute partner for women with excessive desires.
5   *cup and lip*   Proverbial; "many things fall between cup and lip," or, things can go wrong at
    any time. Moll also references the toast she describes earlier in her speech.
6   *Better ... nothing*   A woman is better off if she does something—has sex, presumably—as
    long as the deed remains unspoken, than if she does nothing but is nonetheless the victim
    of a braggart's slander.

For quarrelling wedlocks and poor shifting sisters;[1]
'Tis the best fish he takes. But why, good fisherman,
Am I thought meat for you, that never yet
Had angling rod cast towards me? 'Cause you'll say
100   I'm given to sport,° I'm often merry, jest?   *playfulness*
Had mirth no kindred in the world but lust?
O, shame take all her° friends then! But howe'er   *mirth's*
Thou and the baser world censure my life,
I'll send 'em word by thee, and write so much
105   Upon thy breast,[2] cause thou shalt bear't in mind:
Tell them 'twere base to yield where I have conquered.
I scorn to prostitute myself to a man,
I that can prostitute a man to me![3]
And so I greet thee. [*She draws.*]
LAXTON. [*Laxton draws, in response.*]   Hear me!
MOLL.   Would the spirits
110   Of all my slanders were claspt in thine,
That I might vex an army at one time.[4]

(*They fight. [Moll wounds Laxton.]*)

LAXTON. I do repent me! Hold!
MOLL. You'll die the better Christian then.[5]
LAXTON. I do confess I have wronged thee, Moll.
115   MOLL. Confession is but poor amends for wrong,
      Unless a rope would follow.[6]
LAXTON.   I ask thee pardon.

---

1   *quarrelling wedlocks* Fighting couples; *poor shifting sisters* Single women struggling to
    survive.
2   *write ... breast* Carve on his chest with her sword.
3   *I ... me!* I, who can expose a man to shame, or, who can force a man to lay prostrate before
    me and be at my mercy.
4   *Would ... time* I wish that every slander against me were embodied in you, so I could fight
    them all at once by fighting you.
5   *You'll ... then* Moll treats Laxton's cry of repentance as a confession to God rather than a
    cry for her to stop.
6   *Confession ... follow* Confession does not right your wrongs unless you are hung afterward.
    (Proverbial; "confession of a fault is half amends.")

MOLL. I'm your hired whore, sir!
LAXTON.   I yield both purse and body.
MOLL. Both are mine and now at my disposing.
LAXTON. Spare my life!
MOLL.   I scorn to strike thee basely.
LAXTON. Spoke like a noble girl, i'faith. [*Aside.*] Heart, I think I   120
    fight with a familiar,[1] or the ghost of a fencer. Sh'has wounded
    me gallantly. Call you this a lecherous voyage?[2] Here's blood
    would have served me this seven year in broken heads and cut
    fingers,[3] & it now runs all out together! Pox o'the Three Pigeons!
    I would the coach were here now to carry me to the   125
    chirurgeon's.[4]

(*Exit Laxton.*)

MOLL. If I could meet my enemies one by one thus,
    I might make pretty shift with 'em[5] in time,
    And make 'em know, she that has wit and spirit
    May scorn to live beholding° to her body for meat,°   *obligated / food* 130
    Or for apparel, like your common dame
    That makes shame get her clothes to cover shame.[6]
    Base is that mind that kneels unto her body
    As if a husband stood in awe on's° wife;   *of his*
    My spirit shall be mistress of this house°   *body* 135
    As long as I have time in't.

(*Enter Trapdoor [who does not recognize Moll].*)

                    —Oh,
Here comes my man that would be;[7] 'tis his hour.
Faith, a good well-set fellow, if his spirit

---

1 *familiar* Devilish spirit, typically in service of a witch or sorcerer.
2 *Call ... voyage?* Was this the amorous assignation I intended?
3 *Here's ... fingers* I'm bleeding enough for seven years' worth of minor injuries.
4 *chirurgeon's* Surgeon's.
5 *pretty ... 'em* Deal with them well.
6 *your common ... shame* The common woman who engages in shameful acts so she can buy
    clothes, which then cover her nakedness—her shame.
7 *man ... be* Proposed servant.

Be answerable to his umbles.° He walks stiff,   *inward parts*
140   But whether he will stand to't stiffly, there's the point.[1]
'Has a good calf for't, and ye shall have many a woman
Choose him she means to make her head by his calf;[2]
I do not know their tricks in't.[3] Faith, he seems
A man without; I'll try what he is within.[4]
145   TRAPDOOR. She told me Gray's Inn Fields 'twixt three & four.
I'll fit her mistress-ship with a piece of service;[5]
I'm hired to rid the town of one mad girl.

(*She jostles him.*)

[*To Moll.*] What a pox ails you sir?
MOLL. [*Aside.*] He begins like a gentleman.
150   TRAPDOOR. Heart, is the field so narrow, or your eyesight?

(*She comes towards him.*)

Life, he comes back again!
MOLL. Was this spoke to me, sir?
TRAPDOOR. I cannot tell, sir.
MOLL. Go, you're a coxcomb.[6]
155   TRAPDOOR. Coxcomb?
MOLL. You're a slave.[7]
TRAPDOOR. I hope there's law for you,[8] sir.
MOLL. Yea, do you see, sir?

---

1   *He ... point*   He walks tall, but Moll questions his ability to follow through. Moll's evalu-
    ation of Trapdoor's bravery includes several double entendres on "stiff," "stand to," "stiffly,"
    and "point."
2   *Choose ... calf*   A woman often chooses the man she will marry, who thus becomes the head
    of the couple, by his calf (his looks and bearing).
3   *tricks in't*   Strategy of that approach.
4   *he seems ... within*   He seems to be a man on the outside; I'll test whether he's a man on the
    inside.
5   *fit ... service*   Sarcastic expression; I'll give her some service!
6   *coxcomb*   Fool, ass.
7   *slave*   Subject to another person, low-born.
8   *I hope there's law for you*   I hope you get sued or charged with a crime.

(*Turns his hat.*[1])

TRAPDOOR. Heart, this is no good dealing. Pray, let me know what
house you're of.[2]   160
MOLL. One of the Temple,[3] sir.

(*Fillips*[4] *him.*)

TRAPDOOR. Mass, so methinks.
MOLL. And yet, sometime I lie about Chick Lane.[5]
TRAPDOOR. I like you the worse because you shift your lodging so
often. I'll not meddle with you for that trick, sir.   165
MOLL. A good shift,[6] but it shall not serve your turn.
TRAPDOOR. You'll give me leave to pass about my business, sir?
MOLL. Your business? I'll make you wait on me before I ha' done,
and glad to serve me too.
TRAPDOOR. How, sir, serve you? Not if there were no more men in   170
England.
MOLL. But if there were no more women in England, I hope you'd
wait upon your mistress then.
TRAPDOOR. Mistress?
MOLL. Oh, you're a tried spirit at a push,[7] sir.   175
TRAPDOOR. What would your worship have me do?
MOLL. You a fighter?
TRAPDOOR. No, I praise heaven, I had better grace & more
manners.
MOLL. As how, I pray, sir?   180
TRAPDOOR. Life, 't had been a beastly part of me to have drawn my
weapons upon my mistress. All the world would ha' cried shame
of me[8] for that.

---

1   *Turns his hat*   Impudent gesture.
2   *Pray ... of*   Please, tell me which Inn of Court you are a member of.
3   *Temple*   Either the Inner Temple or Middle Temple; both were Inns of Court.
4   *Fillips*   Strikes with the back of a finger.
5   *Chick Lane*   Rough street in London; it led into the Smithfield livestock market.
6   *shift*   Stratagem.
7   *tried spirit*   Well-tested man (meant sarcastically);   *at a push*   When called upon, in an
    emergency.
8   *cried shame of me*   Condemned me.

MOLL. Why, but you knew me not.

185 TRAPDOOR. Do not say so, mistress. I knew you by your wide
straddle, as well as if I had been in your belly.[1]

MOLL. Well, we shall try you further; i'th'meantime, we give you
entertainment.

TRAPDOOR. Thank your good mistress-ship.

190 MOLL. How many suits have you?

TRAPDOOR. No more suits than backs, mistress.

MOLL. Well if you deserve, I cast off this next week, and you may
creep into't.[2]

TRAPDOOR. Thank your good worship.

195 MOLL. Come, follow me to Saint Thomas Apostles.[3]
I'll put a livery[4] cloak upon your back, the first thing I do.

TRAPDOOR. I follow my dear mistress.

(*Exeunt omnes.*)

[ACT 3, SCENE 2]

(*Enter Mistress Gallipot as from supper, her husband after her.*)

GALLIPOT. What, Pru! Nay, sweet Prudence!

MISTRESS GALLIPOT. What a pruing keep you! I think the baby
would have a teat it kyes[5] so. Pray be not so fond of me; leave
your city humours. I'm vext at you to see how like a calf you come
5 bleating after me.[6]

GALLIPOT. Nay, honey Pru, how does your rising up before all the
table show?[7] And flinging from my friends so uncivilly? Fie, Pru,
fie! Come.

---

1 *as if ... belly* As if I had been born of your womb, or as if I had had sex with you. Trapdoor
continues a line of innuendos from "beastly part," "drawn my weapons," and "straddle."

2 *this* Her suit; *you may creep into't* You may have the suit. Giving castoff clothes to one's
servants was a common practice.

3 *Saint Thomas Apostles* Church in the clothiers' neighborhood in central London.

4 *livery* Official clothing denoting a servant of a particular master.

5 *the baby* Gallipot; *kyes* Cries.

6 *leave ... me* Toss away your city affectations of fondness; it annoys me that you follow me
like a crying calf looking for its mother.

7 *rising ... show?* How does it look when you get up from the table abruptly?

MISTRESS GALLIPOT. Then up and ride,[1] i'faith.

GALLIPOT. Up and ride? Nay my pretty Pru, that's far from my   10
thought, duck.[2] Why mouse, thy mind is nibbling at something,
what is't? What lies upon thy stomach?[3]

MISTRESS GALLIPOT. Such an ass as you! Heyday, you're best turn
midwife, or physician; you're a pothecary already, but I'm none of
your drugs.[4]   15

GALLIPOT. Thou art a sweet drug, sweetest Pru, and the more thou
art pounded, the more precious.[5]

MISTRESS GALLIPOT. Must you be prying into a woman's secrets?[6]
Say ye?

GALLIPOT. Woman's secrets?   20

MISTRESS GALLIPOT. What? I cannot have a qualm come upon me
but your teeth waters[7] 'till your nose hang over it.[8]

GALLIPOT. It is my love, dear wife.

MISTRESS GALLIPOT. Your love? Your love is all words; give me
deeds. I cannot abide a man that's too fond over me—so   25
cookish.[9] Thou dost not know how to handle a woman in her
kind.[10]

GALLIPOT. No Pru? Why, I hope I have handled—

MISTRESS GALLIPOT. Handle a fool's head of your own.—Fie, fie!

---

1   *up and ride*   Go and do what you like, with bawdy implications, which Master Gallipot
    seizes on in his following comment.

2   *Up ... duck*   Playing off of Mistress Gallipot's exclamation, Gallipot jokes that she is asking
    for sex, and insists he's not interested right now;   *duck*   Term of affection—as is "mouse"
    in the following sentence.

3   *What ... stomach?*   Gallipot asks what bothers his wife, but Mistress Gallipot interprets the
    line literally and makes a sexual pun in her response that "such an ass as [Gallipot]" lies on
    her.

4   *you're best ... physician*   You're better off being a physician or a midwife (if you want to get
    physical with me);   *you're a ... drugs*   You're a pharmacist already, but I'm not one of your
    drugs, punning on "drudge" for drug; that is, she refuses to be his servant and submit to
    labor—sexual or otherwise—with him.

5   *pounded ... precious*   Reference to the practice of using a mortar and pestle to break down
    medicinal ingredients, with a bawdy pun on "pounded."

6   *a woman's secrets*   A woman's private thoughts or her private parts.

7   *teeth waters*   Mouth waters; proverbial.

8   *your nose ... it*   You have an inclination; proverbially, "to hang a nose" is to have a
    hankering.

9   *cookish*   Like a cook, fussing over dinner.

10   *in her kind*   According to her nature.

30 GALLIPOT. Ha, ha, 'tis such a wasp! It does me good now to have
her sting me, little rogue.

MISTRESS GALLIPOT. Now fie, how you vex me! I cannot abide
these apron husbands: such cotqueans![1] You overdo your things;
they become you scurvily.[2]

35 GALLIPOT. [Aside.] Upon my life, she breeds.[3] Heaven knows how
I have strained myself to please her, night and day. I wonder why
we citizens should get children so fretful and untoward in the
breeding, their fathers being for the most part as gentle as milch
kine.[4]—Shall I leave thee, my Pru?

40 MISTRESS GALLIPOT. Fie, fie, fie!

GALLIPOT. Thou shalt not be vext no more, pretty kind rogue. Take
no cold, sweet Pru.

(*Exit Master Gallipot.*)

MISTRESS GALLIPOT. As your wit has done.—Now, Master Laxton,
show your head. [*She brings forth a letter.*] What news from you?
45 Would any husband suspect that a woman crying, "Buy any scurvy-grass," should bring love letters amongst her herbs[5] to his wife?
Pretty trick, fine conveyance! Had jealousy a thousand eyes, a silly
woman with scurvy-grass blinds them all.
Laxton, with bays[6]
50 Crown I thy wit for this; it deserves praise.
This makes me affect° thee more; this proves thee wise,   *like, fancy*
'Lack° what poor shift° is love forced to devise?—   *alack / trick*
To th'point.

(*She reads the letter.*)

---

1   *cotqueans* Men who act the housewife; an insult.
2   *scurvily* Poorly, shabbily.
3   *she breeds* I.e., her bad mood indicates she is pregnant.
4   *milch kine* Milk cows.
5   *woman ... scurvy-grass* Street crier advertising that she is selling scurvy-grass, a plant whose
    oil was thought to combat scurvy;   *bring ... herbs* Hide love correspondence in the plants
    being sold.
6   *bays* Leaves from a bay tree, for crowning poets and conquerors.

"O Sweet Creature,"—a sweet beginning!— "pardon my long
absence, for thou shalt shortly be possessed with my presence.   55
Though Demophon was false to Phyllis,[1] I will be to thee as Pan-
da-rus was to Cres-sida;[2] though Aeneas made an ass of Dido,[3]
I will die to thee ere I do so.[4] O sweetest creature, make much
of me, for no man beneath the silver moon shall make more[5]
of a woman than I do of thee. Furnish me therefore with thirty   60
pounds; you must do it of necessity for me. I languish 'till I see
some comfort come from thee, protesting not to die in thy debt,
but rather to live so, as hitherto I have and will.
                                              Thy true Laxton, ever."

Alas, poor gentleman! Troth I pity him.   65
How shall I raise this money? Thirty pound?
'Tis thirty, sure, a three before an O;
I know his threes too well. My childbed linen?[6]
Shall I pawn that for him? Then if my mark[7]
Be known I am undone! It may be thought   70
My husband's bankrupt.[8] Which way shall I turn?
Laxton, what with my own fears, and thy wants,
I'm like a needle 'twixt two adamants.[9]

---

1 *Demophon ... Phyllis* In Greek mythology, Demophon, King of Athens, married the Thra-
cian Phyllis during his trip home from Troy. He left her to go back to Athens, promising he
would return. He instead sailed to Cyprus and settled there, and when he did not return as
he said he would, Phyllis committed suicide.

2 *Pan-da-rus ... Cres-sida* In medieval retellings of the Troilus story, Pandarus is the uncle
to Cressida who arranges for her to meet with her beloved Troilus. Mistress Gallipot, who
stumbles over the names, misses the fact that Laxton has picked out Cressida's pimp rather
than her lover as his stand-in.

3 *Aeneas ... Dido* Aeneas is the lover of Dido, the Queen of Carthage, in *The Aeneid*. Dido
commits suicide after Aeneas, following the bidding of Jupiter via Mercury, leaves her to
continue on his mission to found a new Troy.

4 *die ... so* I will die before I make such a fool out of you, with a pun on "die" as "orgasm."

5 *more* In Laxton's case, make more money.

6 *childbed linen* Fine linen for sheets and bedclothes gotten at the time of the birth of her
children. The quality of such items made them valuable keepsakes.

7 *mark* Embroidered monogram.

8 *Then if ... bankrupt* If anyone recognizes the mark, the person will guess that Mistress
Gallipot sold the linen because Master Gallipot is destitute.

9 *adamants* Very hard minerals, here identified with lodestones (magnets). Mistress Gallipot
uses the idea of a compass; the needle (herself) is pulled in opposite directions by the two
magnetic stones (Gallipot and Laxton).

(*Enter Master Gallipot hastily.*)

GALLIPOT. Nay, nay, wife, the women are all up. [*Aside.*] Ha? How?
75 Reading a'letters? I smell a goose, a couple of capons, and a gam-
mon of bacon from her mother out of the country, I hold my life.
Steal—steal— [*Master Gallipot goes behind Mistress Gallipot to read
over her shoulder.*]
MISTRESS GALLIPOT. Oh, beshrew[1] your heart!
GALLIPOT. What letter's that? I'll see't. (*She tears the letter.*)
80 MISTRESS GALLIPOT. Oh, would thou had'st no eyes to see the
downfall of me and thyself. I'm forever, forever I'm undone.
GALLIPOT. What ails my Pru? What paper's that thou tear'st?
MISTRESS GALLIPOT. Would I could tear
My very heart in pieces! For my soul
85 Lies on the rack of shame that tortures me
Beyond a woman's suffering.
GALLIPOT. What means this?
MISTRESS GALLIPOT. Had you no other vengeance to throw down,
But even in height of all my joys—
GALLIPOT. Dear woman!
MISTRESS GALLIPOT. When the full sea of pleasure and content
90 Seemed to flow over me?
GALLIPOT. As thou desirest
To keep me out of Bedlam,[2] tell what troubles thee!
Is not thy child at nurse fallen sick, or dead?
MISTRESS GALLIPOT. Oh, no!
GALLIPOT. Heavens bless me, are my barns and houses
95 Yonder at Hockley Hole[3] consumed with fire?
I can build more, sweet Pru.
MISTRESS GALLIPOT. 'Tis worse, 'tis worse.
GALLIPOT. My factor broke, or is the *Jonas*[4] sunk?

---

1 *beshrew* Curse.
2 *Bedlam* Bethlehem Hospital in north London, an institution for those deemed mad.
3 *Hockley Hole* Hockley-in-the-Hole, village north of London near Clerkenwell.
4 *My factor broke* Gallipot's broker, or sales agent, gone bankrupt; *Jonas* A ship carrying
Gallipot's goods or in which he has invested.

MISTRESS GALLIPOT. Would all we had were swallowed in
   the waves,
   Rather than both should be the scorn of slaves![1]
GALLIPOT. I'm at my wit's end!   100
MISTRESS GALLIPOT. Oh, my dear husband,
   Where once I thought myself a fixèd star,
   Placed only in the heaven of thine arms,
   I fear now I shall prove a wanderer.
   O, Laxton, Laxton, is it then my fate   105
   To be by thee o'erthrown?
GALLIPOT.   Defend me, wisdom,
   From falling into frenzy!° On my knees,   *madness*
   Sweet Pru, speak! What's that Laxton who so heavy lies
   On thy bosom?[2]
MISTRESS GALLIPOT.   I shall sure run mad.
GALLIPOT. I shall run mad for company, then. Speak to me,   110
   I'm Gallipot thy husband—Pru!—Why Pru,
   Art° sick in conscience for some villainous deed   *are you*
   Thou wert about to act? Didst mean to rob me?
   Tush, I forgive thee. Hast thou on my bed
   Thrust my soft pillow under another's head?   115
   I'll wink at[3] all faults, Pru; 'las that's no more,
   Than what some neighbours near thee have done before.
   Sweet honey Pru, what's that Laxton?
MISTRESS GALLIPOT.   Oh!
GALLIPOT. Out with him.[4]
MISTRESS GALLIPOT.   Oh, he's born to be my undoer.
   This hand which thou call'st thine, to him was given;   120
   To him was I made sure i'th'sight of heaven.[5]

---

1 *scorn of slaves* Object of ridicule for the lowliest members of society.
2 *Laxton ... bosom* Gallipot's inquiry as to who has affected Mistress Gallipot's heart unwit-
   tingly comments on her flirtation with Laxton.
3 *wink at* Close my eyes to.
4 *Out with him* Out with the secret identity.
5 *To him ... heaven* I was pledged to Laxton in marriage under God. A proven betrothal or
   pre-contract could dissolve the Gallipots' marriage, so this is a serious threat (and a lie, on
   Mistress Gallipot's part).

GALLIPOT. I never heard this thunder.

MISTRESS GALLIPOT.   Yes, yes, before
  I was to thee contracted, to him I swore.
  Since last I saw him twelve months three times told
125 The moon hath drawn through her light silver bow,
  For o'er the seas he went, and it was said—
  But Rumour[1] lies—that he in France was dead.
  But he's alive; oh, he's alive! He sent
  That letter to me, which in rage I rent,
130 Swearing with oaths most damnably to have me
  Or tear me from this° bosom. Oh heavens save me!   *Gallipot's*

GALLIPOT. My heart will break. Shamed and undone forever!

MISTRESS GALLIPOT. So black a day, poor wretch, went o'er thee
    never.

GALLIPOT. If thou shouldst wrestle with him at the law,
135 Thou'rt sure to fall; no odd slight, no prevention.[2]
  I'll tell him th'art with child.

MISTRESS GALLIPOT.   Um!

GALLIPOT.   Or give out
  One of my men was ta'en a'bed with thee.

MISTRESS GALLIPOT. Um, um!

GALLIPOT.   Before I lose thee my dear Pru,
  I'll drive it to that push.

MISTRESS GALLIPOT.   Worse, and worse still!
140 You embrace a mischief to prevent an ill.[3]

GALLIPOT. I'll buy thee of him, stop his mouth with gold.
  Think'st thou 'twill do?

MISTRESS GALLIPOT.   Oh, me! Heavens grant it would!
  Yet, now my senses are set more in tune,[4]
  He writ, as I remember in his letter,
145 That he in riding up and down had spent—

---

1 *Rumour* Goddess personifying rumor.

2 *Thou'rt ... prevention* You will lose in court; no strategy at law can stop it.

3 *You ... ill* You embrace one bad thing (a lie about being cuckolded that would shame the
   Gallipots) to prevent another (the dissolution of their marriage).

4 *my senses ... tune* I've come to my senses.

Ere he could find me—thirty pounds. Send that;
Stand° not on thirty with him.   *delay*
GALLIPOT.   Forty, Pru.
Say thou the word, 'tis done. We venture lives
For wealth, but must do more to keep our wives.
Thirty or forty, Pru?   150
MISTRESS GALLIPOT.   Thirty good sweet.
Of an ill bargain let's save what we can,
I'll pay it him with my tears. He was a man,
When first I knew him, of a meek spirit;
All goodness is not yet dried up, I hope.
GALLIPOT. He shall have thirty pound. Let that stop all;   155
Love's sweets taste best when we have drunk down gall.°   *bitterness*

(*Enter Master Tiltyard and his wife, Master Goshawk, and Mistress
Openwork.*)

Godso,° our friends! Come, come, smooth your cheek;   *God's soul*
After a storm the face of heaven looks sleek.
TILTYARD. Did I not tell you these turtles¹ were together?
MISTRESS TILTYARD. [*To Master Gallipot.*] How dost thou sirrah?   160
Why, sister Gallipot!
MISTRESS OPENWORK. Lord, how she's changed!
GOSHAWK. [*To Master Gallipot.*] Is your wife ill, sir?
GALLIPOT. Yes, indeed, la, sir; very ill, very ill, never worse.
MISTRESS TILTYARD. How her head burns; feel how her pulses   165
work.²
MISTRESS OPENWORK. [*To Mistress Gallipot.*] Sister, lie down a little.
That always does me good.
MISTRESS TILTYARD. In good sadness, I find best ease in that too.
Has she laid some hot thing to her stomach?   170
MISTRESS GALLIPOT. No, but I will lay something anon.³

---

1 *turtles* Turtledoves, reputed to mate for life.
2 *pulses work* Pulse beats quickly.
3 *lie down ... anon* All of these remedies have sexual connotations as well as medical ones. To
   "lie down" brings her to bed; the idea of laying "some hot thing" to her stomach implies the
   sex act, especially given "thing" as slang for penis; that she will "lay something anon" implies
   that Mistress Gallipot is eager for sex.

TILTYARD. Come, come, fools, you trouble her. Shall's go, Master
    Goshawk?

GOSHAWK. Yes, sweet Master Tiltyard. [*Apart, with Mistress Open-*
175 *work.*] Sirrah Rosamond, I hold my life Gallipot hath vext his
    wife.

MISTRESS OPENWORK. She has a horrible high colour,[1] indeed.

GOSHAWK. We shall have your face painted with the same red soon
    at night, when your husband comes from his rubbers in a false
180 alley.[2] Thou wilt not believe me that his bowls run with a wrong
    bias?[3]

MISTRESS OPENWORK. It cannot sink into me that he feeds upon
    stale mutton abroad, having better and fresher at home.[4]

GOSHAWK. What if I bring thee where thou shalt see him stand at
185 rack and manger?[5]

MISTRESS OPENWORK. I'll saddle him in's kind[6] and spur him till he
    kick again.

GOSHAWK. Shall thou and I ride our journey,[7] then?

MISTRESS OPENWORK. Here's my hand.

190 GOSHAWK. No more. [*To Master Tiltyard and all.*] Come Master
    Tiltyard, shall we leap into the stirrups with our women and
    amble home?

TILTYARD. Yes, yes.—Come, wife.

MISTRESS TILTYARD. In troth sister, I hope you will do well for all
195 this.

MISTRESS GALLIPOT. I hope I shall. Farewell good sister, sweet
    Master Goshawk.

GALLIPOT. Welcome, brother; most kindly, welcome, sir.[8]

---

1 *She has ... colour* She is very flushed.

2 *We shall ... alley* You'll turn just as red (from anger or embarrassment) when Master Open-
    work's sexual exploits are exposed; *rubbers ... alley* Three matches of bowling in an alley,
    with sexual puns on "rubber," (his rub-hers), "bowl" (balls), and "false alley" (vagina).

3 *that his bowls ... bias* I.e., that he cheats. Bowling balls were weighted to roll according to
    a bias rather than straight.

4 *stale ... home* Old prostitutes outside the home when he has a fresh female (that is, Mistress
    Openwork) waiting for him.

5 *rack and manger* Frame and trough for feeding animals, here signifying the place where
    Master Openwork satisfies his appetites.

6 *in's kind* According to his nature.

7 *ride our journey* Have a getaway together (that is, follow Openwork).

8 *welcome, sir* Gallipot tells them they have been welcome in his home as they go.

OMNES. Thanks, sir, for our good cheer.

(*Exeunt all but [Master] Gallipot and his wife.*)

GALLIPOT.   It shall be so, because a crafty knave   200
Shall not outreach me, nor walk by my door
With my wife arm in arm as 'twere his whore.
I'll give him a golden coxcomb:° thirty pound.   *fool's cap*
Tush, Pru, what's thirty pound? Sweet duck, look cheerily.
MISTRESS GALLIPOT.   Thou art worthy of my heart; thou buy'st it   205
dearly.[1]

(*Enter Laxton muffled [his head wrapped in bandages].*)

LAXTON.   [*Aside.*] 'Uds light,[2] the tide's against me! A pox of your
pothecaryship! Oh, for some glister to set him going![3] 'Tis one of
Hercules's labours[4] to tread one of these city hens[5] because their
cocks are still crowing over them. There's no turning tail here; I
must on.   210
MISTRESS GALLIPOT.   Oh, husband, see, he comes.
GALLIPOT.   Let me deal with him.
LAXTON.   Bless you sir.
GALLIPOT.   Be you blest too, sir, if you come in peace.
LAXTON.   Have you any good pudding-tobacco,[6] sir?   215
MISTRESS GALLIPOT.   Oh, pick no quarrels, gentle sir. My husband
Is not a man of weapon, as you are.
He knows all; I have opened all before him
Concerning you.
LAXTON.   [*Aside.*]   Zounds! Has she shown my letters?
MISTRESS GALLIPOT.   Suppose my case were yours, what would you   220
do?

---

1   *dearly*   Expensively.
2   *'Uds light*   God's light.
3   *glister*   A version of "clyster," an enema or suppository;   *set him going*   Get him out, dis-
tract him.
4   *Hercules's labours*   Extremely difficult tasks. Hercules was charged with twelve extraordinary labors as penance for accidentally killing his wife and children.
5   *tread*   Mate a male bird with a hen;   *city hens*   London wives.
6   *pudding-tobacco*   Tobacco sold in rolls, resembling sausages (puddings).

At such a pinch, such batteries, such assaults,
Of father, mother, kindred, to dissolve
The knot you tied, and to be bound to him?[1]
How could you shift this storm off?

225 LAXTON. [*Aside.*] If I know, hang me.

MISTRESS GALLIPOT. Besides, a story of your death was read
Each minute to me.

LAXTON. [*Aside.*] What a'pox means this riddling?

GALLIPOT. Be wise, sir, let not you and I be tossed

230 On lawyers' pens; they have sharp nibs° and draw   *tips*
Men's very heart-blood from them. What need you sir
To beat the drum of[2] my wife's infamy,
And call your friends together, sir, to prove
Your precontract, when sh'has confest it?

LAXTON.   Um, sir,—

235 Has she confest it?

GALLIPOT.   Sh'has, 'faith, to me, sir,
Upon your letter sending.

MISTRESS GALLIPOT.   I have, I have.

LAXTON. [*Aside.*] If I let this iron cool,[3] call me slave.
    —Do you hear, you, dame Prudence? Think'st thou, vile woman,
I'll take these blows and wink?

MISTRESS GALLIPOT.   Upon my knees—

240 LAXTON. Out, impudence!

GALLIPOT.   Good sir—

LAXTON.   You goatish° slaves,   *lascivious*
No wild fowl to cut up but mine?[4]

GALLIPOT.   Alas, sir,
You make her flesh to tremble. Fright her not;
She shall do reason, and what's fit.[5]

LAXTON.   I'll have thee,
Wert° thou more common than a hospital   *were*

---

1 *At such ... him* In such a difficult position, with my father, mother, and family trying make me break the (fictional) pre-contract and marry Gallipot instead of you.

2 *What need ... drum of* Why do you need to call attention to.

3 *If I ... iron cool* I.e., if I fail to strike while the iron is hot.

4 *No ... mine* There are no other women available but my betrothed?

5 *She shall ... fit* She will proceed with reason and do what is right.

And more diseased.— 245
GALLIPOT. But one word, good sir.
LAXTON. So, sir.
GALLIPOT. I married her, have lain with her, and got
Two children on her body; think but on that.
Have you so beggarly an appetite,
When I upon a dainty dish have fed,
To dine upon my scraps, my leavings?° Ha sir? *leftovers* 250
Do I come near you[1] now, sir?
LAXTON. By'Lady, you touch me.[2]
GALLIPOT. Would not you scorn to wear my clothes sir?
LAXTON. Right, sir.
GALLIPOT. Then pray, sir, wear not her, for she's a garment
So fitting for my body, I'm loath
Another should put it on; you will undo both. 255
Your letter, as she said, complained you had spent
In quest of her, some thirty pound: I'll pay it;
Shall that, sir, stop this gap up 'twixt you two?
LAXTON. Well, if I swallow this wrong,[3] let her thank you.
The money being paid sir, I am gone. 260
Farewell. Oh, women! Happy's he trusts none.[4]
MISTRESS GALLIPOT. Dispatch him hence, sweet husband.
GALLIPOT. Yes, dear wife.
Pray, sir, come in. [*To Mistress Gallipot.*] Ere Master Laxton part,
Thou shalt in wine drink to him.
MISTRESS GALLIPOT. With all my heart—

(*Exit Master Gallipot.*)

How dost thou like my wit? 265
LAXTON. Rarely! That wile
By which the serpent did the first woman beguile

---

1   *come near you*   Affect your opinion.
2   *By'Lady*   By our Lady (Mary), a mild oath;   *you touch me*   You move me or provoke me.
3   *if I ... wrong*   If I keep quiet on this matter.
4   *Happy's ... none*   Happy is he who trusts none.

Did ever since all women's bosoms fill;
You're apple-eaters[1] all, deceivers still.

(*Exit Laxton [and Mistress Gallipot].*)

[ACT 3, SCENE 3]

(*Enter Sir Alexander Wengrave, Sir Davy Dapper, Sir Adam Appleton at one door, and Trapdoor at another door.*)

SIR ALEXANDER. Out with your tale, Sir Davy, to Sir Adam.
A knave is in mine eye, deep in my debt.[2]
SIR DAVY. Nay, if he be a knave, sir, hold him fast.
SIR ALEXANDER. [*Aside, to Trapdoor.*] Speak softly. What egg is there hatching now?[3]
5 TRAPDOOR. A duck's egg, sir; a duck that has eaten a frog.[4] I have crackt the shell, and some villainy or other will peep out presently. The duck that sits is the bouncing ramp,[5] that roaring girl, my mistress; the drake that must tread is your son, Sebastian.
10 SIR ALEXANDER. Be quick.
TRAPDOOR. As the tongue of an oyster wench.[6]
SIR ALEXANDER. And see thy news be true.
TRAPDOOR. As a barber's every Saturday night.[7] Mad Moll—
SIR ALEXANDER. Ah—
15 TRAPDOOR. Must be let in without knocking at your back gate.
SIR ALEXANDER. So—
TRAPDOOR. Your chamber will be made bawdy.
SIR ALEXANDER. Good.
TRAPDOOR. She comes in a shirt of male.

---

1   *apple-eaters*   Like Eve, tempters.
2   *A knave ... debt*   I see a man who is in my debt (an excuse to speak with Trapdoor).
3   *egg* Plan; *hatching now* Progressing now.
4   *duck ... frog* Moll (the "duck") has taken the bait (the "frog").
5   *bouncing* Bellicose, boisterous; *ramp* Bold, wanton woman or tomboy.
6   *oyster wench* Woman who sells oysters, presumably by crying her wares in the street.
7   *As a ... night* As true as the collection of gossip the barber can tell you at the end of the week.

SIR ALEXANDER. How shirt of mail?[1] 20
TRAPDOOR. Yes, sir, or a male shirt, that's to say, in man's apparel.
SIR ALEXANDER. To my son?
TRAPDOOR. Close to your son: your son and her moon will be in
conjunction,[2] if all almanacs lie not. Her black safeguard is
turned into a deep slop, the holes of her upper body to 25
buttonholes, her waistcoat to a doublet, her placket to the ancient
seat of a codpiece, and you shall take 'em both with standing
collars.[3]
SIR ALEXANDER. Art sure of this?
TRAPDOOR. As every throng is sure of a pick-pocket; as sure as a 30
whore is of the clients all Michaelmas Term,[4] and of the pox after
the Term.
SIR ALEXANDER. The time of their tilting?[5]
TRAPDOOR. Three.
SIR ALEXANDER. The day? 35
TRAPDOOR. This.
SIR ALEXANDER. Away, ply it.[6] Watch her.

---

1   *mail*   The connected rings that form mail armor. Alexander is uncertain if "male" or "mail" is meant.
2   *conjunction*   Coupling; having sex. Trapdoor puns on "son" and "sun" and extends his wordplay to make Moll the moon. There is a hint in these lines and those following of Moll's transformation into an apparent male, and in this sense, Moll and Sebastian also form a conjunction of exterior masculinity.
3   *black ... collars*   Trapdoor explains Moll's transformation in terms of clothing, with women's clothing items replaced by men's;   *the holes ... buttonholes*   The eyelets, of her bodice— which would have been fastened and tightened with ties—are turned to buttonholes, as on a men's doublet;   *waistcoat*   Short garment for women, often ornate, which was worn on the upper body and that could be seen from under an outer gown;   *placket*   Slit at the top of a skirt that facilitates dressing and which allows access to an inner pocket or to the wearer's body. "Placket" came to mean "woman" and "codpiece" to mean "man";   *standing collars*   Large, fashionable collars that were stiffened and stood up, off the shoulders. There is an additional bawdy pun on "standing" indicating Moll's masculinization.
4   *Michaelmas Term*   Michaelmas Term (autumn) was the busiest of the terms of the law courts in London, and Trapdoor jokes that the influx of young gentleman for term time would have meant an influx in business for whores.
5   *tilting*   Jousting term for a hard charge by a jouster against an opponent or target (perhaps with a bawdy suggestion that both Moll and Sebastian have "lances").
6   *ply it*   Apply yourself, do as I ask.

TRAPDOOR. As the devil doth for the death of a bawd,[1] I'll watch
  her; do you catch her.
40 SIR ALEXANDER. She's fast;[2] here, weave thou the nets. Hark!
TRAPDOOR. They are made.
SIR ALEXANDER. I told them thou didst owe me money: hold it up,
  maintain 't.[3]
TRAPDOOR. Stiffly; as a Puritan does contention.[4] [*Aloud, as if in an*
45 *argument.*] Fox, I owe thee not the value of a halfpenny halter![5]
SIR ALEXANDER. Thou shalt be hanged in't ere thou 'scape so! Varlet,
  I'll make thee look through a grate![6]
TRAPDOOR. I'll do't presently: through a tavern grate. Drawer![7] Pish!

(*Exit Trapdoor.*)

SIR ADAM. Has the knave vext you, sir?
SIR ALEXANDER.   Askt him my money;
50 He swears my son received it. Oh, that boy
  Will ne'er leave heaping sorrows on my heart,
  'Till he has broke it quite.
SIR ADAM.   Is he still wild?
SIR ALEXANDER. As is a Russian bear.
SIR ADAM.   But he has left
  His old haunt with that baggage?[8]
SIR ALEXANDER.   Worse still and worse,
55 He lays on me his shame, I on him my curse.
SIR DAVY. My son Jack Dapper then shall run with him
  All in one pasture.[9]
SIR ADAM.   Proves your son bad too, sir?

---

1 *bawd* Pimp or madam; *devil ... bawd* The devil watches so as to be ready to take the
  bawd to hell.
2 *fast* Trapped.
3 *them* Sir Adam and Sir Davy; *maintain 't* Support my lie (so that we avoid suspicion).
4 *as a ... contention* Reference to the Puritans' dogged and serious pursuit of religious con-
  troversies.
5 *halter* Noose.
6 *grate* Bars on a window, as in a prison.
7 *Drawer* One who draws liquor and serves at a tavern, a tapster.
8 *that baggage* That trashy strumpet, i.e., Moll.
9 *in one pasture* In the same place.

Sir Davy. As villainy can make him. Your Sebastian
'Dores but on one drab,[1] mine on a thousand.
A noise of fiddlers,[2] tobacco, wine, and a whore,   60
A mercer that will let him take up[3] more,
Dice, and a water spaniel with a duck; oh,
Bring him abed with these![4] When his purse jingles,
Roaring boys follow at's tail. Fencers and ningles[5]—
Beasts Adam ne'er gave name to[6]—these horse-leeches suck   65
My son. He being drawn dry, they all live on smoke.
Sir Alexander. Tobacco?
Sir Davy.   Right, but I have in my brain
A windmill going that shall grind to dust
The follies of my son and make him wise,
Or a stark° fool. Pray, lend me your advice.   *unmitigated* 70
Both. That shall you, good Sir Davy.
Sir Davy.   Here's the springe°   *trap*
I ha' set to catch this woodcock[7] in: an action
In a false name—unknown to him—is entered
I'th'Counter[8] to arrest Jack Dapper.
Both.   Ha, ha, he!
Sir Davy. Think you the Counter cannot break him?   75
Sir Adam.   Break him?
Yes, and break's heart too, if he lie there long.
Sir Davy. I'll make him sing a counter-tenor,[9] sure.

---

1   *drab*   Prostitute or slut.
2   *noise of fiddlers*   Company of violin players (musicians).
3   *take up*   Buy on credit, even though he is in debt.
4   *Bring ... these!*   Deliver him of these; to bring a pregnant woman abed means to guide her
    through childbirth.
5   *ningles*   Ingles, or close male friends. "Ningles" can also carry a derogatory suggestion of
    same-sex male lovers, especially subservient, younger ones.
6   *Adam ... name to*   Reference to Genesis 2.19–20.
7   *woodcock*   Popular game bird, or a fool likely to be tricked or trapped. "A spring to catch a
    woodcock" is proverbial.
8   *action ... false name*   Legal action, or suit, for debt prosecution, which has been ordered
    against Jack by Sir Davy, though he has done so under an assumed name; *Counter*   Prison
    for debtors. Sir Davy and Sir Alexander are speaking about the Wood Street Counter, one of
    two counters in the city of London.
9   *counter-tenor*   High-pitched male voice part sung in contrast to a principal melody. The
    pun on "counter" implies that Jack will develop his singing voice while in prison begging
    for money and that he will be symbolically castrated by his father.

SIR ADAM. No way to tame him like it; there he shall learn
  What money is indeed, and how to spend it.
80 SIR DAVY. He's bridled there.
  SIR ALEXANDER.   Ay, yet knows not how to mend it.
  Bedlam cures not more madmen in a year
  Than one of the Counters does; men pay more dear
  There for their wit than anywhere. A Counter,
  Why 'tis an university! Who not sees?
85 As scholars there, so here men take degrees,
  And follow the same studies—all alike.
  Scholars learn first logic and rhetoric;
  So does a prisoner. With fine honeyed speech,
  At 's first coming in he doth persuade, beseech
90 He may be lodged with one that is not itchy,
  To lie in a clean chamber, in sheets not lousy;[1]
  But when he has no money, then does he try,
  By subtle logic, and quaint sophistry,
  To make the keepers trust him.
  SIR ADAM.   Say they do.
95 SIR ALEXANDER. Then he's a graduate.
  SIR DAVY.   Say they trust him not.
  SIR ALEXANDER. Then is he held a freshman and a sot,
  And never shall commence, but being still barred
  Be expulst from the Master's Side to th'Twopenny Ward,
  Or else i'th'Hole,[2] be plac't.
  SIR ADAM.   When, then, I pray,
100 Proceeds° a prisoner?   *advances, graduates*
  SIR ALEXANDER.   When, money being the theme,
  He can dispute with his hard creditors' hearts

---

1 *lousy* Infested with lice.
2 *th'Twopenny ... i'th'Hole* The Counters had different quarters for incarceration depending
  on how much one could pay (prisoners were to pay their jailers even while they could not
  pay their debts). Prisoners often moved down levels as they grew more poor, as from the
  Knight's Ward to the Master's Ward (hence the "Master of Arts" that Sir Alexander explains
  is to be had at the Counter) to the "Two-penny Ward" and finally the "Hole." The Hole was
  reputed to be the worst, darkest part of the Wood Street Counter and was full of the poorest
  and most hopeless debtors.

And get out clear, he's then a Master of Arts.[1]
Sir Davy send your son to Wood Street College;[2]
A gentleman can nowhere get more knowledge.

SIR DAVY. There gallants study hard.   105

SIR ALEXANDER.   True: to get money.

SIR DAVY. 'Lies by th'heels i'faith. Thanks, thanks; I ha' sent
For a couple of bears shall paw[3] him.

(*Enter Sergeant Curtalax and Yeoman Hanger.*)

SIR ADAM.   Who comes yonder?

SIR DAVY. They look like puttocks;[4] these should be they.

SIR ALEXANDER.   I know 'em;
They are officers. Sir, we'll leave you.

SIR DAVY.   My good knights,
Leave me. You see I'm haunted now with sprites.°   *spirits* 110

BOTH. Fare you well, sir.

(*Exeunt Alex[ander] and Adam.*)

CURTALAX. [*To Hanger.*] This old muzzle chops[5] should be he, by
the fellow's description. [*To Sir Davy.*] —Save you sir.

SIR DAVY. Come hither you mad varlets! Did not my man tell you
I watcht here for you?   115

CURTALAX. One in a blue coat,[6] sir, told us that in this place an old
gentleman would watch for us—a thing contrary to our oath, for
we are to watch for every wicked member in a city.

SIR DAVY. You'll watch, then, for ten thousand. What's thy name,
honesty?   120

CURTALAX. Sergeant Curtalax, I, sir.

SIR DAVY. An excellent name for a sergeant, *Curtalax.*

---

1 *money ... Arts* Money being the topic of the debate ("dispute") to be settled between Jack
   Dapper and his creditors, when he can pay them or, more likely, convince them to forgive
   his debts, he will have completed his Counter education.

2 *Wood Street College* Wood Street Counter.

3 *bears* Officers; in this case, Curtalax and Hanger; *paw* Arrest.

4 *puttocks* Literally, birds of prey; here, greedy petty officers of law.

5 *muzzle chops* Man with a conspicuously large or projecting mouth and nose.

6 *blue coat* Servant in livery, in this case, one of Sir Davy's servants.

Sergeants indeed are weapons of the law.
When prodigal ruffians far in debt are grown,
125 Should not you cut them, citizens were o'erthrown.
Thou dwell'st hereby in Holborn, Curtalax?
CURTALAX. That's my circuit, sir; I conjure most in that circle.[1]
SIR DAVY. And what young toward° welp° is this? *promising / puppy*
HANGER. Of the same litter: his yeoman,[2] sir. My name's Hanger.
130 SIR DAVY. Yeoman Hanger.
One pair of shears sure cut out both your coats;[3]
You have two names most dangerous to mens' throats.
You two are villainous loads on gentlemen's backs;
Dear ware,[4] this Hanger and this Curtalax.
135 CURTALAX. We are as other men are, sir. I cannot see but he who
makes a show of honesty and religion, if his claws can fasten to
his liking,[5] he draws blood. All that live in the world are but great
fish and little fish and feed upon one another. Some eat up whole
men; a sergeant cares but for the shoulder of a man.[6] They call us
140 knaves and curs,[7] but many times he that sets us on worries more
lambs one year than we do in seven.[8]
SIR DAVY. Spoke like a noble Cerberus. Is the action entered?
HANGAR. His name is entered in the book of unbelievers.[9]
SIR DAVY. What book's that?
145 CURTALAX. The book where all prisoners' names stand; and not one
amongst forty when he comes in, believes to come out in haste.

---

1 *circuit* Jurisdiction; *conjure ... circle* Compel or constrain by charge offenders in that
   given area. Curtalax plays on the idea of conjuring magic spirits in a circle.
2 *yeoman* Assistant, servant.
3 *One pair ... coats* You're very similar; a variation on the idea of "cut from the same cloth."
4 *Dear ware* Expensive or valuable goods.
5 *he ... religion* One who makes an effort to appear to be God-fearing and truthful; *if ...
   liking* If his grip takes hold.
6 *the shoulder of a man* Place where a sergeant might grab hold of a suspect. The sergeant
   does not devour whole his victim, since he turns the victim over to others after doing and
   getting his part. Shoulder cuts typically include some of the best meat, which here is the
   Sergeant's reward.
7 *knaves and curs* Villains and dogs.
8 *worries ... seven* Devours more men in one year than we catch in seven. This suggests that
   the sergeants prosecute mildly and in small numbers compared to the greedy creditors who
   completely ruin men.
9 *book of unbelievers* Record of arrests, here opposed to St. Peter's Book of Life, which is
   supposed to record believers desiring entrance to heaven, not criminals to be tried.

SIR DAVY. Be as dogged[1] to him as your office allows you to be.
BOTH. Oh, sir!
SIR DAVY. You know the unthrift Jack Dapper.
CURTALAX. Aye, aye, sir, that gull? As well as I know my yeoman. 150
SIR DAVY. And you know his father too, Sir Davy Dapper?
CURTALAX. As dammed a usurer as ever was among Jews.[2] If
he were sure his father's skin would yield him any money, he
would—when he dies—flay it off and sell it to cover drums for
children at Bartholomew Fair.[3] 155
SIR DAVY. [Aside.] What toads are these to spit poison on a man to
his face! [To them.] Do you see, my honest rascals? Yonder grey-
hound is the dog he hunts with; out of that tavern Jack Dapper
will sally.[4] Sa, sa! Give the Counter! On! Set upon him!
BOTH. We'll charge him upo'th'back,[5] sir. 160
SIR DAVY. Take no bail. Put mace enough into his caudle![6] Double
your files![7] Traverse your ground![8]
BOTH. Brave, sir!
SIR DAVY. Cry arm, arm, arm![9]
BOTH. Thus, sir. 165

[*They attempt—poorly—to make ready, following Sir Davy's
commands.*]

---

1 *dogged* Malicious, obstinate.
2 *usurer* Moneylender who charges interest, especially one with rates over the legal ten per-
   cent; *Jews* Slur indicating usurers. In the early modern world, Jews were associated with
   usury because Christians were not supposed to engage in moneylending at interest, while
   moneylending was one of few means of earning a living available to Jews. In practice, Christians often engaged in moneylending—and Jews were expelled from England in 1290 and
   not formally accepted back into the nation until 1657—but the prejudicial and pejorative
   association persisted.
3 *Bartholomew Fair* Cloth fair held at Smithfield in London on or around the feast day
   of St. Bartholomew (24 August). Many consumer goods were sold at the fair for popular
   consumption, especially trinkets and toys for children.
4 *sally* To set out, often boldly, i.e., as one would at the beginning of a hunt or military
   operation.
5 *charge him upo'th'back* Approach him from behind.
6 *mace ... caudle* Literally, "put enough spice into his warm gruel and drink." The mace was
   also the sergeant's weapon of office, so the pun suggests that the arrest order will shake Jack
   up, possibly through physical force.
7 *Double your files* Order for marching troops to make twice as many columns.
8 *Traverse your ground* Cross the same patch of ground again and again.
9 *Cry ... arm* Order men to take up arms!

SIR DAVY. There boy! There boy, away! Look to your prey my true
English wolves, and—and so, I vanish.

(*Exit S*[*ir*] *Davy.*)

CURTALAX. Some warden of the sergeants begat this old fellow,[1]
upon my life. Stand close.

170 HANGAR. Shall the ambuscado[2] lie in one place?

CURTALAX. No, nook thou[3] yonder.

[*They hide.*]
(*Enter Moll*[*, still in men's clothes,*] *and Trapdoor.*)

MOLL. Ralph—

TRAPDOOR. What says my brave captain, male and female?

MOLL. This Holborn is such a wrangling[4] street.

175 TRAPDOOR. That's because lawyers walk to and fro in't.

MOLL. Here's such jostling, as if every one we met were drunk and
reeled.

TRAPDOOR. Stand, mistress; do you not smell carrion?[5]

MOLL. Carrion? No, yet I spy ravens.[6]

180 TRAPDOOR. Some poor wind-shaken gallant will anon fall into
sore labour, and these men midwives must bring him to bed i'the
counter. There all those that are great with child, with debts, lie
in.[7]

MOLL. Stand up.[8]

---

1 *warden* Overseeing officer; *warden ... fellow* Sir Davy's father must be a warden of the
sergeants (because he has such impressive knowledge of the drill commands).

2 *ambuscado* Ambush.

3 *nook thou* Hide yourself.

4 *Holborn* Main artery from the west leading into the city of London, with two of the Inns
of Court—Lincoln's Inn and Gray's Inn—close by; *wrangling* Noisy, full of quarreling
and talk.

5 *carrion* Putrefying flesh, dead body, or more generally anything rotting or corrupted.

6 *ravens* Opportunistic birds of prey who also eat carrion, i.e., Curtalax and Hanger.

7 *There ... debts* In the Counter, debtors wait to be delivered of their burdensome debts; *lie
in* Undergo labor in the childbed, here with the assistance of the sergeants as midwives.

8 *Stand up* Be ready. In the next line Trapdoor implies that Moll has ordered him to get an
erection.

TRAPDOOR. Like your new maypole.[1]   185
HANGAR. Whist! Whew!
CURTALAX. Hump, no![2]
MOLL. Peeping? It shall go hard, huntsmen, but I'll spoil your
    game. They look for all the world like two infected maltmen[3]
    coming muffled up in their cloaks in a frosty morning to   190
    London.
TRAPDOOR. A course, Captain; a bear comes to the stake.[4]

(*Enter Jack Dapper and Gull.*)

MOLL. It should be so, for the dogs[5] struggle to be let loose.
HANGAR. [*Signals to Curtalax.*] Whew!
CURTALAX. [*Answers.*] Hemp!   195
MOLL. Hark, Trapdoor, follow your leader.
DAPPER. Gull?
GULL. Master?
DAPPER. Did'st ever see such an ass as I am, boy?
GULL. No by my troth, sir. To lose all your money, yet have false 200
    dice of your own![6] Why 'tis as I saw a great fellow used t'other
    day: he had a fair sword and buckler, and yet a butcher dry beat
    him with a cudgel.[7]
MOLL AND TRAPDOOR. [*To Curtalax.*] Honest sergeant! [*To Dapper
    and Gull.*] Fly, fly, Master Dapper! You'll be arrested else.   205

---

1 *maypole* Tall pole decorated with flowers, painted with stripes, and raised on a green for
   traditional May Day celebrations, which usually included a ceremonial dance around it.
2 *Whist … no!* Signal exchange between Hanger and Curtalax. Hanger asks if they should
   ambush Moll and Trapdoor, and Curtalax says no.
3 *maltmen* Men who make grain for distilling, used in producing beer, vinegar, and other
   foodstuffs. Maltmen were considered particularly susceptible to plague because they transported malt into cities and took soiled rags, which were used for fertilizing fields, back to
   the country.
4 *a bear* Jack Dapper; *to the stake* In bearbaiting contests, the bear was chained to a stake
   and set upon by dogs.
5 *the dogs* Curtalax and Hanger.
6 *false dice* Altered dice for cheating; *To lose … your own* To have the ability to cheat, yet
   still lose all your money.
7 *dry beat* Severely beat, hit with so-called "dry blows," which do not draw blood despite
   their force; *cudgel* Club or short stick used to beat someone.

DAPPER. Run, Gull, and draw!

GULL. Run, master! Gull follows you!

(*Exit Dapper and Gull.*)

CURTALAX. [*To Moll.*] I know you well enough; you're but a whore
to hang upon any man.

210 MOLL. Whores then are like sergeants: so now hang you. [*To Trapdoor.*] Draw, rogue, but strike not: for a broken pate, they'll keep
their beds and recover twenty marks damages.[1]

CURTALAX. You shall pay for this rescue! [*To Hanger.*] Run down
Shoe Lane[2] and meet him.

215 TRAPDOOR. Shoo! Is this a rescue, gentlemen, or no?[3]

MOLL. Rescue? A pox on 'em, Trapdoor. Let's away.
I'm glad I have done perfect° one good work today.   *complete, sound*
If any gentleman be in scrivener's bands,[4]
Send but for Moll; she'll bail him,[5] by these hands.

(*Exeunt.*)

[ACT 4, SCENE 1]

(*Enter Sir Alexander Wengrave solus.*)

SIR ALEXANDER. Unhappy in the follies of a son,
Led against judgment, sense, obedience,
And all the powers of nobleness and wit—
Oh, wretched father!

---

1   *broken pate* Head injury, broken skull; *keep their beds* Stay in bed; *recover ... damages* Sue for twenty marks for their pains. Moll warns Trapdoor not to strike them because
the rascals will benefit from the injury as much as they will suffer.

2   *Shoe Lane* Street outside the city wall in Clerkenwell that ran parallel to the Fleet River; it
connected Fleet Street and Holborn. Curtalax assumes that if Hanger runs down Shoe Lane
he might be able to catch up with Dapper, who has presumably run down a parallel street
toward Fleet Street.

3   *Is this a ... or no?* Trapdoor suggests that to make this a true rescue he and Moll would have
had to seize Dapper from the sergeants; merely warning him would not qualify.

4   *scrivener* Professional clerk who drew up legal documents or worked as a money
broker; *bands* Bond for a debt, contract, or agreement. To be in a scrivener's bands is to
be trapped in a legal agreement.

5   *bail him* Liberate him.

(*Enter Trapdoor.*)

Now, Trapdoor, will she come? 5
TRAPDOOR. In men's apparel, sir. I am in her heart now,
And share in all her secrets.
SIR ALEXANDER. Peace, peace, peace!
[*Sir Alexander handing Trapdoor a watch.*] Here, take my German
watch, hang't up in sight,
That I may see her hang in English[1] for't.
TRAPDOOR. I warrant you for that now, next sessions rids her,[2] sir. 10
This watch will bring her in better than a hundred constables.
SIR ALEXANDER. Good Trapdoor, say'st thou so? Thou cheer'st my
heart
After a storm of sorrow.—My gold chain too:
Here, take a hundred marks in yellow links.

[*Sir Alexander hands Trapdoor a gold chain.*]

TRAPDOOR. That will do well to bring the watch to light,[3] sir, 15
And worth a thousand of your headborough's[4] lanterns.
SIR ALEXANDER. Place that o'the court-cupboard,[5] let it lie
Full in the view of her thief-whorish eye.

[*Trapdoor places the chain and the watch on the cupboard.*]

TRAPDOOR. She cannot miss it, sir, I see 't so plain,
That I could steal 't myself. 20
SIR ALEXANDER. Perhaps thou shalt, too—
That or something as weighty. What she leaves,

---

1   *in English*   Under English law.
2   *sessions*   Period of meetings of the criminal court;   *next sessions rids her*   You'll be free of
    her after the next sessions.
3   *That will ... watch to light*   The links will call attention to the watch, but with a pun on
    "watch" (meaning officers of the night watch) and on "links" (meaning torches, which
    would provide light for the officers).
4   *headborough*   Parish officer who acts as a constable or a member of the night watch.
5   *court-cupboard*   Moveable cabinet or sideboard.

Thou shalt come closely° in, and filch away,   *secretly*
And all the weight upon her back I'll lay.[1]
TRAPDOOR. You cannot assure that, sir.
SIR ALEXANDER.   No? What lets° it?   *stops*
25 TRAPDOOR. Being a stout° girl, perhaps she'll desire pressing;[2]   *lively*
Then all the weight must lie upon her belly.
SIR ALEXANDER. Belly or back I care not, so I've one.[3]
TRAPDOOR. You're of my mind for that, sir.
SIR ALEXANDER. Hang up my ruff band with the diamond at it,
30   It may be she'll like that best.

[*Trapdoor hangs the ruff with diamond in view.*]

TRAPDOOR. [*Aside.*] It's well for her that she must have her choice;
he thinks nothing too good for her. [*To Sir Alexander.*] If you hold
on this mind a little longer, it shall be the first work I do to turn
thief myself. Would do a man good to be hanged when he is so
35   well provided for.
SIR ALEXANDER. So, well said. All hangs well, would she hung so
   too!
The sight would please me more than all their glisterings:° *glittering*
Oh, that my mysteries° to such straits should run,   *skills*
That I must rob myself to bless my son!

(*Exeunt.*)

(*Enter Sebastian, with Mary Fitzallard like a page, and Moll.*)

40 SEBASTIAN. Thou hast done me a kind office,° without touch *service*
Either of sin or shame, our loves are honest.
MOLL. I'd scorn to make such shift[4] to bring you together else.

---

1   *all the weight* The full force of the law (via the accusation of theft);   *lay* Put to her, with
    added sexual innuendo.
2   *pressing* Form of torture involving placing a heavy weight on a criminal and continuing to
    add weight until the accused confessed or died. There is a continued sexual implication.
3   *Belly ... one* As long as we catch Moll, I don't care how we do it (or as long as I have sex, I
    do not care if I lay on a woman's belly or her back).
4   *shift* Work, or change of clothes.

SEBASTIAN. Now have I time and opportunity
  Without all fear to bid thee welcome, love.

([*Sebastian and Mary*] *kiss.*)

MARY. Never with more desire and harder venture.   45
MOLL. How strange this shows one man to kiss another.
SEBASTIAN. I'd kiss such men to choose° Moll;   *by choice*
  Methinks a woman's lip tastes well in a doublet.
MOLL. Many an old madam has the better fortune then,
  Whose breaths grew stale before the fashion came.   ·50
  If that will help 'em, as you think 'twill do,
  They'll learn in time to pluck on the hose too.[1]
SEBASTIAN. The older they wax,[2] Moll. Troth,°   *in truth*
  I speak seriously:
  As some have a conceit their drink tastes better
  In an outlandish° cup than in our own,[3]   *strange* 55
  So methinks every kiss she gives me now
  In this strange form is worth a pair of two.[4]
  Here we are safe, and furthest from the eye
  Of all suspicion. This is my father's chamber,
  Upon which floor he never steps 'till night.   60
  Here he mistrusts° me not, nor I his coming.   *suspects*
  At mine own chamber he still pries° unto me;   *keeps prying*
  My freedom is not there at mine own finding,
  Still checkt and curbed. Here he shall miss his purpose.[5]
MOLL. And what's your business, now you have your mind, sir?   65
  At your great suit° I promised you to come;   *request*

---

1 *Whose breaths grew ... hose too* If what you say is true, many madams who grew old before
  the fad for masculine clothes (and are therefore no longer alluring in themselves) will now
  be able to make money by putting on men's breeches. Though some prostitutes did wear
  masculine attire, Moll's response to Sebastian is facetious.
2 *The ... wax* The older the madams get, the more masculine clothing they'll need to seem
  attractive.
3 *some have ... own* Some think their drink tastes better in a strange cup than in a familiar
  one (meaning that a man will be more interested in his lover if she is dressed in a strange
  way even if, as in this case, she appears to be a man).
4 *worth a pair of two* Worth double.
5 *My freedom ... purpose* In my chamber, I am not free to do as I like, but here in my father's
  chamber, he is unable to monitor me.

I pitied her for name's sake, that a Moll°   *Mary*
Should be so crost° in love, when there's so many   *impeded*
That owes nine lays apiece, and not so little.¹—
70   My tailor fitted her,° how like you his work?   *Mary*
SEBASTIAN. So well, no art can mend it for this purpose.
But to thy wit and help we're chief in debt,
And must live still° beholding.°   *always / indebted*
MOLL.   Any honest pity
I'm willing to bestow upon poor ringdoves.²
75   SEBASTIAN. I'll offer no worse play.
MOLL.   Nay, an you should, sir,
I should draw first and prove the quicker man.³ [*Moll draws her
weapon.*]
SEBASTIAN. Hold, there shall need no weapon at this meeting;
But 'cause thou shalt not loose thy fury idle,
Here, take this viol, [*Sebastian hands Moll a viol da gamba.*⁴] run
upon the guts⁵
80   And end thy quarrel singing.
MOLL.   Like a swan above bridge;
For, look you, here's the bridge, and here am I.⁶
SEBASTIAN. Hold on, sweet Moll.
MARY. I've heard her much commended, sir, for one that was ne'er
taught.
85   MOLL. I'm much beholding to 'em. Well, since you'll needs put us
together, sir, I'll play my part as well as I can. It shall ne'er be said

---

1   *when there's so ... little*   When there are so many Molls who have excesses of lovers. The
precise meaning is uncertain: it may refer to other Molls (here, prostitutes) having nine
lodgings—places to have sex—apiece for their business.
2   *ringdoves*   Literally, wood pigeons; here meaning the pitiable young lovers.
3   *an you ... man*   If you were to deal with me dishonestly, I would draw my weapon first and
be faster than you.
4   *viol da gamba*   Viol played with the instrument held upright and between the knees, simi-
larly to modern cello technique.
5   *run ... guts*   Run the bow across the strings, which would have been made of animal gut.
Sebastian suggests a non-violent resolution to Moll's fury.
6   *Like a swan ... I*   A pun: just as a swan may be above a bridge over a body of water, Moll's
fingers are above the bridge of the viol. Swans were supposed to sing before their deaths.

I came into a gentleman's chamber and let his instrument hang by the walls.[1]

SEBASTIAN. Why, well said Moll, i'faith. It had been a shame for that gentleman, then, that would have let it hung still and ne'er offered thee it.   90

MOLL. There it should have been still, then, for Moll; for though the world judge impudently of me, I ne'er came into that chamber yet where I took down the instrument myself.[2]

SEBASTIAN. Pish, let 'em prate abroad![3] Thou'rt here where thou art known and loved. There be a thousand close dames that will call the viol an unmannerly instrument for a woman, and therefore talk broadly of thee, when you shall have them sit wider[4] to a worse quality.   95

MOLL. Pish, I ever fall a sleep and think not of 'em, sir, and thus I dream.   100

SEBASTIAN. Prithee, let's hear thy dream, Moll.

MOLL. ([*Moll sings*] *the song and plays the viol.*)

I dream there is a mistress,
    And she lays out the money,
She goes unto her sisters,
    She never comes at any.[5]   105

(*Enter Sir Alexander behind them.*)

---

1   *It ... walls*   Double-entendre implying that Moll would never enter a gentleman's chamber and leave without making full use of him sexually.

2   *I ne'er ... myself*   I.e., I have never initiated social or sexual displays in a gentleman's chambers.

3   *let ... abroad*   Let the world outside chatter about you.

4   *close dames*   Secretive, private, strict women;   *unmannerly*   Impolite. One must place the viol between the legs to play, and it was therefore deemed inappropriate for women;   *talk broadly*   Gossip openly, extensively;   *sit wider*   Playing on Moll parting her legs for the viol, Sebastian implies that those that would speak ill of Moll are sexually loose themselves.

5   *goes ... any*   The woman goes to her sisters/friends (or, possibly, prostitutes), and does not come into any money or approach any men. The song is ambiguous; but it seems to indicate that this housewife spends time with other women—possibly prostitutes, possibly friends—and does not try to engage with men or prostitute herself (or, if she does, she is not successful).

She says she went to th' Burse for patterns,[1]
You shall find her at Saint Kathern's,[2]
And comes home with never a penny.

110 SEBASTIAN. That's a free mistress 'faith.
SIR ALEXANDER. [*Aside.*] Ay, Ay. I like her that sings it—one of
thine own choosing.
MOLL. But shall I dream again?

[*Moll sings again.*]

Here comes a wench will brave° ye,   *challenge*
115   Her courage was so great.
She lay with one o'the Navy,
    Her husband lying i'the Fleet.°   *Fleet Prison*
Yet oft with him she caviled,[3]
    I wonder what she ails—
120 Her husband's ship lay gravelled,°   *beached*
    When hers could hoise up° sails.   *raise up*
Yet she began like all my foes,
    To call whore first;[4] for so do those—
A pox of all false tails![5]

125 SEBASTIAN. Marry, amen say I.
SIR ALEXANDER. [*Aside.*] So say I, too.
MOLL. Hang up the viol now, sir; all this while I was in a dream.[6]
    One shall lie rudely then,[7] but being awake, I keep my legs

---

1   *Burse*   Royal Exchange, a center for trading merchants and for commercial shopping;
    patterns   Designs and instructions for garments; alternatively, patrons—people who would
    pay the woman for a service.
2   *Saint Kathern's*   East London neighborhood around St. Katherine's, the poor women's hos-
    pital. The area was well known for its taverns and bawdy houses; hence the woman in the
    song likely spends all her money frivolously instead of on the goods she says she was to buy
    at the burse.
3   *with ... caviled*   She bickered or argued with him over silly things.
4   *To call whore first*   To call me a whore before I called her one.
5   *false tails*   False women (extended from "tail" meaning "vagina") or false tales.
6   *all this ... dream*   I was in a reverie while singing and playing.
7   *One shall ... then*   While sleeping it is acceptable for one to lie with her legs apart.

together. [*Sebastian hangs up the viol.*] —A watch: what's o'clock,
here?   130
SIR ALEXANDER. [*Aside.*] Now, now, she's trapt!
MOLL. Between one and two; nay, then I care not. A watch and a
    musician are cousin-germans in one thing: they must both keep
    time well,[1] or there's no goodness in 'em. The one else deserves to
    be dasht against a wall, and tother to have his brains knockt out   135
    with a fiddle case. [*Moll notices the gold chain and the ruff.*]
    What? A loose chain and a dangling diamond!
    Here were a brave° booty for an evening-thief now.   *splendid, showy*
    There's many a younger brother[2] would be glad
    To look twice in at a window for't,   140
    And wriggle in and out, like an eel in a sandbag.[3]
    Oh, if men's secret youthful faults should judge 'em,
    'Twould be the general'st execution
    That e'er was seen in England.[4]
    There would be but few left to sing the ballads![5] There would be   145
    so much work, most of our brokers would be chosen for hang-
    men. A good day for them; they might renew their wardrobes of
    free cost[6] then.
SEBASTIAN. [*To Mary.*] This is the roaring wench must do us good.[7]
MARY. [*To Sebastian.*] No poison, sir, but serves us for some use,[8]   150
    Which is confirmed in her.
SEBASTIAN. [*To All.*]   Peace, peace—
    'Foot,° I did hear him, sure, where'er he be.   *God's foot*

---

1 *cousin-germans* Closely allied like relatives; can also refer to first cousins; *they must ...
   time well* The watch must be correct and the musician must be steady in tempo.
2 *younger brother* One who (unlike his older brothers) does not stand to inherit any con-
   siderable fortune or land.
3 *eel in a sandbag* Proverbial: one who is crafty and slippery. Here, Moll imagines that the
   younger brother must find a way by craft to wriggle in and steal the treasures in the window.
4 *if ... England* If men were judged by the things they did in secret as youths, there would
   be the most widespread punishment (execution) in all England.
5 *left to ... the ballads* Left alive to sing the songs of others' exploits, as Moll has just done.
6 *brokers* Intermediaries, second hand clothes-dealers in this case; *renew ... cost* Get
   many new clothes for free (from the people they execute). Hangmen would receive the
   clothes of those they executed.
7 *must do us good* That will help us.
8 *No poison ... use* Proverbial, from "One poison expels another"; they will use Moll to undo
   Alexander's ills.

MOLL. Who did you hear?

SEBASTIAN.   My father—
  'Twas like a sigh of his; I must be wary.

155 SIR ALEXANDER. [*Aside.*] No, will't not be? Am I alone so wretched
  That nothing takes?[1] I'll put him to his plunge for't.[2]

  [*Sebastian spies Sir Alexander.*]

SEBASTIAN. Life, here he comes. [*Aloud to Moll.*] Sir, I beseech you
    take it,
  Your way of teaching does so much content me,
  I'll make it four pound, here's forty shillings, sir.
160 I think I name it right. [*Aside to Moll, handing her money.*] Help
    me, good Moll.
  Forty in hand.

MOLL.   Sir, you shall pardon me,
  I have more of the meanest scholar I can teach:
  This pays me more than you have offered yet.[3]

SEBASTIAN. At the next quarter,
165 When I receive the means my father 'lows° me.   allows
  You shall have t'other forty.

SIR ALEXANDER. [*Aside.*]   This were well now,
  Were 't to a man, whose sorrows had blind eyes,
  But mine behold his follies and untruths
  With two clear glasses.

  [*Alexander comes forward, addressing Sebastian.*]

                    —How now?

SEBASTIAN.   Sir.

SIR ALEXANDER. [*Indicating Moll.*]   What's he there?[4]
170 SEBASTIAN. You're come in good time, sir. I've a suit to you;
    I'd crave your present kindness.

SIR ALEXANDER.   What is he there?

---

1 *nothing takes* Nothing works.
2 *I'll ... for't* I'll push him into difficulty for this.
3 *I have ... offered yet* The poorest of my students pays me more, while you've never offered
   this much before and I question your ability to pay the balance. (Forty shillings is half of
   the promised four pounds.)
4 *What's he there* Who's that?

SEBASTIAN. A gentleman, a musician, sir, one of excellent fingering.[1]
SIR ALEXANDER. Ay, I think so. [*Aside.*] I wonder how they scapt her.[2]
SEBASTIAN. H'as the most delicate stroke,[3] sir.
SIR ALEXANDER. [*Aside.*] A stroke indeed, I feel it at my heart.   175
SEBASTIAN. Puts down all your famous musicians.
SIR ALEXANDER. [*Aside.*] Ay, a whore may put down a hundred of 'em.
SEBASTIAN. Forty shillings is the agreement, sir, between us.
   Now, sir, my present means mounts but to half on't.
SIR ALEXANDER. And he stands upon the whole.[4]   180
SEBASTIAN. Ay, indeed does he, sir.
SIR ALEXANDER. [*Aside.*] And will do still; he'll ne'er be in other tale.[5]
SEBASTIAN. Therefore I'd stop his mouth, sir, an I could.
SIR ALEXANDER. Hum, true. [*Aside.*] There is no other way indeed,
   His folly hardens, shame must needs succeed.   185
   [*To Moll.*] Now, sir, I understand you profess music.
MOLL. I am a poor servant to that liberal science, sir.
SIR ALEXANDER. Where is it you teach?
MOLL. Right against Clifford's Inn.[6]
SIR ALEXANDER. Hum, that's a fit place for it; you have many   190
   scholars.[7]
MOLL. And some of worth, whom I may call my masters.
SIR ALEXANDER. [*Aside.*] Ay, true, a company of whoremasters.[8]
   [*To Moll.*] You teach to sing, too?
MOLL. Marry, do I, sir.   195

---

1 *fingering* Placement of one's fingers on the viol's frets while playing, also suggesting stealing or sexual touching.
2 *I wonder ... her* I wonder how it could be that Moll did not steal the watch and the chain.
3 *stroke* Bow stroke, with a double entendre suggesting sexual touch (though the following line also puns upon "stroke" as an apoplectic attack).
4 *stands* Waits for, and bawdily, has an erection; *whole* Whole sum, and bawdily, hole.
5 *he'll ... tale* He'll never accept another reckoning of the account; *tale* Tally or account, with a possible pun on tale with "tail," slang for "genitals."
6 *Clifford's Inn* One of the Inns of Chancery, associated with the Inner Temple, where men trained in the lower offices of the law as attorneys and solicitors.
7 *scholars* Students or clients.
8 *whoremasters* Those who hire prostitutes.

SIR ALEXANDER. I think you'll find an apt scholar of my son, especially for pricksong.[1]

MOLL. I have much hope of him.

SIR ALEXANDER. [*Aside.*] I am sorry for't, I have the less for that.

200 [*To Moll.*] You can play any lesson?

MOLL. At first sight, sir.

SIR ALEXANDER. There's a thing called "The Witch,"[2] can you play that?

MOLL. I would be sorry anyone should mend me in't.[3]

205 SIR ALEXANDER. [*Aside.*] Ay, I believe thee. Thou hast so bewitcht my son,

　　No care will mend the work that thou hast done.

　　I have bethought myself since my art fails,

　　I'll make her policy the art to trap her.

　　Here are four angels markt with holes[4] in them

210 　　Fit for his crackt[5] companions. Gold he will give her;

　　These will I make induction to her ruin,[6]

　　And rid shame from my house, grief from my heart.

　　[*To Sebastian, giving angels.*] Here, son, in what you take content

　　　and pleasure,

　　Want shall not curb you. Pay the gentleman

215 　　His latter half in gold.

SEBASTIAN. 　　　　　　　I thank you, sir.

SIR ALEXANDER. [*Aside.*] Oh, may the operation on't, end three:

　　In her, life; shame in him; and grief in me.[7]

(*Exit Alexander.*)

---

1 *pricksong* Sheet music or written charts rather than music imitated by ear, with a bawdy pun on "prick."

2 *"The Witch"* May refer to a specific ballad, or it could be a name chosen to imply that Moll has wicked power over Sebastian.

3 *I would ... in't* I doubt anyone could play the song better than I could; *mend* Correct, improve.

4 *markt with holes* Tampered with, clipped, or filed and marked. If a coin were cracked at the edge, it could no longer pass as legal tender. Tampering with coins in this way was highly illegal; defacing coins could be prosecuted as treason.

5 *crackt* Of flawed moral character.

6 *These ... ruin* I will cause her ruin through these coins.

7 *may the ... me* May this plan result in three things: that Moll will be executed, that Sebastian will stop bringing me shame, and that I will stop feeling grief.

SEBASTIAN. [*Gives money to Moll.*] Faith, thou shalt have'em. 'Tis
  my father's gift;
Never was man beguiled with better shift.[1]
MOLL. He that can take me for a male musician,   220
  I cannot choose but make him my instrument
  And play upon him![2]

(*Exeunt omnes.*)

[ACT 4, SCENE 2]

(*Enter Mistress Gallipot and Mistress Openwork.*)

MISTRESS GALLIPOT. Is then that bird of yours, Master Goshawk, so
  wild?
MISTRESS OPENWORK. A goshawk, a puttock: all for prey. He angles
  for fish, but he loves flesh better.
MISTRESS GALLIPOT. Is't possible his smooth face should have   5
  wrinkles in't, and we not see them?[3]
MISTRESS OPENWORK. Possible? Why, have not many handsome
  legs in silk stockings villainous splay feet for all their great
  roses?[4]
MISTRESS GALLIPOT. Troth, sirrah, thou say'st true.   10
MISTRESS OPENWORK. Didst never see an archer, as thou'ast walkt
  by Bunhill,[5] look asquint when he drew his bow?
MISTRESS GALLIPOT. Yes, when his arrows have fline toward Islington, his eyes have shot clean contrary towards Pimlico.[6]

---

1 *Never ... shift* Never was a man tricked with a better ploy.
2 *I ... him* See *Hamlet* 3.2, in which Hamlet accuses Rosencrantz and Guildenstern, "You
  would play upon me; you would seem to know / my stops."
3 *Is't ... them?* Is it possible this youth is older than he seems, and we don't see it?
4 *villainous splay feet* Ugly, clumsy feet that turn outward; *great roses* Decorative rose
  knots on shoes.
5 *Bunhill* Part of the recreation fields north of London, and the site of a legendary archery
  contest featuring Robin Hood.
6 *Pimlico* Tavern in Hoxton that was known for its ale and as a place of resort. Hoxton was
  to the northwest while Islington was to the northeast, so the archer lets his arrow go in one
  direction and looks in the opposite.

15   MISTRESS OPENWORK. For all the world, so does Master Goshawk
     double with[1] me.

     MISTRESS GALLIPOT. Oh, fie upon him! If he double once, he's not
     for me.

     MISTRESS OPENWORK. Because Goshawk go in a shag-ruff band,
20   with a face sticking up in't which shows like an agate set in a
     cramp-ring,[2] he thinks I'm in love with him.

     MISTRESS GALLIPOT. 'Las, I think he takes his mark amiss in thee.

     MISTRESS OPENWORK. He has, by often beating into me, made me
     believe that my husband kept a whore.

25   MISTRESS GALLIPOT. Very good.

     MISTRESS OPENWORK. Swore to me that my husband this very
     morning went in a boat, with a tilt over it, to the Three Pigeons at
     Brentford, and his punk[3] with him under his tilt.

     MISTRESS GALLIPOT. That were wholesome!

30   MISTRESS OPENWORK. I believed it; fell a-swearing at him, cursing
     of harlots, made me ready to hoise up sail and be there as soon as
     he.

     MISTRESS GALLIPOT. So, so.

     MISTRESS OPENWORK. And for that voyage, Goshawk comes hither
35   incontinently.[4] But, sirrah, this water-spaniel dives after no duck
     but me:[5] his hope is having me at Brentford to make me cry
     quack.[6]

     MISTRESS GALLIPOT. Art sure of it?

     MISTRESS OPENWORK. Sure of it? My poor innocent Openwork
40   came in as I was poking[7] my ruff; presently hit I him i'the teeth
     with the Three Pigeons.[8] He forswore all, I up and opened all,
     and now stands he—in a shop hard by—like a musket on a

---

1   *double with* Deceive, act duplicitously toward.

2   *agate* Quartz mineral variety, often banded and multi-colored, that was frequently used
    for jewelry; *cramp-ring* Ring considered a charm against cramps.

3   *tilt* Awning; *punk* Prostitute.

4   *incontinently* Immediately.

5   *water-spaniel ... me* Goshawk, like a dog, is single minded in his pursuit of his prey:
    Mistress Openwork.

6   *his hope ... quack* His intention is to bring me to Brentford where he hopes to have sex
    with me.

7   *poking* Crimping the folds of a ruff with a special poking stick.

8   *presently ... Pigeons* As soon as he came in, I confronted him with the tale of his trip to the
    Three Pigeons.

rest,[1] to hit Goshawk i'the eye when he comes to fetch me to the boat.

MISTRESS GALLIPOT. Such another lame gelding[2] offered to carry 45
me through thick and thin—Laxton, sirrah—but I am rid of him now.

MISTRESS OPENWORK. Happy is the woman can be rid of 'em all!
'Las, what are your whisking[3] gallants to our husbands? Weigh
'em rightly man for man. 50

MISTRESS GALLIPOT. Troth, mere shallow things.[4]

MISTRESS OPENWORK. Idle, simple things, running heads.[5] And
yet, let 'em run over us never so fast: we shop-keepers—when all's
done—are sure to have 'em in our purse-nets[6] at length, and when
they are in, Lord, what simple animals they are. 55

MISTRESS OPENWORK. Then they hang head.

MISTRESS GALLIPOT. Then they droop.

MISTRESS OPENWORK. Then they write letters.

MISTRESS GALLIPOT. Then they cog.[7]

MISTRESS OPENWORK. Then they deal underhand with us, and we 60
must ingle with our husbands a-bed, and we must swear they are
our cousins and able to do us a pleasure at court.[8]

MISTRESS GALLIPOT. And yet when we have done our best, all's but
put into a riven dish:[9] we are but frumpt at[10] and libelled upon.

MISTRESS OPENWORK. Oh, if it were the good Lord's will there 65
were a law made, no citizen should trust any of 'em all!

(*Enter Goshawk.*)

---

1   *hard by*   Nearby;   *musket ... rest*   Early seventeenth-century gun supported by a pole with
    an iron, u-shaped holder.
2   *gelding*   Castrated male—a term used in reference to horses more often than to people. The
    insult refers to Laxton's name and his apparent "lack of stones" (testicles).
3   *whisking*   Active and brisk.
4   *things*   The gallants; but also in a double entendre, penises.
5   *running heads*   Easily distracted, changeable people.
6   *purse-nets*   Bag-shaped nets used for catching rabbits and other small game; there is as well
    an implicit comparison between "purse-nets" and women's sexual anatomy.
7   *cog*   Cheat, deceive.
8   *ingle*   Fondle, caress, wheedle;   *cousins*   Kin, close relatives;   *able ... court*   Able to do
    us a favor with an official.
9   *riven dish*   Cloven, broken dish.
10 *frumpt at*   Scoffed at, mocked.

MISTRESS GALLIPOT. Hush, sirrah! Goshawk flutters.

GOSHAWK. How now, are you ready?

MISTRESS OPENWORK. Nay, are you ready? A little thing you see
70 makes us ready.[1]

GOSHAWK. Us? Why, must she make one i'the voyage?

MISTRESS OPENWORK. Oh, by any means. Do I know how my
husband will handle me?

GOSHAWK. [*Aside.*] 'Foot, how shall I find water to keep these two
75 mills going?[2] [*To them.*] Well since you'll needs be clapt under
hatches, if I sail not with you both till all split, hang me up at
the main yard, & duck me.[3] [*Aside.*] It's but liquoring them both
soundly, & then you shall see their cork heels fly up high, like two
swans when their tails are above water, and their long necks under
80 water, diving to catch gudgeons.[4] [*To them.*] Come, come! Oars
stand ready! The tide's with us, on with those false faces. [*Wives
put on masks.*] Blow winds, and thou shalt take thy husband,
casting out his net to catch fresh salmon at Brentford.[5]

MISTRESS GALLIPOT. I believe you'll eat of a cod's head of your own
85 dressing before you reach half-way thither.[6]

GOSHAWK. So, so, follow close. Pin as you go. [*They move toward an
exit.*]

(*Enter Laxton muffled.*)

---

1 *A little ... ready* We are almost ready, with a pun on "thing" meaning "penis."

2 *how ... going?* How will I find the energy to have sex with both of these women?

3 *you'll ... hatches* You'll be kept below deck; *all split* Torn to pieces or wrecked; *main
yard* Spar on a ship's mast on which the mainsail is extended; *duck me* Plunge me
under the water; *Well since ... duck me* Goshawk claims that if the boat were to wreck, he
would accept the traditional punishments of being hoisted up on the yard or being thrown
overboard. The lines suggest a pledge to do his best to satisfy them sexually, even if it wrecks
him, or to submit to punishment.

4 *liquoring ... soundly* Getting them very drunk; *cork heels* Fashionable shoes with
cork heels; figuratively, "cork-heeled" meant light-heeled or wanton; *like two swans ...
gudgeons* Simile imagining the women in outrageous sexual positions, like swans diving
for fish, with posteriors high up and heads at their feet underwater.

5 *thou shalt ... Brentford* You will overtake your husband looking for fresh prostitutes at
Brentford.

6 *cod's head* Stupid fellow or blockhead; *dressing* preparation; *you'll eat ... thither* You'll
expose yourself as a fool before you get halfway to Brentford.

LAXTON. [*To Mistress Gallipot.*] Do you hear?[1]

MISTRESS GALLIPOT. Yes, I thank my ears.

LAXTON. I must have a bout with your pothecaryship.[2]

MISTRESS GALLIPOT. At what weapon?   90

LAXTON. I must speak with you.

MISTRESS GALLIPOT. No.

LAXTON. No? You shall.

MISTRESS GALLIPOT. Shall? Away soust sturgeon, half-fish, half-flesh![3]   95

LAXTON. 'Faith, gib,[4] are you spitting? I'll cut your tail, puss-cat for this.

MISTRESS GALLIPOT. 'Las poor *Laxton*, I think thy tail's cut already.[5] Your worst![6]

LAXTON. If I do not[7]—   100

(*Exit Laxton.*)

GOSHAWK. Come, ha'you done?

(*Enter Master Openwork.*)

[*To Mistress Openwork.*] S'foot, Rosamond, your husband!

OPENWORK. How now? Sweet Master Goshawk, none more welcome.

I have wanted[8] your embracements. When friends meet,

The music of the spheres[9] sounds not more sweet,   105

---

1   *Do you hear?*   Laxton wants to know if he can be heard over his muffling.

2   *bout ... pothecaryship*   Fight with your husband.

3   *soust sturgeon*   Drunk fish;   *half-fish, half-flesh*   Neither one thing or the other, referring to the proverb "Neither fish nor flesh nor good red herring"; the implication is, again, that Laxton has been gelded and is less than a man.

4   *gib*   Cat—usually a male cat, castrated—or a cat-like personality; a term of reproach when applied to a woman.

5   *thy ... cut already*   You're already castrated.

6   *Your worst!*   Do your worst!

7   *If ... not*   See if I do not.

8   *wanted*   Missed.

9   *music of the spheres*   Beautiful harmony created by the resonances of celestial bodies in alignment.

Than does their conference. Who is this? Rosamond? Wife?
How now sister?
GOSHAWK.   Silence if you love me.
OPENWORK. Why maskt?
MISTRESS OPENWORK.   Does a mask grieve you sir?
OPENWORK.   It does.
MISTRESS OPENWORK. Then you're best get you a-mumming.[1]
110 GOSHAWK. [*To Mistress Openwork*.] S'foot you'll spoil all.
MISTRESS GALLIPOT. May not we cover our bare faces with masks
As well as you cover your bald heads with hats?
OPENWORK. No masks; why, they're thieves to beauty that rob eyes
Of admiration in which true love lies.
115 Why are masks worn? Why good? Or why desired?
Unless by their gay covers wits are fired
To read the vil'st looks.[2] Many bad faces—
Because rich gems are treasured up in cases—
Pass by their privilege current;[3] but as caves
120 Damn misers' gold, so masks are beauties' graves.[4]
Men ne'er meet women with such muffled eyes,
But they curse her that first did masks devise,
And swear it was some beldam.[5] Come, off with't.
MISTRESS OPENWORK. I will not.
125 OPENWORK. Good faces maskt are jewels kept by sprites.[6]
Hide none but bad ones, for they poison men's sights;
Show them as shop-keepers do their 'broidered stuff:[7]
By owl-light.[8] Fine wares cannot be open enough.

---

1   *get you a-mumming*   Get ready to perform like a mummer, a masked, mute participant in
    a celebratory festival or play; be quiet.
2   *by their ... vil'st looks*   The masks' attractive exteriors fire up men to look at otherwise ugly
    faces.
3   *Many ... current*   Ugly faces hidden behind masks pass for good, because as with riches kept
    in cases, people assume that what is concealed is valuable;   *current*   Genuine.
4   *but ... graves*   But, as treasure is wasted when hidden by the miserly in caves, so is it wrong
    to hide beauty behind masks.
5   *Men ... beldam*   When men meet women who hide behind masks, they curse the woman
    who first invented masks and swear she was an old hag.
6   *kept by sprites*   Kept away by spirits.
7   *'broidered stuff*   Cheap fabrics that have been embroidered to make them seem more fine.
8   *owl-light*   Dim light, nightfall.

Prithee, sweet Rose, come strike this sail.[1]

MISTRESS OPENWORK. Sail?

OPENWORK. Ha?

Yes, wife, strike sail, for storms are in thine eyes. 130

MISTRESS OPENWORK. They're here, sir, in my brows,[2] if any rise.

OPENWORK. Ha, brows? [*To Mistress Gallipot.*] What says she,
    friend? Pray tell me why
    Your two flags were advanced:[3] the comedy?
    Come, what's the comedy?

MISTRESS GALLIPOT. *Westward Ho.*[4]

OPENWORK. How?

MISTRESS OPENWORK. 'Tis *Westward Ho*, she says.[5] 135

GOSHAWK. Are you both mad?

MISTRESS OPENWORK. Is't market day at Brentford, and your ware
    Not sent up yet?[6]

OPENWORK. What market day? What ware?

MISTRESS OPENWORK. A pie with three pigeons in't; 'tis drawn and
    stays your cutting up.[7]

GOSHAWK. As you regard my credit— 140

OPENWORK. Art mad?

MISTRESS OPENWORK. Yes, lecherous goat! Baboon![8]

OPENWORK. Baboon? Then toss me in a blanket.[9]

MISTRESS OPENWORK. [*To Mistress Gallipot.*] Do I it well?[10]

MISTRESS GALLIPOT. [*To Mistress Openwork.*] Rarely.°   *excellently* 145

---

1   *strike this sail* Lower the sails, take off your mask.

2   *in my brows* In my forehead (where cuckold's horns would be located).

3   *two flags ... advanced* London playhouses flew flags to indicate they were showing plays.

4   *Westward Ho* 1604 play by Thomas Dekker and John Webster that featured city wives going on an excursion to Brentford with their gallant suitors. "Westward Ho!" was also a cry to hire a boat to go west on the river.

5   *'Tis ... says* Mistress Openwork responds as though Openwork's "How?" is a mispronunciation of "Ho," which she then corrects.

6   *Is't market ... up yet?* Is it the day of the market at Brentford, and your goods are not yet ready?

7   *stays your cutting up* Is waiting to be served; i.e., your out-of-town mistresses are ready and waiting for you.

8   *goat! Baboon!* Goats and baboons were considered lustful creatures.

9   *toss ... blanket* Rough punishment in which someone is bounced up in the air repeatedly by means of a blanket held by the punishers.

10 *Do ... well?* Am I doing a good job of acting my part of the angry wife?

GOSHAWK. Belike, sir, she's not well; best leave her.

OPENWORK.   No,
I'll stand the storm now, how fierce soe'er it blow.

MISTRESS OPENWORK. Did I for this lose all my friends?[1] Refuse
Rich hopes and golden fortunes to be made
150   A stale[2] to a common whore?

OPENWORK.   This does amaze me.

MISTRESS OPENWORK. Oh God, oh God! Feed at reversion now?
A strumpet's leaving?[3]

OPENWORK.   Rosamond!

GOSHAWK. [Aside.] I sweat; would I lay in Cold Harbor.[4]

MISTRESS OPENWORK. Thou hast struck ten thousand daggers
through my heart!

155   OPENWORK. Not I, by heaven, sweet wife.

MISTRESS OPENWORK. Go, devil, go! That which thou swear'st by
damns thee.

GOSHAWK. [Aside to Mistress Openwork.] 'Sheart will you undo me?

MISTRESS OPENWORK. [To Mister Openwork.] Why stay you here?
The star by which you sail,
Shines yonder above Chelsea; you lose your shore.[5]
160   If this moon light you, seek out your light whore. [6]

OPENWORK. Ha?

MISTRESS GALLIPOT. Pish! Your western pug![7]

GOSHAWK. [Aside.]   Zounds! Now hell roars!

---

1   *my friends* My relatives and connections.

2   *stale* Lover whose devotion is ridiculed for the amusement of others or rivals and, in this
case, for the amusement of a common prostitute.

3   *reversion* Remains or leftovers; *leaving* Cast-off.

4   *Cold Harbor* Generally speaking, a place of refuge or asylum, a shelter, inn, or place of
entertainment. Specifically, Cold Harbour was a great house near London Bridge held by
the Earl of Shrewsbury. John Stow in *A Survey of London* (1603) details that the last earl
built a number of tenements on the site, "now letten out for great rents, to people of all
sorts" (1.237). Cold Harbour was then, as George Walter Thornbury attests in *Old and New
London*, a "haunt of poverty" (2.17) and a place of sanctuary.

5   *Chelsea* District on the north side of the Thames, to the west of the city and on the way
to Brentford; a likely place to stop and pick up a prostitute, who is here imagined as the
guiding "star" toward which Openwork navigates; *you lose your shore* Get going or you'll
lose the ability to find your shore—your rendezvous—in the dark.

6   *light whore* Wanton woman, while punning on "light" as moonlight.

7   *western pug* Chelsea harlot.

MISTRESS OPENWORK. With whom you tilted in a pair of oars[1]
    This very morning.
OPENWORK.   Oars?
MISTRESS OPENWORK.   At Brentford, sir.
OPENWORK.   Rack° not my patience! Master Goshawk,   *torture*
    Some slave has buzzed this into her, has he not?   165
    I run a-tilt in Brentford with a woman?
    'Tis a lie!
    What old bawd tells thee this? 'Sdeath° 'tis a lie.   *God's death*
MISTRESS OPENWORK. 'Tis one[2] to thy face shall justify
    All that I speak.   170
OPENWORK.   'Ud'soul,[3] do but name that rascal.
MISTRESS OPENWORK. No, sir, I will not.
GOSHAWK. [*Aside.*]   Keep thee there, girl. [*To them.*]—Then!
OPENWORK. [*To Mistress Gallipot.*] Sister, know you this varlet?
MISTRESS GALLIPOT.   Yes.
OPENWORK.   Swear true;
    Is there a rogue so low damned? A second Judas?[4]
    A common hangman? Cutting a man's throat?
    Does it to his face? Bite me behind my back?[5]   175
    A cur-dog? Swear if you know this hell-hound![6]
MISTRESS GALLIPOT. In truth I do.
OPENWORK.   His name?
MISTRESS GALLIPOT.   Not for the world,
    To have you to stab him.
GOSHAWK. [*Aside.*]   Oh, brave girls! Worth gold.
OPENWORK. A word, honest Master Goshawk.
    ([*Master Openwork*] draw[*s*] out his sword.)
GOSHAWK.   What do you mean, sir?
OPENWORK. Keep off, and if the devil can give a name   180

---

1 *With ... oars* With whom you boated, with a pun on "tilt" as the boat's covering and "tilt-
    ing" as jousting or sexual intercourse. The wordplay in this exchange also reflects the early
    modern pronunciation of "whores" as a homophone for "oars."
2 *one* Someone who.
3 *'Ud'soul* God bless my soul.
4 *second Judas* Someone as much of a traitor to a friend as Judas Iscariot, the disciple who
    betrayed Jesus.
5 *Bite ... back* Slander me behind my back.
6 *cur-dog* Ill-bred, snappish dog; *hell-hound* Cerberus.

To this new fury,[1] holla° it through my ear,   *shout*
Or wrap it up in some hid character.[2]
I'll ride to Oxford, and watch out mine eyes,
But I'll hear the brazen head speak;[3] or else
185   Show me but one hair of his head or beard,
That I may sample it. If the fiend I meet
In mine own house, I'll kill him—the street,
Or at the church door—there, 'cause he seeks to untie
The knot God fastens,[4] he deserves most to die!
190   MISTRESS OPENWORK. [*To Mistress Gallipot.*] My husband titles
him.[5]
OPENWORK.   Master Goshawk, pray, sir,
Swear to me that you know him or know him not,
Who makes me at Brentford to take up a petticoat[6]
Beside my wife's.
GOSHAWK.   By heaven, that man I know not.
MISTRESS OPENWORK. Come, come, you lie!
GOSHAWK. [*To Mistress Openwork.*]   Will you not have all out?[7]
195   [*To Openwork.*] By heaven, I know no man beneath the moon
Should° do you wrong, but if I had his name,   *would*
I'd print it in text letters.[8]
MISTRESS OPENWORK.   Print thine own then.
Did'st not thou swear to me he kept his whore?

---

1   *fury*   In Roman and Greek mythology, a tormenting or avenging spirit, female in form. Three main furies are often invoked—Tisiphone (punishment), Alecto (endless), and Megaera (jealous rage)—and perhaps the "new fury" would be a fourth.
2   *hid character*   Secret code.
3   *I'll ride ... speak*   I'll get the answer from Roger Bacon's enchanted bronze head, as in Robert Greene's *Friar Bacon and Friar Bungay* (1587–92?); *watch out mine eyes*   Stay awake (unlike Friar Bacon, who falls asleep and misses the head's proclamation).
4   *The knot God fastens*   The marriage knot.
5   *titles him*   Calls him what he is.
6   *Who makes ... a petticoat*   Who says that at Brentford I lift a woman's petticoat—i.e., have sex with her. The phrase has an added irony because Master Openwork is a sempster who would "take up" garments; i.e., tighten, shorten, or pleat them.
7   *Will ... out?*   Perhaps an aside to quiet Mistress Openwork, or a feigned statement to make Goshawk look like he has no secrets.
8   *text letters*   Capital letters.

MISTRESS GALLIPOT. And that in sinful Brentford they would
    commit
That which our lips did water at,¹ sir?—Ha?   200
MISTRESS OPENWORK. Thou spider, that hast woven thy cunning
    web
In mine own house t'ensnare me: hast not thou
Suck't nourishment even underneath this roof,
And turned it all to poison, spitting it
On thy friend's face, my husband—he, as t'were sleeping—   205
Only to leave him ugly to mine eyes,
That they might glance on thee?²
MISTRESS GALLIPOT.   Speak, are these lies?
GOSHAWK. Mine own shame me confounds.
MISTRESS OPENWORK.   No more, he's stung.
Who'd think that in one body there could dwell
Deformity and beauty, heaven and hell?   210
Goodness, I see, is but outside; we all set,
In rings of gold, stones that be counterfeit.
I thought you none.³
GOSHAWK.   Pardon me.
OPENWORK.   Truth, I do.
This blemish grows in nature,° not in you,   *human nature*
For man's creation stick even moles in scorn   215
On fairest cheeks.—Wife, nothing is perfect born.
MISTRESS OPENWORK. I thought you had been born perfect.
OPENWORK. What's this whole world but a gilt rotten pill?⁴
For at the heart lies the old core still.
I'll tell you, Master Goshawk, ay, in your eye   220
I have seen wanton fire;⁵ and then to try
The soundness of my judgment, I told you
I kept a whore—made you believe 'twas true—

---

1   *water at* Salivate at—the women would be enticed by the thought of sex with their own
    husbands.
2   *turned ... thee?* Did you not take the sweetness offered to you and turn it to "poison"—
    your slanders of Master Openwork—which you then spat on Openwork to disfigure him
    and make me look more favorably on you?
3   *I ... none* I thought you were the real gem.
4   *gilt rotten pill* Rotten core covered by a golden shell.
5   *in ... fire* I have seen lechery in the way that you look at others.

Only to feel how your pulse beat, but find
225 The world can hardly yield a perfect friend.¹
Come, come, a trick° of youth, and 'tis forgiven;   *indiscretion*
This rub° put by, our love shall run more even.   *impediment*
MISTRESS OPENWORK. You'll deal upon men's wives no more?
GOSHAWK. No.—You teach me a trick for that.
230 MISTRESS OPENWORK. Troth do not; they'll o'erreach thee.²
OPENWORK. Make my house yours, sir, still.
GOSHAWK.   No.
OPENWORK.   I say you shall.
Seeing, thus besieged, it holds out, 'twill never fall.³

(*Enter Master Gallipot and Greenwit like a summoner [wearing a wig]; Laxton, muffled, aloof off.*⁴)

OMNES. How now?
GALLIPOT. [*To Greenwit.*] With me, sir?
235 GREENWIT. [*To Gallipot.*] You, sir. I have gone snuffling up and down by your door this hour to watch for you.
MISTRESS GALLIPOT. What's the matter, husband?
GREENWIT. I have caught a cold in my head,⁵ sir, by sitting up late in the Rose Tavern, but I hope you understand my speech.
240 GALLIPOT. So, sir.
GREENWIT. I cite you by the name of Hippocrates Gallipot, and you by the name of Prudence Gallipot, to appear upon *Crastino*—do you see—*Crastino sancti Dunstani*, this Easter Term, in Bow Church.⁶
245 GALLIPOT. Where, sir? What says he?

---

1 *to try ... friend* To test my judgment of your lechery, I told you I kept a whore in order to see how you would react, and found your friendship lacking and my judgment correct.
2 *they'll ... thee* They'll defeat you.
3 *Seeing ... fall* Having seen how my house and marriage have survived this attack, I know they will never collapse.
4 *summoner* Officer who serves citations or summonses to ecclesiastical court; *muffled, aloof off* Standing off to the side with his face covered.
5 *cold in my head* Greenwit pretends he has a cold to disguise his voice.
6 *Crastino sancti Dunstani* 20 May, the day after St. Dunstan's Day (19 May); *Easter Term* The spring law term, April–May; *Bow Church* St. Mary Le Bow, in Cheapside, central London. Bow Church housed the Court of Arches—the Ecclesiastical Court for parishes under the Archbishop of London—that heard marital cases.

GREENWIT. Bow: Bow Church, to answer to a libel of precontract[1]
on the part and behalf of the said Prudence and another. You're
best, sir, take a copy of the citation,[2] 'tis but twelvepence. [*Offers
citation.*]

OMNES. A citation?

GALLIPOT. You pocky-nosed rascal, what slave fees you to this?[3]   250

LAXTON. Slave? [*Laxton joins the others; he speaks aside to Goshawk.*] I
ha' nothing to do with you, do you hear, sir?

GOSHAWK. [*Aside to Laxton.*] Laxton is't not?—What vagary[4] is this?

GALLIPOT. [*To Laxton.*] Trust me, I thought, sir, this storm long ago
had been full laid, when, if you be remembered, I paid you the   255
last fifteen pound, besides the thirty you had first; for then you
swore—

LAXTON. Tush, tush, sir, oaths.
Truth yet I'm loath to vex you. Tell you what;
Make up the money I had an hundred pound,[5]   260
And take your bellyful of her.[6]

GALLIPOT.   An hundred pound?

MISTRESS GALLIPOT. What, a hundred pound? He gets none! What,
a hundred pound?

GALLIPOT. Sweet Pru, be calm. The gentleman offers thus:
If I will make the moneys that are past
A hundred pound, he will discharge all courts   265
And give his bond never to vex us more.[7]

MISTRESS GALLIPOT. A hundred pound? 'Las; take, sir, but
threescore.[8]
[*Aside to Laxton.*] Do you seek my undoing?

LAXTON.   I'll not bate° one sixpence.   *give up*

---

1 *libel of precontract* Charge that Gallipot married Mistress Gallipot when she was officially
   betrothed to another.
2 *citation* Summons to court.
3 *pocky-nosed* Syphilitic; *what slave ... this* What rascal employs you to deliver this summons?
4 *vagary* Capricious action, eccentric ploy.
5 *Make ... pound* Bring the total payment to one hundred pounds.
6 *take your ... of her* You can have as much as you want of her.
7 *discharge ... more* Rescind all lawsuits and sign a document pledging no legal action
   against us.
8 *threescore* Sixty.

[*Aside to Mistress Gallipot.*] I'll maul you, puss, for spitting.

MISTRESS GALLIPOT. [*Aside to Laxton.*]   Do thy worst!

270   [*Aloud.*] Will fourscore stop thy mouth?

LAXTON.   No.

MISTRESS GALLIPOT.   You're a slave!

Thou cheat, I'll now tear money from thy throat.

Husband, lay hold on yonder tawny-coat.[1]

GREENWIT. Nay, gentlemen, seeing your women are so hot,[2]

I must lose my hair in their company, I see.

[*Greenwit removes his wig.*]

275 MISTRESS OPENWORK. His hair sheds off, and yet he speaks not so
much

In the nose[3] as he did before.

GOSHAWK.   He has had

The better chirurgeon.[4]—Master Greenwit,

Is your wit so raw as to play no better a part

Than a summoner's?

GALLIPOT.   I pray, who plays

280 *A Knack to Know an Honest Man* in this company?[5]

MISTRESS GALLIPOT. Dear husband, pardon me. I did dissemble,

Told thee I was his precontracted wife,

When letters came from him for thirty pound,

I had no shift but that.

GALLIPOT.   A very clean shift,

---

1   *tawny-coat* Officer of the ecclesiastical court.

2   *so hot* So angry, but also punning on the idea that they are syphilitic. Syphilis resulted in hair loss, as he jokes about in his next line when taking off his wig.

3   *In the nose* Mistress Openwork confirms that Greenwit no longer sounds like he has a cold.

4   *He has ... better chirurgeon* The person who attached the fake nose for Greenwit proves the better surgeon, as that doctor did a good job curing him. Fake noses, like wigs, were commonly worn by victims of syphilis.

5   *A Knack ... Man* 1596 play, the counterpart to the earlier *A Knack to Know a Knave* (1594); *who plays ... this company* Who would attempt to find an honest man among those present?

But able to make me lousy.¹—On.°   *go on* 285
MISTRESS GALLIPOT.   Husband, I plucked—
When he had tempted me to think well of him—
Gelt feathers² from thy wings, to make him fly
More lofty.
GALLIPOT.   O'the top of you, wife.³—On.
MISTRESS GALLIPOT. He having wasted them, comes now for more,
Using me as a ruffian doth his whore,   290
Whose sin keeps him in breath.⁴ By heaven, I vow,
Thy bed he never wronged more than he does now.
GALLIPOT. My bed? Ha, ha! Like enough, a shop-board will serve
To have a cuckold's coat cut out upon;⁵
Of that we'll talk hereafter. [*To Laxton.*] You're a villain.   295
LAXTON. Hear me but speak, sir, you shall find me none.
OMNES. Pray, sir, be patient and hear him.
GALLIPOT.   I am
Muzzled for biting, sir, use me how you will.
LAXTON. The first hour that your wife was in my eye,
Myself with other gentlemen sitting by   300
In your shop tasting smoke,⁶ and speech being used
That men who have fairest wives are most abused
And hardly scapt the horn,⁷ your wife maintained
That only such spots in city dames were stained
Justly but by men's slanders.⁸ For her own part,   305
She vowed that you had so much of her heart,
No man by all his wit, by any wile,

---

1 *A very ... lousy* A clean trick (punning on shift as an undergarment), but one that makes
   me dirty or itchy with lice.
2 *Gelt feathers* Golden feathers; money.
3 *O'the ... wife* To fly over top of you, wife; an implication that Laxton has had sex with
   Mistress Gallipot.
4 *as a ruffian ... breath* Like the whore whose fornication gives the pimp a living (just as
   Gallipot's money keeps Laxton going).
5 *shop-board* Counter for transactions or where goods are displayed in a shop, or in this case,
   where a tailor cuts and sews garments; *a shop-board ... upon* My bed need not have been
   used to cuckold me, and a table in the shop could have worked well enough.
6 *tasting smoke* Smoking.
7 *scapt the horn* Escaped being cuckolded.
8 *That ... slanders* That city dames' reputations are spotted justly only when their indiscretions have not been fabricated by men.

Never so fine spun, should yourself beguile,
Of what in her was yours.[1]

GALLIPOT.   Yet, Pru, 'tis well.

310   Play out your game at Irish,[2] sir. Who wins?

MISTRESS OPENWORK. The trial is when she comes to bearing.[3]

LAXTON. I scorned one woman, thus, should brave°   *challenge*
    all men,
    And, which more vext me, a she-citizen.[4]
    Therefore I laid siege to her. Out she held,

315   Gave many a brave repulse, and me compelled
    With shame to sound retreat[5] to my hot lust.
    Then seeing all base desires raked up in dust,[6]
    And that to tempt her modest ears I swore
    Ne'er to presume again,[7] she said her eye

320   Would ever give me welcome honestly;
    And—since I was a gentleman—if it run low,
    She would my state relieve, not to o'erthrow
    Your own and hers;[8] did so. Then, seeing I wrought
    Upon her meekness,° me she set at naught;[9]   *kindness*

325   And yet to try if I could turn that tide,[10]
    You see what stream I strove with. But, sir, I swear
    By heaven and by those hopes men lay up there,
    I neither have nor had a base intent
    To wrong your bed. What's done is merriment.

330   Your gold I pay back with this interest.

---

1 *No man ... yours* No man had enough wit or means to trick Gallipot out of owning his
    wife's heart.

2 *Play ... at Irish* Finish your story; *Irish* Game resembling backgammon.

3 *bearing* Particular move in Irish at the end of the game that involved removing a piece
    from the board; here, with a secondary meaning of bearing a child or bearing the weight of
    a man during sex.

4 *she-citizen* City woman, usually married to a citizen. The title of "citizen" was awarded to
    men who had achieved membership in their guild and been granted the freedom of the City
    of London.

5 *sound retreat* Fully back down.

6 *raked up in dust* Gathered together and covered by dust.

7 *to tempt ... again* I swore I would not think I could tempt her ears again.

8 *She would ... hers* She would give me help as she could as long as it did not upset your
    well-being.

9 *me ... naught* She considered me nothing, scorned me.

10 *turn that tide* Change her mind.

When I had most power to do't, I wronged you least.

GALLIPOT. If this no gullery° be, sir—   *trickery*

OMNES.   No, no, on my life.

GALLIPOT. Then, sir, I am beholden—not to you wife,

But Master Laxton, to your want° of doing ill,   *lack*

Which it seems you have not. Gentlemen,   335

Tarry° and dine here all.   *stay*

OPENWORK.   Brother, we have a jest

As good as yours to furnish out¹ a feast.

GALLIPOT. We'll crown our table with it. Wife brag no more

Of holding out: who most brags is most whore.²

(*Exeunt omnes.*)

[ACT 5, SCENE 1]

(*Enter Jack Dapper, Moll, Sir Beauteous Ganymede, and Sir Thomas Long.*)

JACK DAPPER. But prithee Master Captain Jack, be plain and perspicuous with me: was it your Meg of Westminster's courage that
rescued me from the Poultry puttocks,³ indeed?

MOLL. The valor of my wit, I ensure you, sir, fetcht you off bravely
when you were i'the forlorn hope among those desperates.⁴ Sir   5
Beauteous Ganymede here and Sir Thomas Long heard that
cuckoo—my man Trapdoor—sing the note of your ransom from
captivity.⁵

---

1 *furnish out* Provide for.

2 *Wife ... whore* Wife, do not brag of excessively putting off a suitor; whoever brags most of
such a deed is the most corrupt.

3 *perspicuous* Easily understood; *Meg of Westminster* Woman of sixteenth-century London who supposedly fought disguised as a man during the Anglo-French wars of the mid-six-
teenth century. The name also more generally referred to mannish or tall women; *Poultry*
puttocks Bailiffs of the Poultry Counter. Poultry Street and the Counter located there near
Cheapside were named for the poultry market; this enables word play on "puttocks," the
descriptor already applied to Curtalax and Hanger in 3.3.

4 *fetcht you off* Delivered you from your would-be captors; *desperates* Reckless men willing to go to any length to win.

5 *cuckoo* Bird, or fool; *sing ... captivity* Make the warning that allowed Dapper to escape.

SIR BEAUTEOUS. Ud's so,[1] Moll, where's that Trapdoor?

10 MOLL. Hanged, I think, by this time. A justice in this town that speaks nothing but "Make a *mittimus*, away with him to New-gate!" used that rogue like a firework to run upon a line betwixt him and me.[2]

OMNES. How, how?

15 MOLL. Marry, to lay trains of villainy to blow up my life! I smelt the powder, spied what linstock gave fire to shoot against the poor captain of the galley-foist, & away slid I my man, like a shovel-board shilling.[3] He struts up and down the suburbs, I think, and eats up whores, feeds upon a bawd's garbage.[4]

20 SIR THOMAS. Sirrah, Jack Dapper.

JACK DAPPER. What say'st, Tom Long?

SIR THOMAS. Thou hadst a sweet-faced boy, hail-fellow with thee to[5] your little Gull. How is he spent?[6]

JACK DAPPER. Troth, I whistled the poor little buzzard off o'my fist,

25 because when he waited upon me at the ordinaries, the gallants hit me i'the teeth still and said I lookt like a painted alderman's tomb, and the boy at my elbow like a death's head.[7] Sirrah Jack,[8] Moll—

---

1 *Ud's so* God save my soul.

2 *mittimus* Justice of the Peace's warrant for committing someone to custody; *New-gate* Newgate Prison, located next to the Old Bailey, London's criminal court; *used ... me* Used Trapdoor to track me, as though he were leaving a trail of gunpowder directly to me.

3 *powder* Explosive or gunpowder; *linstock* Staff that would hold a lit match; *gal-ley-foist* Barge of state, like that of the Lord Mayor of London. The image presents Moll as the captain of a barge, narrowly escaping explosions showering the barge; *shovel-board shilling* Shilling used in a game that involved sliding coins into position along a polished board. Moll implies that she pushed Trapdoor and herself out of danger.

4 *He ... garbage* Trapdoor haunts the suburbs, becoming a pimp for whores, whom he exploits as he consumes ("eats up") their incomes.

5 *hail-fellow* Intimate associate; *to* In, as.

6 *How ... spent?* How is he employed? How is he consumed by you?

7 *whistled ... fist* Sent Gull off as though he were an inferior hawk perched on my hand; *hit ... teeth* Reproached me, made fun of me; *painted alderman's tomb* Decorative effigy marking the tomb of an important person; *alderman* Chief representative of a London ward in government; *death's head* Representation of a skull or figure of death, serving as a *momento mori* (Latin: reminder of death).

8 *Jack* Alternative name for Moll, who is often referred to by this name while in men's clothing.

MOLL. What says my little Dapper?

SIR BEAUTEOUS. Come, come. Walk and talk, walk and talk.   30

JACK DAPPER. Moll and I'll be i'the midst.

MOLL. These knights shall have squires' places[1] belike, then. Well,
Dapper what say you?

JACK DAPPER. Sirrah Captain, mad Mary, the gull my own father—
Dapper, Sir Davy—laid these London boot-halers, the catch-   35
poles,[2] in ambush to set upon me.

OMNES. Your father? Away,[3] Jack!

JACK DAPPER. By the tassels of this handkercher, 'tis true! And what
was his warlike stratagem, think you? He thought, because a
wicker cage tames a nightingale, a lousy prison could make an ass   40
of me.

OMNES. A nasty plot.

JACK DAPPER. Ay; as though a counter, which is a park in which all
the wild beasts of the city run head by head, could tame me.[4]

(*Enter the Lord Noland.*)

MOLL. Yonder comes my Lord Noland.   45

OMNES. Save you, my lord.

LORD NOLAND. Well met, gentlemen all, good Sir Beauteous Ganymede, Sir Thomas Long. And how does Master Dapper?

JACK DAPPER. Thanks, my lord.

MOLL. No tobacco, my lord?   50

LORD NOLAND. No, faith, Jack.[5]

JACK DAPPER. My Lord Noland, will you go to Pimlico with us? We
are making a boon voyage to that nappy[6] land of spice-cakes.

---

1   *knights*   Beauteous and Ganymede;   *squires' places*   Position of attendants, on either side
of Moll and Jack.

2   *boot-halers*   Brigands, highwaymen;   *catchpoles*   Petty officers, sergeants.

3   *Away*   Go on, no way!

4   *could tame me*   Could reform me.

5   *Jack*   I.e., Moll.

6   *nappy*   Intoxicating or heady; here, the feeling is likely caused by strong ale offered at the
Pimlico Tavern.

LORD NOLAND. Here's such a merry ging, I could find in my heart
55   to sail to the World's End[1] with such company. Come gentlemen,
let's on.

JACK DAPPER. Here's most amorous[2] weather, my lord.

OMNES. Amorous weather?

(*They walk.*)

JACK DAPPER. Is not "amorous" a good word?

(*Enter Trapdoor like a poor soldier with a patch o'er one eye, and
Tearcat with him, all tatters.[3]*)

60   TRAPDOOR. [*To Tearcat.*] Shall we set upon the infantry, these troops
of foot?[4] Zounds, yonder comes Moll, my whorish master &
mistress. Would I had her kidneys between my teeth.

TEARCAT. I had rather have a cow heel.[5]

TRAPDOOR. Zounds, I am so patcht up, she cannot discover me.[6]
65   We'll on.

TEARCAT. *Alla corago[7]* then.

TRAPDOOR. Good your honours and worships, enlarge the ears of
commiseration, and let the sound of a hoarse military organ-pipe
penetrate your pitiful bowels to extract out of them so many small
70   drops of silver[8] as may give a hard straw-bed lodging to a couple
of maimed soldiers.

---

1   *ging*   Gang or group, derived from nautical usage meaning a crew of a boat;   *World's
End*   Another tavern, but also suggesting that Noland would go to the ends of the earth
with such company.
2   *amorous*   Lovely, though the word also carried its modern meanings of loving or sexual.
3   *all tatters*   Wearing tattered clothing, in rags.
4   *the infantry ... of foot*   These enemy foot soldiers (meaning Moll and her friends).
5   *cow heel*   Cow's foot stewed until jellied.
6   *patcht up ... discover me*   Wearing so many velvet patches on my face—including the eye
patch—that Moll will not recognize me. Velvet patches were used to conceal blemishes and
to cover scars and wounds, so soldiers (or pretend soldiers) might wear several.
7   *Alla corago*   Have courage ("corago" is a slang imitation of the Italian *coraggio*).
8   *drops of silver*   Coins.

JACK DAPPER. Where are you maimed?

TEARCAT. In both our nether limbs.

MOLL. Come, come, Dapper, lets give 'em something. 'Las poor
men, what money have you? By my troth, I love a soldier with my   75
soul.

SIR BEAUTEOUS. [*To Moll.*] Stay, stay. [*To Trapdoor and Tearcat.*]
Where have you served?

SIR THOMAS. In any part of the Low Countries?[1]

TRAPDOOR. Not in the Low Countries, if it please your manhood,   80
but in Hungary against the Turk at the Siege of Belgrade.[2]

LORD NOLAND. Who served there with you, sirrah?

TRAPDOOR. Many Hungarians, Moldavians, Valachians, and Tran-
sylvanians, with some Sclavonians,[3] and retiring home, sir, the
Venetian galleys took us prisoners, yet freed us, and suffered us to   85
beg up and down the country.

JACK DAPPER. You have ambled all over Italy then.

TRAPDOOR. Oh, sir, from Venice to Roma, Vecchio, Bononia,
Romania, Bolonia, Modena, Piacenza, and Tuscana, with all her
cities, as Pistoia, Valteria, Mountepulchena, Arrezzo, with the   90
Siennois,[4] and diverse others.

MOLL. Mere rogues. Put spurs to 'em once more.

JACK DAPPER. [*To Tearcat.*] Thou look'st like a strange creature, a fat
butterbox,[5] yet speak'st English. What art thou?

---

1 *Low Countries* Areas of northern Europe whose inhabitants spoke Dutch; often considered the area of present-day Belgium and the Netherlands, but sometimes the reference
includes parts of northern France and western Germany. English soldiers served in the Low
Countries during the Anglo-Spanish War (1585–1604) in support of the Dutch resistance
to Hapsburg Spain (1568–1648, or the Eighty Years' War).

2 *Siege of Belgrade* Belgrade was conquered by Sultan Suleiman in a great Ottoman victory
in 1522. Trapdoor would have to be more than one hundred years old to have participated
in the sixteenth-century battle.

3 *Valachians* Walachians of Walachia, a Romanian people; *Sclavonians* People of Slavic
origin.

4 *Venice ... Arrezzo* Long list of Italian place-names, including two names for the same
place (Bononia and Bolonia); *Siennois* People of Sienna, the province that is home to
Montepulciano.

5 *butterbox* Dutchman (term of abjection).

95 TEARCAT. *Ick, mine here? Ick bin den ruffling Tearcat, den brave*
soldado. Ick bin dorick all Dutchlant gueresen. Der shellum das meere
ine beasa, ine woert gaeb. Ick slaag vin stroakes ou tom cop, dastick,
den hundred touzun devil halle; frollick mine here.[1]

SIR BEAUTEOUS. Here, here, let's be rid of their jabbering—

[*Sir Beauteous starts to give money.*]

100 MOLL. Not a cross[2] Sir Beauteous.—You base rogues, I have taken
measure of you better than a tailor can, and I'll fit you, as you—
monster with one eye—have fitted me.[3]
TRAPDOOR. Your worship will not abuse a soldier!
MOLL. Soldier? Thou deserv'st to be hanged up by that tongue
105 which dishonours so noble a profession. Soldier, you skeldering[4]
varlet? Hold, stand; there should be a trapdoor hereabouts.

([*Moll*] *pull*[*s*] *off his patch.*)

TRAPDOOR. The balls of these glaziers of mine—mine eyes—shall
be shot up and down in any hot piece of service for my invincible
Mistress.
110 JACK DAPPER. I did not think there had been such knavery in black
patches as now I see.

---

1 *Ick... here* Tearcat offers a mix of English and Dutch in imitation of a foreign soldier and
offers up a messy proclamation that is garbled at best. The spelling of the original text has
been preserved. He says, roughly, "I, my lord? I am the ruffling Tearcat, the brave soldier. I
have been through all Dutch-land [or Deutschland—Germany; possibly a deliberate con-
flation of Dutchlant and Deutschland]. The rascal who has done me wrong, I gave it to him.
I hit him with strokes on the head, enough for a hundred thousand devils. [Be] merry, my
lord!"
2 *cross* Coin with a cross imprint.
3 *I have ... me* Moll means she will size them up as they have sized up her—that is, they have
mistakenly taken her as a fool, and she'll measure them accordingly, like a tailor measures
and fits clothes.
4 *skeldering* Begging or swindling, especially by pretending to be a wounded or decommis-
sioned soldier.

MOLL. Oh, sir, he hath been brought up in the Isle of Dogs and can both fawn like a spaniel, and bite like a mastiff,[1] as he finds occasion.

LORD NOLAND. [*To Tearcat.*] What are you, sirrah? A bird of this feather too?   115

TEARCAT. A man beaten from the wars, sir.

SIR THOMAS. I think so, for you never stood to fight.[2]

JACK DAPPER. What's thy name, fellow soldier?

TEARCAT. I am called, by those that have seen my valor, Tearcat.   120

OMNES. Tearcat?

MOLL. A mere whip-jack, and that is, in the common-wealth of rogues, a slave that can talk of sea-fight, name all your chief Pirates, discover[3] more countries to you than either the Dutch, Spanish, French, or English ever found out; yet indeed, all his ser-   125
vice is by land, and that is to rob a fair,[4] or some such venturous exploit. Tearcat! Foot, sirrah! I have your name, now I remember me, in my book of horners—horns for the thumb,[5] you know how.

TEARCAT. No indeed, Captain Moll—for I know you by sight—I   130
am no such nipping Christian, but a maunderer upon the pad,[6] I confess; and meeting with honest Trapdoor here, whom you had cashiered from bearing arms, out at elbows under your colours, I instructed him in the rudiments of roguery and by my map

---

1 *Isle of Dogs* Peninsula to the east of the city along the Thames that serves as a refuge for criminals and debtors lying low. *The Isle of Dogs* was also the name of a suppressed 1597 play; *spaniel* Friendly, subservient hunting dog; *mastiff* Large dog who will bite when a threat is perceived.

2 *never ... fight* Ran away rather than fought.

3 *whip-jack* Vagabond or beggar; *discover* Make known, reveal, with the implication of falsifying in this case.

4 *to rob a fair* To steal goods or money at a fair; the only risks he ever takes are to commit petty thievery.

5 *book of horners* List of thieves and criminals; *horns for the thumb* Thimble-like tools worn on the thumb and used by cutpurses. Horn-thumb was a slang term for pickpocket, and there is an additional play on cuckolding in the phrase.

6 *nipping Christian* Thief, cutpurse; *maunderer* Professional beggar; *upon the pad* On the road, the highway.

135 made him sail over any country you can name, so that now he can
maunder better than myself.[1]

JACK DAPPER. So then, Trapdoor, thou art turned soldier now.

TRAPDOOR. Alas, sir, now there's no wars, 'tis the safest course of life
I could take.

140 MOLL. I hope then you can cant, for by your cudgels, you, sirrah,
are an upright man.[2]

TRAPDOOR. As any walks the highway I assure you.

MOLL. And Tearcat what are you? A wild rogue, an angler, or a
ruffler?[3]

145 TEARCAT. Brother to this upright man, flesh and blood, ruffling
Tearcat is my name, and a ruffler is my style, my title, my
profession.

MOLL. Sirrah, where's your doxy?[4] Halt not with me.[5]

OMNES. Doxy, Moll? What's that?

150 MOLL. His wench.

TRAPDOOR. My doxy? I have, by the solomon, a doxy that carries
a kinchin-mort in her slate at her back, besides my dell and my
dainty wild dell, with all whom I'll tumble this next darkman's in
the strommel, and drink ben booze, and eat a fat, gruntling cheat,

155 a cackling cheat, and a quacking cheat.[6]

---

1 *cashiered ... arms* Dismissed from service; *out ... colours* Wearing tattered livery; *instructed ... myself* Taught him all the different countries of the world on a map, so
that he can beg better than I can.

2 *can cant* Can speak in a special jargon, canting language, that was attributed to thieves
and vagabonds, especially in sixteenth- and seventeenth-century rogue literature; *upright
man* Big, strong, sturdy vagrant, second-in-command of a group of beggars and thieves.
Many of the strange and foreign-seeming slang words offered in the dialogue that follows
are from cant talk.

3 *wild rogue* Someone born and bred in criminal life who excels at villainy, often as a thief
and beggar; *angler* Pickpocket or thief who steals via a long pole, like a fishing rod; *ruffler* Vagabond typically operating under the guise of a soldier; rufflers are near the top of
the supposed underworld hierarchy, along with upright men, as described in rogue literature.

4 *doxy* Common female rogue, usually one who has lost her virginity and keeps company
with an upright man as his mistress or harlot.

5 *Halt ... me* Do not stop talking.

6 *by the solomon* By the mass; *kinchin-mort ... slate* Little girl carried on her mother's
back in a sheet; *dell* Young woman yet to be spoiled by an upright man; *dainty wild
dell* Young, virginal woman born into the rogue life; *tumble* Have sex with; *darkman's* Night; *strommel* Straw; *ben booze* Good drink; *gruntling cheat* Fat pig;
cackling cheat Hen; *quacking cheat* Duck.

JACK DAPPER. Here's old[1] cheating.

TRAPDOOR. My doxy stays for me in a boozing ken,[2] brave Captain.

MOLL. He says his wench stays for him in an alehouse. [*To Trapdoor and Tearcat.*] You are no pure rogues.

TEARCAT. Pure rogues? No, we scorn to be pure rogues, but if you   160
come to our libken, or our stalling ken, you shall find neither him
nor me a queer cuffin.[3]

MOLL. So, sir, no churl of you.

TEARCAT. No, but a ben cove, a brave cove, a gentry cuffin.[4]

LORD NOLAND. Call you this canting?[5]   165

JACK DAPPER. Zounds, I'll give a schoolmaster half a crown a week
and teach me this peddler's French.[6]

TRAPDOOR. Do but stroll, sir, half a harvest with us, sir, and you
shall gabble your bellyful.

MOLL. [*To Trapdoor.*] Come, you rogue, cant with me.   170

SIR THOMAS. Well said Moll!—Cant with her sirrah, and you shall
have money; else not a penny.

TRAPDOOR. I'll have a bout, if she please.

MOLL. Come on, sirrah.

TRAPDOOR. Ben mort, shall you and I heave a booth, mill a ken, or   175
nip a bung? And then we'll couch a hogshead under the ruffmans,
and there you shall wap with me, & I'll niggle with[7] you.

MOLL. Out, you damned impudent rascal!

TRAPDOOR. Cut benar whids, and hold your fambles and your
stamps![8]   180

LORD NOLAND. Nay, nay, Moll! Why art thou angry? What was his
gibberish?

---

1 *old* Experienced, practiced.

2 *boozing ken* Alehouse.

3 *libken* House where thieves and beggars sleep; *stalling ken* House where stolen goods are received; *queer cuffin* Churlish fellow.

4 *ben cove* Good chap; *brave cove* Stout, splendid fellow; *gentry cuffin* Gentleman.

5 *canting* Speaking in the secret jargon of thieves and professional beggars.

6 *half a crown* Coin valued at 2s. 6d.; *and* To; *peddler's French* Name for canting language.

7 *Ben ... you* Most of this passage is translated by Moll below; *heave a booth, mill a ken* Taken together as "to rob a house" by Moll; "heave a booth" is more directly to rob a booth, which could be a temporary dwelling (tent) or a market stall; *wap with* Have sex with; *niggle with* Have sex with.

8 *Cut ... stamps* Speak good words, and hold your hands and your legs.

MOLL. Marry this my Lord says he: "Ben mort"—good wench—
"shall you and I heave a booth, mill a ken, or nip a bung?" Shall
185   you and I rob a house, or cut a purse?
OMNES. Very Good.
MOLL. "And then we'll couch a hogshead under the ruffmans":
And then we'll lie under a hedge.
TRAPDOOR. That was my desire, captain, as 'tis fit a soldier should
190   lie.[1]
MOLL. And there you shall wap with me, and I'll niggle with you,
and that's all.
SIR BEAUTEOUS. Nay, nay Moll what's that wap?
JACK DAPPER. Nay teach me what niggling is, I'd fain be niggling.
195 MOLL. Wapping and niggling is all one, the rogue my man can tell
you.
TRAPDOOR. 'Tis fadoodling,[2] if it please you.
SIR BEAUTEOUS. This is excellent, one fit[3] more good Moll.
MOLL. Come, you rogue, sing with me.

[*They sing.*]

The Song.

200 MOLL. A gage° of ben° Rom-booze°		*quart pot / good / wine*
In a boozing ken° of Rom-vile.°		*alehouse / London*
TEARCAT. Is benar° then a caster,°		*better / cloak*
Peck,[4] pannam,° lap,° or poplar,°	*bread / buttermilk / porridge*	
Which we mill° in Deuce-a-ville.°		*rob / the country*
205 MOLL AND TEARCAT. Oh, I would lib° all the lightmans.°		*lie / day*
Oh I would lib all the darkmans,°		*night*
By the solomon° under the ruffmans.°	*the mass / bushes, hedges*	
By the solomon in the harmans.°		*stocks*
TEARCAT. And scour the queer cramp-ring,[5]		

---

1   *lie* Spend the night; sleep under a hedge.
2   *fadoodling* Another word for having sex.
3   *fit* Part of a song or poem; a canto.
4   *Peck* Food or meat.
5   *scour ... cramp-ring* Wear fetters.

And couch° till a pallyard° docked my dell,[1] *lie down / beggar* 210
So[2] my boozy nab° might skew° Rom-booze well *head / hold*
Avast,° to the pad,° let us bing,° *hold fast / road / go*
Avast, to the pad, let us bing.

OMNES. Fine knaves i'faith.

JACK DAPPER. The grating of ten new cart-wheels and the gruntling 215
of five hundred hogs coming from Romford[3] market, cannot
make a worse noise than this canting language does in my ears.
Pray, my Lord Noland, let's give these soldiers their pay.

SIR BEAUTEOUS. Agreed, and let them march.

LORD NOLAND. Here, Moll. 220

MOLL. [*To Trapdoor and Tearcat.*] Now I see that you are stalled to
the rogue[4] and are not ashamed of your professions. Look you,
my Lord Noland here, and these gentlemen, bestows upon you
two, two bords and a half: that's two shillings sixpence.

[*Moll gives the rogues money.*]

TRAPDOOR. Thanks to your lordship. 225

TEARCAT. Thanks, heroical captain.

MOLL. Away.

TRAPDOOR. We shall cut ben whids[5] of your masters- and mistress-ship, wheresoever we come.

MOLL. [*Aside to Trapdoor.*] You'll maintain, sirrah, the old justice's 230
plot[6] to his face.

TRAPDOOR. Else trine me on the cheats:[7] hang me.

MOLL. Be sure you meet me there.

TRAPDOOR. Without any more maundering,[8] I'll do't. Follow, brave
Tearcat. 235

---

1 *docked my dell* Had sex with my girl.
2 *So* So long that.
3 *Romford* Market town northeast of London.
4 *stalled ... rogue* Committed to the life of a rogue; installed as a rogue.
5 *cut ben whids* Speak well of.
6 *maintain* Tell the truth about; *the old justice's plot* Sir Alexander's plan.
7 *Else ... cheats* If not, hang me on the gallows.
8 *maundering* Grumbling, or in cant talk, begging.

TEARCAT. *I prae, sequor.*[1] Let us go, mouse.

(*Exeunt they two, manet*[2] *the rest.*)

LORD NOLAND. Moll, what was in that canting song?
MOLL. Troth my Lord, only a praise of good drink—the only milk
which these wild beasts love to suck—and thus it was:

240   A rich cup of wine,
Oh, it is juice divine,
More wholesome for the head
Than meat, drink, or bread.
To fill my drunken pate
245   With that, I'd sit up late.
By the heels would I lie,
Under a lousy hedge die,
Let a slave have a pull
At my whore, so I be full
250   Of that precious liquor[3]—

And a parcel of such stuff my Lord, not worth the opening.[4]

(*Enter a Cutpurse very gallant, with four or five men after him, one
with a wand.*[5])

LORD NOLAND. What gallant comes yonder?
SIR THOMAS. Mass, I think I know him; 'tis one of Cumberland.[6]
1 CUTPURSE. [*Aside to his Gang.*] Shall we venture to shuffle in
255   amongst yon heap of gallants, and strike?[7]

---

1 *I prae, sequor* Latin: Go on before, I follow.
2 *manet* Remain.
3 *A rich ... liquor* Moll's translation is not entirely accurate, but here resembles a rhyming
    song. It's not clear if Moll desires to edit the song, or just prefers this verse version.
4 *opening* Explaining.
5 *wand* Cane or walking stick.
6 *Cumberland* County in the North of England.
7 *shuffle ... strike?* Infiltrate this group of gallants and rob them?

2 CUTPURSE. 'Tis a question whether there be any silver shells
amongst them, for all their satin outsides.[1]

CUTPURSES. Let's try.

MOLL. Pox on him. A gallant? Shadow me. I know him: 'tis one
that cumbers[2] the land indeed. If he swim near to the shore of any   260
of your pockets, look to your purses.

GENTLEMEN. Is't possible?[3]

MOLL. This brave fellow is no better than a foist.

GENTLEMEN. Foist? What's that?

MOLL. A diver[4] with two fingers: a pickpocket. All his train study   265
the figging law, that's to say, cutting of purses and foisting.[5]
One of them is a nip;[6] I took him once i'the twopenny gallery at
the Fortune.[7] Then there's a cloyer, or snap,[8] that dogs any new
brother in that trade, and snaps will have half in any booty. He
with the wand is both a stale,[9] whose office is to face a man i'the   270
streets whilst shells are drawn by another, and then with his
black conjuring rod in his hand, he, by the nimbleness of his eye
and juggling stick, will, in cheaping a piece of plate[10] at a gold-
smith's stall, make four or five rings mount from the top of his
caduceus,[11] and, as if it were at leapfrog, they skip into his hand   275
presently.

2 CUTPURSE. Zounds, we are smoke't![12]

ALL CUTPURSES. Ha?[13]

---

1   whether ... outsides   Whether they have any money, regardless of their fancy clothes.
2   cumbers   Troubles, encumbers.
3   Is't possible   Is it possible such gallants are thieves?
4   diver   One who dives into pockets to steal from them.
5   train   Gang; figging law   Way of the cutpurse; foisting   Picking pockets.
6   nip   Cutpurse.
7   took him   Caught him; twopenny ... Fortune   Mid-priced gallery seats at the Fortune
    Theater, a playhouse near Finsbury Fields, to the west of Shoreditch and north of Crip-
    plegate. The Roaring Girl was first played at the Fortune in 1611, so this line may be espe-
    cially effective for the theater audience.
8   cloyer, or snap   One who horns in on the gains of the other thieves and cutpurses and
    demands a share.
9   stale   Decoy; accomplice.
10 cheaping   Bargaining over; plate   Gold vessels or utensils.
11 caduceus   In Greek and Roman mythology, the wand carried by Hermes or Mercury (a
    trickster god associated with thieves), featuring two serpents encircling a staff.
12 smoke't   Discovered, known.
13 Ha?   Presumably, all the other cutpurses make an exclamation of surprise and confusion.

2 CUTPURSE. We are boiled![1] Pox on her! See Moll, the roaring
280   drab.[2]
1 CUTPURSE. All the diseases of sixteen hospitals boil[3] her! Away!

[*Moll stops the thieves before they can exit.*]

MOLL. Bless you, sir.
1 CUTPURSE. And you, good sir.
MOLL. Dost not ken[4] me, man?
285   1 CUTPURSE. No, trust me sir.
MOLL. Heart, there's a knight to whom I'm bound for many
    favours, lost his purse at the last new play i'the Swan[5]—seven
    angels in't. Make it good, your best;[6] do you see? No more.
1 CUTPURSE. A synagogue[7] shall be called, Mistress Mary. Disgrace
290   me not; *pacus palabros,*[8] I will conjure for you.[9] Farewell.

[*Exeunt Cutpurses.*]

MOLL. Did not I tell you my Lord?
LORD NOLAND. I wonder how thou cam'st to the knowledge of
    these nasty villains.
SIR THOMAS. And why do the foul mouths of the world call thee
295   Moll Cutpurse? A name, methinks, damned and odious.
MOLL. Dare any step forth to my face and say,
    "I have ta'en thee doing so,[10] Moll"? I must confess,
    In younger days, when I was apt to stray,
    I have sat amongst such adders, seen their stings—
300   As any here might—and in full playhouses

---

1   *boiled*   Betrayed, cooked.
2   *drab*   Slut, prostitute.
3   *boil*   Agitate, infect, or give boils to her.
4   *ken*   Know.
5   *Swan*   Bankside amphitheater playhouse.
6   *Make ... best*   Your best interest is to "make it good," meaning to give back the money.
7   *synagogue*   Meeting of thieves (for investigating the lost angels).
8   *pacus palabros*   Few words, a mistaken version of the Spanish *pocas palabras*. Proverbial: "few words show wise men."
9   *I will ... you*   I will make this entreaty for you, or I will make the stolen goods appear as if by magic.
10   *I ... doing so*   I have seen you cutting purses or picking pockets.

Watcht their quick-diving hands, to bring to shame
Such rogues, and in that stream met an ill name.[1]
When next, my Lord, you spy any one of those,
So he be in his art a scholar,[2] question him.
Tempt him with gold to open the large book 305
Of his close villainies, and you yourself shall cant
Better than poor Moll can, and know more laws
Of cheaters, lifters, nips, foists, puggards, curbers,[3]
Withal the devil's blackguard,[4] than it is fit
Should be discovered to a noble wit.[5] 310
I know they have their orders, offices,
Circuits and circles, unto which they are bound,
To raise their own damnation in.[6]

JACK DAPPER. How dost thou know it?

MOLL. As you do. I show it you; they to me show it. 315
Suppose, my lord, you were in Venice.

LORD NOLAND.   Well.

MOLL. If some Italian pander there would tell
All the close tricks of courtesans, would not you
Harken to such a fellow?

LORD NOLAND.   Yes.

MOLL.   And here,
Being come from Venice, to a friend most dear 320
That were to travel thither, you would proclaim
Your knowledge in those villainies to save
Your friend from their quick danger: Must you have
A black ill name, because ill things you know?
Good troth my lord, I am made Moll Cutpurse so. 325

---

1 *I have sat ... name* To expose the crimes of rogues, I traveled in their circles, and so I
   acquired a bad reputation, even if undeserved.
2 *in his art a scholar* Expertly learned in his profession.
3 *cheaters* Dishonest gamblers, those with false dice or false deals; *lifters* Thieves;
   nips Cutpurses; *foists* Pickpockets; *puggards* Thieves; *curbers* Thieves who steal
   with the aid of a long, hooked pole: they reach through windows and pull out items.
4 *devil's blackguard* Devil's servants or a guard of devil's attendants dressed in black.
5 *than ... wit* Than it is appropriate for a nobleman to know.
6 *they have ... damnation in* Thieves and cutpurses operate in their own social circles and
   circuits, and make their own fall (damnation) in so doing. The image plays on the idea of a
   necromancer conjuring evil spirits in a magic circle.

How many are whores in small ruffs and still looks?[1]
How many chaste, whose names fill Slander's books?
Were all men cuckolds, whom gallants in their scorns
Call so, we should not walk for goring horns.[2]
330   Perhaps for my mad going[3] some reprove me;
I please myself, and care not else who loves me.
OMNES. A brave mind, Moll, i'faith!
SIR THOMAS. Come, my Lord, shall's to the ordinary?
LORD NOLAND. Ay, 'tis noon, sure.
335   MOLL. Good my lord, let not my name condemn me to you, or to
the world. A fencer, I hope, may be called a coward; is he so for
that? If all that have ill names in London were to be whipt, and to
pay but twelve pence apiece to the beadle, I would rather have his
office than a constable's.[4]
340   JACK DAPPER. So would I, Captain Moll. 'Twere a sweet tickling[5]
office, i'faith!

(*Exeunt.*)

[ACT 5, SCENE 2]

(*Enter Sir Alexander Wengrave, Goshawk, and Greenwit, and others.*)

SIR ALEXANDER. My son marry a thief? That impudent girl
Whom all the world stick their worst eyes upon?
GREENWIT. How will your care prevent it?
GOSHAWK.   'Tis impossible.
They marry close;° they're gone, but none knows whither.   *secretly*
5   SIR ALEXANDER. Oh, gentlemen, when has a father's heartstrings

---

1   *small ruffs* Narrow ruffs, perhaps with the small pleats favored by Puritans;   *still looks* Meek and serious countenances.
2   *Were ... horns* If all the men reputed to be cuckolds were so, we would be gored by horns anywhere we walked.
3   *mad going* Zany ways, strange doings.
4   *If ... constable's* If everyone who had a bad name—not everyone who is guilty of a crime—in London were to be whipped and have to pay twelve pence to the beadle, I would rather be a beadle than a constable (who outranks the beadle) because I'd get that income.
5   *tickling* Pleasant, gratifying.

Held out so long from breaking?

(*Enter a servant.*)

                                Now, what news, sir?
SERVANT. They were met upo'th'water an hour since, sir,
Putting in towards the Sluice.[1]
SIR ALEXANDER.   The Sluice? come gentlemen,
'Tis Lambeth[2] works against us.

[*Exit servant.*]

GREENWIT.   And that Lambeth
Joins more mad matches than your six wet towns,   10
Twixt that and Windsor Bridge, where fares lie soaking.[3]
SIR ALEXANDER. Delay no time, sweet gentlemen: to Blackfriars![4]
We'll take a pair of oars[5] and make after 'em.

(*Enter Trapdoor.*)

TRAPDOOR. Your son, and that bold masculine ramp, my mistress,
Are landed now at Tower.[6]   15
SIR ALEXANDER.   Heyday! At Tower?
TRAPDOOR. I heard it now reported.
SIR ALEXANDER.   Which way,[7] gentlemen,

---

1   *Sluice* Embankment intended to control the flooding in Lambeth Marsh, located across the Thames from Westminster and just outside Lambeth Palace.

2   *Lambeth* Marshy borough where Lambeth Marsh was located. It was the property of the Archbishop of Canterbury and outside of London's jurisdiction.

3   *wet towns* Towns on the Thames between Lambeth and Windsor Bridge, near London but not subject to the city's laws. Londoners might go there to elope, avoiding the rigors of pre-marriage publicity required by typical marriage ceremonies, or to have adulterous affairs; *fares* Customers hiring water transportation; *soaking* Taking hot baths to treat their venereal diseases.

4   *Blackfriars* Area on the north side of the Thames and location of Blackfriars Stairs, one of the water gates to the river.

5   *pair of oars* Boat for hire.

6   *Tower* Referring to Tower Wharf or Tower Stairs, landing areas near the Tower of London in the east.

7   *Which way* Alexander is torn between going west toward Lambeth, or going east toward the Tower.

Shall I bestow my care? I'm drawn in pieces
Betwixt deceit and shame.

(*Enter Sir [Guy] Fitzallard.*)

SIR GUY.   Sir Alexander,
You're well met, and most rightly served;
20 My daughter was a scorn¹ to you.
SIR ALEXANDER.   Say not so, sir.
SIR GUY. A very abject,° she, poor gentlewoman!   *lowly person*
Your house had been dishonoured.² Give you joy, sir,
Of your son's gaskin-bride.³ You'll be a grandfather shortly
To a fine crew of roaring sons and daughters;
25 'Twill help to stock the suburbs passing well, sir.
SIR ALEXANDER. Oh, play not with the miseries of my heart!
Wounds should be drest and healed, not vext, or left
Wide open to the anguish of the patient,
And scornful air⁴ let in; rather let pity
30 And advice charitably help to refresh° 'em.   *heal*
SIR GUY. Who'd place his charity so unworthily,
Like one that gives alms to a cursing beggar?
Had I but found one spark of goodness in you
Toward my deserving child, which° then grew fond   *who*
35 Of your son's virtues, I had eased° you now.   *relieved*
But I perceive both fire of youth and goodness
Are raked up in the ashes of your age,⁵
Else no such shame⁶ should have come near your house,
Nor such ignoble sorrow touch your heart.

---

1 *scorn* Object of mockery or contempt.
2 *Your ... dishonoured* Marrying my daughter would have brought dishonor to your family. Sir Guy mockingly agrees with Sir Alexander's earlier assessment of Mary, pointing out how much better for his reputation it would be to have Mary rather than Moll for a daughter-in-law.
3 *gaskin-bride* Bride wearing breeches; galligaskins are wide-legged breeches.
4 *scornful air* Harsh and potentially diseased air negatively affecting healing. It was believed that wounds would heal better if they were covered and that air could carry sickness and contamination.
5 *raked ... age* Smothered by the detritus of age.
6 *such shame* Moll being married to Sebastian.

SIR ALEXANDER. If not for worth,[1] for pity's sake assist me!   40
GREENWIT. You urge a thing past sense; how can he help you?
  All his assistance is as frail as ours,
  Full as uncertain. Where's the place that holds 'em?
  One brings us water-news;[2] then comes another
  With a full-charged mouth, like a culverin's voice,   45
  And he reports[3] the Tower. Whose sounds are truest?
GOSHAWK. [*To Sir Guy.*] In vain you flatter him.[4]—Sir Alexander—
SIR GUY. I flatter him? Gentlemen, you wrong me grossly.
GREENWIT. [*Aside to Goshawk.*] He does it well,[5] i'faith.
SIR GUY.   Both news are false,
  Of Tower or water: they took no such way yet.   50
SIR ALEXANDER. Oh, strange! Hear you this gentlemen? Yet more
  plunges![6]
SIR GUY. They're nearer than you think, for yet more close
  Than if they were further off.
SIR ALEXANDER.   How am I lost
  In these distractions!
SIR GUY.   For your speeches, gentlemen,
  In taxing me for rashness: 'fore° you all,   *in front of*   55
  I will engage my state to half his wealth,[7]
  Nay, to his son's revenues, which are less,[8]
  And yet nothing at all till they come from him,[9]
  That I could—if my will stuck to my power—
  Prevent this marriage yet, nay, banish her   60

---

1 *If not for worth* Even if I don't deserve it.
2 *Where's ... 'em?* Where are Sebastian and Moll?; *water-news* News of where Moll and Sebastian put in at the river.
3 *full-charged* A full-charged gun is packed with powder and ready to fire; *culverin* Small cannon or gun; *reports* Pun on report as the sound of a gun firing and to deliver news.
4 *In vain ... him* Uselessly, you encourage Sir Alexander with your implied ability to help.
5 *He ... well* Sir Guy plays his part well.
6 *plunges* Difficulties, with a play on falling into water.
7 *engage ... wealth* Pledge from my entire estate against the value of half of Alexander's wealth.
8 *to his son's ... less* Against the worth of Sebastian's income, which is smaller.
9 *And yet nothing ... him* In fact, Sebastian is worth nothing until Alexander gives that income to him.

Forever from his thoughts, much more his arms.[1]

SIR ALEXANDER. Slack not this goodness,[2] though you heap upon me

Mountains of malice and revenge hereafter!

I'd willingly resign up half my state to him,

65 So he would marry the meanest drudge I hire.[3]

GREENWIT. [*To Sir Alexander.*] He talks impossibilities, and you believe 'em!

SIR GUY. I talk no more than I know how to finish;

My fortunes else are his that dares stake with me.[4]

The poor young gentleman I love and pity,

70 And to keep shame from him—because the spring

Of his affection[5] was my daughter's first,°   *first love*

Till his° frown blasted all—do but estate him   *Sir Alexander's*

In those possessions which your love and care

Once pointed out for him,[6] that he may have room,

75 To entertain fortunes of noble birth,[7]

Where now his desperate wants[8] casts him upon her;°   *Moll*

And if I do not, for his own sake chiefly,

Rid him of this disease[9] that now grows on him,

I'll forfeit my whole state, before these gentlemen.[10]

80 GREENWIT. [*To Sir Alexander.*] Troth, but you shall not undertake

such matches;°   *bets*

We'll persuade° so much with you.   *urge*

SIR ALEXANDER. [*To Sir Guy, giving ring.*]   Here's my ring;

He will believe this token. 'Fore these gentlemen,

I will confirm it fully: all those lands,

---

1   *Prevent ... arms*   Prevent Sebastian and Moll's marriage even now and ensure that Sebastian will never think on Moll again, let alone embrace her.

2   *Slack ... goodness*   Do not lessen this kindness.

3   *I'd ... hire*   I'd willingly sign over half of my estate to Sebastian if he would marry my lowliest servant (rather than Moll).

4   *I talk ... me*   I only start what I can finish; I bet my whole fortune on it.

5   *spring ... affection*   Sebastian's youthful love.

6   *do ... him*   Only advocate for you (Alexander) to grant Sebastian legal title to the revenues you had originally appointed for him.

7   *entertain ... birth*   Invite the attentions of gentlewomen.

8   *his desperate wants*   Sebastian's financial desperation (because he has been disinherited).

9   *this disease*   Moll, or financial dependency.

10   *before these gentlemen*   As witnessed by these gentlemen.

My first love 'lotted° him,[1] he shall straight possess   *allotted*
In that refusal.[2]   85
SIR GUY.   If I change it not,[3]
Change me into a beggar!
GREENWIT.   Are you mad, sir?
SIR GUY. 'Tis done.°   *agreed*
GOSHAWK.   Will you undo° yourself by doing,   *wreck*
And show a prodigal trick[4] in your old days?
SIR ALEXANDER. 'Tis a match[5] gentlemen.
SIR GUY.   Ay, ay, sir, ay.
I ask no favour, trust to you for none;   90
My hope rests in the goodness of your son.

(*Exit* [*Sir Guy*] *Fitzallard.*)

GREENWIT. [*Aside to Goshawk.*] He holds it up well yet.
GOSHAWK. [*Aside to Greenwit.*]   Of an old knight i'faith.
SIR ALEXANDER. Cursed be the time I laid his first love barren,[6]
Willfully barren, that before this hour
Had° sprung forth fruits of comfort and of honour;   *would have*   95
He loved a virtuous gentlewoman.

(*Enter Moll* [*in men's clothes*].)

GOSHAWK. Life, here's Moll.
GREENWIT. Jack!
GOSHAWK.   How dost thou, Jack?
MOLL.   How dost thou, gallant?
SIR ALEXANDER. [*To Moll.*] Impudence, where's my son?
MOLL.   Weakness, go look° him!   *look for*
SIR ALEXANDER. Is this your wedding gown?   100
MOLL.   The man talks monthly.°   *like a lunatic*

---

1   *all ... him*   All the land and holdings he was originally to inherit.
2   *In that refusal*   If he refuses Moll.
3   *If ... not*   If I don't prevent the marriage to Moll.
4   *show a prodigal trick*   Turn reckless and make yourself poor.
5   *'Tis a match*   It's a deal.
6   *laid ... barren*   Obstructed Sebastian's quest for his first love (Mary).

Hot broth and a dark chamber[1] for the knight;
I see he'll be stark mad at our next meeting.

(*Exit Moll.*)

GOSHAWK. Why, sir, take comfort now, there's no such matter:
No priest will marry her, sir, for° a woman   *as*
105 Whilst that shape's on,[2] and it was never known,
Two men were married and conjoined in one.
Your son hath made some shift° to love another.   *plan, trick*
SIR ALEXANDER. Whate'er she be, she has my blessing with her.
May they be rich and fruitful, and receive
110 Like comfort to their issue[3] as I take in them.
He's pleased me now, marrying not this;°   *Moll*
Through a whole world he could not choose amiss![4]
GREENWIT. Glad you're so penitent for your former sin, sir.
GOSHAWK. Say° he should take a wench with her   *let's say*
smock-dowry:[5]
115 No portion° with her, but her lips and arms?   *dowry*
SIR ALEXANDER. Why? Who thrive better, sir? They have most
blessing,
Though other have more wealth, and least repent:
Many that want most know the most content.[6]
GREENWIT. Say he should marry a kind youthful sinner.[7]
120 SIR ALEXANDER. Age will quench that, any offence but theft
And drunkenness—nothing but death can wipe away;[8]
Their sins are green, even when their heads are gray.[9]

---

1 *Hot ... chamber* Seventeenth-century treatments for madness.
2 *Whilst ... on* While she is dressed in men's clothing.
3 *Like comfort ... issue* The same happiness from their children.
4 *Through ... amiss* Sebastian could choose any other woman in the world but Moll and choose well.
5 *smock-dowry* Dowry of only the bride's underclothes.
6 *Though ... content* Though others have more wealth and don't feel the need to repent for their sins, those who have the least are the most happy.
7 *kind youthful sinner* Young woman with sexual experience.
8 *Age ... away* Age will stop such promiscuity as well as any sin except theft and drunkenness; those haunt one into old age.
9 *Their ... gray* Their (drunkards' and thieves') sins remain fresh, even while they grow old.

Nay I despair not now, my heart's cheered, gentlemen:
No face can come unfortunately to me.[1]

(*Enter a Servant.*)

Now, sir, your news?   125
SERVANT.   Your son with his fair bride
   Is near at hand.
SIR ALEXANDER.   Fair may their fortunes be!
GREENWIT.   Now you're resolved,° sir, it was never she?   *convinced*
SIR ALEXANDER.   I find it in the music of my heart.

(*Enter Moll [dressed as a bride], maskt, in Sebastian's hand,[2] and [Sir Guy] Fitzallard.*)

See where they come.
GOSHAWK.   A proper lusty° presence, sir.   *joyful, cheerful*
SIR ALEXANDER.   Now has he pleased me right. I always counseled   130
   him
   To choose a goodly personable creature.
   Just of her pitch° was my first wife, his mother.   *height, size*
SEBASTIAN.   Before I dare discover° my offence,   *reveal*
   I kneel for pardon.

[*Sebastian kneels.*]

SIR ALEXANDER.   My heart gave it thee,
   Before thy tongue could ask it.   135
   Rise; thou hast raised my joy to greater height
   Than to that seat where grief dejected it.[3]

[*Sebastian rises.*]

Both welcome to my love and care forever!
Hide not my happiness too long; all's pardoned.

---

1   *No ... to me*   No prospective bride will look bad to me now.
2   *in Sebastian's hand*   Holding Sebastian's hand.
3   *dejected it*   Threw it down.

140   Here are our friends.—Salute° her, gentlemen.   *greet with a kiss*

(*They unmask her.*)

OMNES. Heart, who? This Moll?[1]
SIR ALEXANDER. Oh, my reviving shame! Is't I must live,
   To be struck blind? Be it the work of sorrow,
   Before age take't in hand![2]
SIR GUY.   Darkness and death!
145   Have you deceived me thus? Did I engage
   My whole estate for this?
SIR ALEXANDER.   You askt no favour,
   And you shall find as little. Since my comforts
   Play false with me, I'll be as cruel to thee
   As grief to fathers' hearts.[3]
MOLL.   Why, what's the matter with you?
150   'Less° too much joy should make your age forgetful?   *unless*
   Are you too well, too happy?
SIR ALEXANDER.   With a vengeance!
MOLL. Methinks you should be proud of such a daughter—
   As good a man as your son.
SIR ALEXANDER.   Oh, monstrous impudence!
MOLL. You had no note° before: an   *distinction*
   unmarkt° knight;   *unremarked*
155   Now all the town will take regard on you,
   And all your enemies fear you for my sake.
   You may pass where you list,° through crowds most thick,   *like*
   And come off[4] bravely with your purse unpickt.

---

1 *Heart … Moll?* Editors are uncertain of the original line, "Heart, who this *Moll.*" and several different versions of the line have been used. I follow Paul A. Mullholland's reasoning that "this" suggests "this is." I consider the line to show the reaction of surprise upon learning that the masked bride is Moll after all, now in women's wedding clothes. Alternatively, as this line is spoken by all, different expressions could be simultaneously uttered: "Who?" "This?" "Moll?"

2 *Is't … hand* Must I live to be blinded? Sorrow blinds me now, before old age could.

3 *Since … hearts* Since I feel I have been tricked and my relief proven false, I'll be merciless in demanding your whole estate, just as my grief is merciless.

4 *come off* Escape, leave. In martial practice, the phrase means to leave the field of combat, here figured as the crowded street.

You do not know the benefits I bring with me:
No cheat dares work upon you, with thumb or knife,[1]   160
While you've a roaring girl to° your son's wife.   *as*
SIR ALEXANDER. A devil rampant![2]
SIR GUY. [*To Sir Alexander.*]   Have you so much charity
    Yet to release me of my last rash bargain,
    An I'll give in your pledge?[3]
SIR ALEXANDER.   No, sir, I stand to't.
I'll work upon advantage, as all mischiefs   165
    Do upon me.[4]
SIR GUY.   Content: bear witness all, then,
His° are the lands, and so contention ends.   *Sebastian's*
Here comes your son's bride, 'twixt two noble friends.

(*Enter the Lord Noland and Sir Beauteous Ganymede, with Mary*
Fitzallard between them, the citizens [*Masters Tiltyard, Openwork,*
and Gallipot] *and their wives with them.*)

MOLL. [*To Sir Alexander.*] Now are you gulled as you would be;[5]
    thank me for't,
    I'd a forefinger in't.   170
SEBASTIAN.   Forgive me father,
Though there before your eyes my sorrow feigned,
This° still was she for whom true love complained.   *Mary Fitzallard*
SIR ALEXANDER. Blessings eternal and the joys of angels,
Begin your peace here to be signed[6] in heaven!
How short my sleep of sorrow seems now to me,   175
To° this eternity of boundless comforts   *compared to*
That finds no want but utterance and expression.[7]
[*To Lord Noland.*] My lord, your office here appears so honourably,

---

1 *with ... knife*   With a thumb for picking your pocket or a knife for cutting your purse.
2 *rampant*   Unchecked or wild; the term is often also used to describe a position taken by
   animals in heraldic images: standing or rearing with forelegs or paws in the air.
3 *Have you ... pledge?*   Are you kind enough to let me out of my wager if I give back your
   ring?
4 *I'll ... me*   I'll work with whatever advantage I can get, since evilness takes advantage of me.
5 *gulled ... be*   Tricked as you would like to be.
6 *to be signed*   To be made official.
7 *comforts ... expression*   Comforts that lack nothing except words to express their greatness.

So full of ancient° goodness, grace, and worthiness,   *venerable, long-known*
180   I never took more joy in sight of man,
     Than in your comfortable° presence now.   *supportive*
LORD NOLAND. Nor I more delight in doing grace to virtue,
     Than in this worthy gentlewoman, your son's bride,
     Noble Fitzallard's daughter, to whose honour
185   And modest° fame° I am a servant vowed;   *pure / reputation*
     So is this knight. [*Indicating Sir Beauteous.*]
SIR ALEXANDER.   Your loves make my joys proud.
     [*To Servant.*] —Bring forth those deeds of land my care laid
     ready—

[*Servant gets deeds.*]

     [*To Sir Guy.*] And which, old knight, thy nobleness may
          challenge,°   *claim*
     Joined with thy daughter's virtues, whom I prize now
190   As dearly as that flesh I call mine own.
     [*To Mary.*] Forgive me worthy gentlewoman, 'twas my blindness.
     When I rejected thee, I saw thee not;
     Sorrow and willful rashness grew like films[1]
     Over the eyes of judgment, now so clear
195   I see the brightness of thy worth appear.
MARY. Duty and love may I deserve in those,°   *your eyes*
     And all my wishes have a perfect close.
SIR ALEXANDER. That tongue can never err, the sound's so sweet.
     [*To Sebastian, giving deeds.*] Here, honest son, receive into thy
     hands
200   The keys of wealth, possession of those lands
     Which my first care provided;[2] they're thine own.
     Heaven give thee a blessing with 'em! The best joys
     That can in worldly shapes to man betide°   *befall*
     Are fertile lands and a fair fruitful bride,

---

1 *films* Unhealthy and possibly fatal growths on the eyes, potentially indicative of disease.
    Films were also thought to be the cause of increasing blindness or darkness perceived by a
    dying person, as referenced in the following lines' assertion of "brightness" restored.
2 *my first care provided* Alexander originally set aside these deeds for Sebastian.

Of which I hope thou'rt sped.°   *furnished* 205
SEBASTIAN.   I hope so too, sir.
MOLL. Father and son, I ha'done you simple service[1] here.
SEBASTIAN. For which thou shalt not part, Moll, unrequited.
SIR ALEXANDER. Thou art a mad girl, and yet I cannot now
  Condemn thee.
MOLL.   Condemn me? Troth, an° you should, sir,   *if*
  I'd make you seek out one to hang in my room:[2]   210
  I'd give you the slip at gallows and cozen° the people. *deceive, cheat*
  [*To Lord Noland.*] Heard you this jest my Lord?
LORD NOLAND.   What is it Jack?
MOLL. He was in fear his son would marry me,
  But never dreamt that I would ne'er agree!
LORD NOLAND. Why? Thou had'st a suitor once, Jack; when wilt   215
  marry?
MOLL. Who, I, my lord? I'll tell you when i'faith:
  When you shall hear
  Gallants void from sergeants' fear,[3]
  Honesty and truth unslandered,
  Woman manned,[4] but never pandered,°   *prostituted* 220
  Cheaters booted, but not coacht,[5]
  Vessels older ere they're broacht.[6]
  If my mind be then not varied,°   *changeable, uncertain*
  Next day following, I'll be married.
LORD NOLAND. This sounds like doomsday!   225
MOLL.   Then° were marriage best, *at doomsday*
  For if I should repent, I were soon at rest.[7]

---

1 *simple service* Modest description of good work.
2 *in my room* In my place.
3 *Gallants ... fear* Gallants not afraid of sergeants arresting them (for debt).
4 *manned* Provided with, or married to, a man.
5 *Cheaters ... coacht* Thieves and rogues able to live—to afford boots—but not rich enough
  to hire coaches.
6 *Vessels ... broacht* Girls allowed to reach maturity before they are made to have sex (or,
  literally, liquor or wine casks allowed to sit longer before they are tapped). Proverbial: "The
  woman is the weaker vessel."
7 *if I should ... rest* Reference to the proverb "Marry today repent tomorrow." Doomsday
  would be a good day for the marriage because she would quickly be dead (at rest); there is
  then no time to repent, or regret, the marriage.

SIR ALEXANDER. [*To Moll.*] In troth tho'art a good wench; I'm sorry now
The opinion was so hard I conceived of thee.
Some wrongs I've done thee.

(*Enter Trapdoor.*[1])

TRAPDOOR.   Is the wind there now?[2]
230   'Tis time for me to kneel and confess first,
For fear it come too late and my brains feel it.[3]
[*To Moll.*] Upon my paws,[4] I ask you pardon mistress.
MOLL.   Pardon? For what sir? What has your rogueship done now?
TRAPDOOR. I have been from time to time hired to
    confound° you,   *defeat, deceive*
235   By this old gentleman.
MOLL.   How?
TRAPDOOR.   Pray forgive him—
But, may I counsel you, you should never do't.[5]
Many a snare to entrap your worship's life
Have I laid privily—chains, watches, jewels—
And when he saw nothing could mount you up,[6]
240   Four hollow-hearted angels he then gave you,
By which he meant to trap you, I to save you.
SIR ALEXANDER. To all which, shame and grief in me cry guilty.
Forgive me; now I cast the world's eyes from me,
And look upon thee freely with mine own:[7]
245   I see the most of many wrongs before thee
Cast from the jaws of Envy and her people,

---

1   *Enter Trapdoor*   Trapdoor seems to enter unseen by the others, while Moll speaks with Sir Alexander. Mullholland speculates that Trapdoor may enter through a trapdoor in the stage.
2   *Is ... now?*   How are things going now? Have Moll and Alexander become friendly?
3   *For fear ... it*   For fear that my involvement with Alexander will be discovered before I can confess it, and I am beaten on the head.
4   *Upon my paws*   On hands and knees, dog-like.
5   *But ... do't*   But, if I may say so, you should never forgive him.
6   *mount you up*   Put you on the gallows.
7   *cast ... own*   Reject the way the world looks at you (Moll) and look instead with an open mind and my own eyes.

And nothing foul but that.¹ I'll never more
Condemn by common voice,° for that's the whore   *opinion, rumor*
That deceives man's opinion, mocks his trust,
Cozens his love, and makes his heart unjust.   250
MOLL. [*Showing coins.*] Here be the angels, gentlemen; they were
   given me
As a musician. I pursue no pity;
Follow the law. An° you can cuck me,² spare not;   *if*
Hang up my viol by me, and I care not.
SIR ALEXANDER. So far I'm sorry, I'll thrice double 'em³   255
To make thy wrongs amends.—
Come worthy friends, my honourable lord,°   *Noland*
Sir Beauteous Ganymede, and noble Fitzallard,
And you kind gentlewomen,⁴ whose sparkling presence
Are glories set in marriage, beams° of society,   *looks or rays* 260
For all your loves give lustre to my joys.
The happiness of this day shall be remembered,
At the return of every smiling spring;
In my time now 'tis born,⁵ and may no sadness
Sit on the brows of men upon that day,   265
But as I am, so all go pleased away!⁶

[*Exeunt.*]

---

1 *from the jaws ... her people* From the mouth of the deadly sin of Envy and her followers.
   Envy appeared again in Thomas Heywood and Thomas Dekker's *Troia-Nova Triumphans*
   (1612), a Lord Mayor's pageant, which featured Envy attacking Virtue, with "fellowes and
   followers of Envy: As Ignorance, Sloth, Oppression, Disdain, &c." with a company of ugly
   helpers bearing black bows and arrows; *nothing foul but that* The only thing foul about
   Moll is what is said about her.
2 *cuck me* Punish me by cucking, a public punishment carried out by strapping the mal-
   efactor (usually a woman) into a "cucking stool" (a chair) and then ducking the chair and
   person into the water, often repeatedly.
3 *I'll ... 'em* I will give you three times twice the original number of angels—twenty-four.
4 *gentlewomen* Originally "gentlewoman" in the text; many editors have changed, following
   Alexander Dyce, "gentlewoman" to "gentlewomen," which might agree better with "Are
   glories set in marriage" that follows in the next line and which could help explain why the
   citizens' wives are on stage in this scene. This change also whisks away all of the wives' past
   marital indiscretions in the happy ending.
5 *'tis born* This happiness is born by me.
6 *as I am ... away* As I am happy, I hope everyone leaves happy too! The line also serves as
   the cue for exit.

EPILOGUE

[*Enter Epilogue.*[1]]

MOLL. A painter, having drawn with curious° art   *skillful, careful*
  The picture of a woman—every part,
  Limned° to the life—hung out the piece to sell.   *painted*
  People, who passed along, viewing it well,
5 Gave several° verdicts on it. Some dispraised   *different*
  The hair; some said the brows too high were raised;
  Some hit her o'er the lips, misliked their colour;
  Some wisht her nose were shorter; some, the eyes fuller;
  Others said roses on her cheeks should grow,
10 Swearing they lookt too pale, others cried no.
  The workman still,° as fault was found, did mend it, *constant, silent*
  In hope to please all; but, this work being ended,
  And hung open at stall,° it was so vile,   *booth or stand*
  So monstrous, and so ugly, all men did smile
15 At the poor painter's folly. Such we doubt°   *fear*
  Is this our comedy. Some perhaps do flout
  The plot, saying, 'tis too thin, too weak, too mean;° *lowly*
  Some for the person° will revile the scene, *character (i.e., Moll)*
  And wonder, that a creature of her being
20 Should be the subject of a poet, seeing
  In the world's eye, none weighs so light;[2] others look
  For all those base tricks published in a book—
  Foul as his brains they flowed from—of cutpurses,
  Of nips and foists, nasty, obscene discourses,
25 As full of lies, as empty of worth or wit,
  For any honest ear, or eye unfit.
  And thus,
  If we to every brain that's humorous°   *capricious*
  Should fashion scenes, we, with the painter, shall
30 In striving to please all, please none at all.
  Yet for such faults, as either the writer's wit,

---

1 *Epilogue* The epilogue is usually assigned to Moll.
2 *In ... light* In the eyes of society, no one has so little worth as Moll; *weighs* Placing
 something on a balance to assess it, with lightness indicating lesser value.

Or negligence of the actors do commit,
Both° crave your pardons: if what both have done,　*writers and actors*
Cannot full° pay° your expectation,　　　　　　　*fully / fulfill*
The Roaring Girl herself, some few days hence,　　　　　　35
Shall on this stage, give larger recompense;[1]
Which mirth that you may share in, herself does woo you,[2]
And craves this sign: your hands[3] to beckon her to you.

FINIS.

—1611

1　*Roaring ... recompense*　Moll will come and perform on the stage herself, to make it up to you.
2　*Which ... you*　Moll woos you to come back and share the mirth of her future performance.
3　*your hands*　Your applause.

In Context

A. On Mary Frith's Life

1. from the Consistory Court of London Correction Book, 27 January 1611/12[1]

Consistory Courts are the ecclesiastical courts for each diocese, and until the mid-nineteenth century, Consistory Courts in the Church of England held jurisdiction over matters of probate and matrimony, including matters of sexual morality. The following record comes from Mary Frith's examination in one such court before the Bishop of London, John King, in January of 1611/12. Her crime was having circulated in the middle aisle of St. Paul's on Christmas Day, wearing a man's cloak and her skirts tucked in to resemble breeches. Frith admits to this act, and was apparently willing to confess to drunkenness and association with London's criminals and "lewd company." However, she maintains the assertion that she was guiltless of sexual crimes and of enticing other women to bad behavior.

This document has been of most interest to drama scholars because it also records Frith's earlier transgressions from the spring of 1611, for which she served time in Bridewell Prison. Bridewell Prison and Hospital was established in the late sixteenth century as a place of correction and for housing the city's poor and orphaned children. It was especially known as place for disorderly women, who served by doing hard labor and who were sometimes publicly whipped while stripped to the waist. The "crimes" for which Frith was sent to Bridewell include a visit to the Fortune Theater, where she appeared in public wearing men's attire and carrying a sword, sat on the stage with men, and performed a song. Whether these details confirm the promise made in *The Roaring Girl's* epilogue that Mad Moll would appear on the same stage "some few days hence" (35), is still uncertain, but they give us a better picture of Mary Frith.

---

1   *1611/12*   England did not accept the Gregorian calendar and mark 1 January as the New Year until 1752; thus, officially this was January of 1611 for the English, but we would think of it as 1612.

This day & place the said Mary appeared personally & then & there voluntarily confessed that she had long frequented all or most of the disorderly & licentious places in this City as namely she had usually in the habit[1] of a man resorted to alehouses, taverns, tobacco shops, & also to playhouses there to see plays & prizes & namely being at a play about three quarters of a year since at the Fortune in man's apparel & in her boot & with a sword by her side, she told the company there present that she thought many of them were of opinion that she was a man, but if any of them would come to her lodging they should find that she is a woman & some other immodest & lascivious speeches she also used at that time. And also sat there upon stage in the public view of all the people there present in man's apparel & played upon her lute & sang a song. And she further confessed that she hath for this long time past usually blasphemed & dishonoured the name of God by swearing & cursing & by tearing God out of his kingdom if it were possible, & hath also usually associated herself with ruffianly swaggering & lewd company as namely with cutpurses, blasphemous drunkards, & others of bad note & most dissolute behaviour with whom she hath to the great shame of her sex often times (as she said) drunk hard & distempered her head with drink. And she further confessed that since she was punished for the misdemeanours aforementioned in Bridewell, she was since upon Christmas day at night taken in Paul's Church with her petticoat tucked up about her in the fashion of a man with a man's cloak on her to the great scandal of diverse persons who understood the same & to the disgrace of all womanhood. ... And she sayeth & protesteth that she is heartily sorry for her foresaid licentious & dissolute life & giveth her earnest promise to carry & behave herself ever from hence forward honestly soberly & womanly & resteth ready to undergo any censure or punishment for her misdemeanours aforesaid in such manner & form as shall be assigned her by the Lord Bishop of London, her ordinary.[2]

---

1 *habit* Attire.

2 *Bishop of London* Leader of the London Diocese of the Church of England, John King became bishop in September 1611, and his processor, George Abbot, would likely have heard Frith's earlier cases; *ordinary* Someone who has immediate jurisdiction in the matter of an ecclesiastical case, such as the bishop of a diocese.

And then she being pressed to declare whether she had not been dishonest of her body & hath not also drawn other women to lewdness by her persuasions & by carrying herself like a bawd,[1] she absolutely denied that she was chargeable with either of these imputations, and thereupon his Lordship thought fit to remand her to Bridewell from whence she now came until he might further examine the truth of the misdemeanours enforced against her without laying as yet any further censure upon her.

2. The Last Will and Testament of Mary Markham, Alias Mary Frith (1659)

A transcript of Mary Frith's will survives in the records of probate held by the National Archives in London. Frith died a widow on 26 July 1659, predeceased by an estranged husband, Lewknor Markham. The will was composed on 6 June 1659 and proved just two days before her death. In the will, she leaves some small estate to surviving relatives—members of the Robinson family—and her niece, Frances Edmonds, who is made the will's executor.[2] Frith indicates a wish to be buried in the church or churchyard of her parish church, St. Bride's in Fleet Street, and indeed Edmonds was able to secure her burial in the church on 10 August 1659.

In the name of God Amen

I, Mary Markham, alias Frith, of the parish of St. Bride, alias Bridget, in Fleet Street London, Widow, being aged and sick and weak in body but of good mind and memory and understanding, for all which I do most humbly thank my most gracious and merciful creator for the quieting of my mind and the settling of the small part and remainder

---

1 *bawd* Procuress or pimp.

2 At 20 pounds and 12 pence, the inheritance Frith left to the Robinsons was substantial enough, but it is far short of the 100-pound fortune reported in the 1662 anonymous biography *The Life and Death of Mrs. Mary Frith, Commonly Called Moll Cutpurse*. The dubious biography supposes that Mary had 1,500 pounds prior to her death, but gave away all but 100 pounds to her friends, the cavaliers. Of her remaining fortune, she distributed some in the form of specially made rings to her close companions and friends, as well as gave 30 pounds to her maids, and the rest of her money, goods, and moveables to her "Kinsman Frith" a shipmaster—or so says the story.

of that mean estate which it hath pleased God of his great mercy and goodness to lend to me in this world of sorrows, do make this my last Will and Testament in manner and form following.

(That is to say) First, I do give and bequeath my soul into the hands of my most gracious Creator, who by his only power breathes the breath of life into me, hoping and confidently believing that all my manifold and grievous sins are and shall be fully pardoned and washed away in, by, and through the shedding and pouring out of the most precious blood and the bitter sufferings and passion of my most blessed Redeemer and Saviour Jesus Christ and that after this transitory and mortal life is ended my soul and body shall be reunited and enjoy everlasting bliss and felicity with him in his heavenly kingdom forever and ever, Amen. My body I leave unto the Earth whence it came to be decently buried in Christian burial within the parish Church or Churchyard of St. Bride's aforesaid in such sort and manner as my Executrix hereafter named, shall think most fitting.

Item,[1] I give unto my kinsman Abraham Robinson twenty pounds of lawful money of England and give unto James Robinson, father of the same Abraham, twelve pence. All the rest and remainder of all my personal estate whatsoever my just debts by me owing and my legacies in this my Will given and bequeathed being first paid and discharged, I fully and wholly give and bequeath the same unto my niece and kinswoman Frances Edmonds, wife of George Edmonds, with my will and desires that they shall be and remain unto her own sole use, benefit, and behoof[2] so long as she liveth. And I do make the said Frances Edmonds sole executrix of this, my last Will and Testament.

In witness whereof I, the said Mary Markham, alias Frith, have hereunto set my hand and seal the sixth day of June in the year of our Lord God one thousand six hundred fifty nine. The mark[3] of Mary Markham, alias Frith, subscribed, sealed, and published by her the said Mary Markham, alias Frith, as and for her last Will and Testament in the presence of us, Richard Hulet, Ralph Warfeild, Abraham Robinson.

---

1 *Item* Also.
2 *behoof* Utility, advantage.
3 *mark* "X" or cross conveying Mary's signature. The use of a mark indicates that she was not able to write her name.

This Will was proved[1] at London before the Right Worshipful William Meynck, Doctor of Laws, Master Keeper or Commissary of the Prerogative Court of Canterbury[2] lawfully constituted the four and twentieth day of July in the year of our Lord God according to the computation of Church of England one thousand six hundred and sixty. By the oath of Frances Edmonds the sole executrix named in the said Will to whom administration of all and singular the goods, chattels, and debts of the said deceased are granted and committed, she being first sworn truly to administer the same according to the tenor and effect of the said Will.

---

1 *proved* Verified by the Church. The part of the will providing this verification, considered the "probate clause," officially granted power to the will's executor.
2 *Prerogative Court of Canterbury* Court that was responsible for the proving of wills for much of southern England and Wales until civil probate courts were created in 1858. The court was located in London, but was under the jurisdiction of the Archbishop of Canterbury.

B. On Theater, Gender, and Cross-Dressing

1. from Stephen Gosson, *Plays Confuted in Five Actions, Proving that they are not to be suffered in a Christian Commonweal* (1582)

Stephen Gosson (1554–1625) was an opponent of the commercial theater at the time of its rise in London. He, along with Philip Stubbes (c. 1555–1610) and William Prynne (1600–69), engaged in lively tirades in print against the sins of stage plays. His first anti-theatrical attack, *The School of Abuse* (1579), inaugurated the sixteenth-century debate over theater and its morality—or lack thereof, in his opinion. Thomas Lodge (1558–1625), a gentleman studying at Lincoln's Inn, answered the pamphlet in a defense of theater, and Gosson's *Plays Confuted in Five Actions* (1582) rebutted Lodge and continued the attack. One of Gosson's main complaints is that theatrical performance openly embraced lying, which was made even more dangerous in its sinful requirement that young men were to play the parts of women. For Gosson, not only was the acting of the lady's part a sinful and dangerous form of dishonesty, it also required the audience to engage in hypocrisy and break God's commandments by embracing the lie of cross-dressing.

... Whatsoever he be that looketh narrowly into our stage plays, or considereth how, and which ways they are represented, shall find more filthiness in them, than players dream of. The Law of God very straightly forbids men to put on women's garments, garments are set down for signs distinctive between sex & sex; to take unto us those garments that are manifest signs of another sex is to falsify, forge, and adulterate, contrary to the express rule of the word of God, which forbiddeth it by threatening a curse unto the same.

All that do so are abomination unto the Lord,[1] which way I beseech you shall they be excused, that put on, not the apparel only, but the

---

1 *All ... Lord* Deuteronomy 22.5: "The woman shall not wear that which pertaineth unto the man, neither shalt a man put on a woman's raiment: for all that do so, are abomination unto the Lord thy God."

gait, the gestures, the voice, the passions of a woman? All which like the wreathings[1] and winding of a snake, are flexible to catch, before they speed; and bind up cords when they have possession. Some there are that think this commandment of God to be restrained to them, that go abroad in women's attire and use it for juggling, to shadow[2] adultery.

These interpreters, like unto narrow-mouthed vessels, will receive nothing without loss, except it be slenderly poured in according to the straightness of their own making. These men must understand, that, that can bear no excuse, which God condemneth, such is the integrity, uniformity, and simplicity of truth that it is ever like itself, it never carrieth two faces in one hood, that thing is nowhere, nor at anytime lawful by the word of God which is not ever, and everywhere lawful. ...

Nevertheless, we will wade somewhat further in this point, and see whether by the philosophers themselves it may be suffered. I trust they will grant me that every lie is sin, for the devil is the father of all lies, as oft as ever he lyeth, he speaketh of his own.[3] Aristotle in the thickest fog of his ignorance concerning God, pronounceth a lie to be nought of itself, and to be fled.[4] Let us therefore consider what a lie is, a lie is *Actus cadens super indebitam materiam*,[5] an act executed where it ought not. This act is discerned by outward signs, every man must show himself outwardly to be such as in deed he is. Outward signs consist either in words or gestures; to declare ourselves by words or gestures to be otherwise than we are, is an act executed where it should not, therefore a lie.

The proof is evident, the consequent is necessary, that in stage plays for a boy to put on the attire, the gesture, the passions of a

---

1 *wreathings* Writhings, contortions, or otherwise actions of twisting on oneself.

2 *juggling* Deceiving; *shadow* Keep dark, cover.

3 *father ... own* See John 8.44: "Ye are of your father the devil, and the lusts of your father ye will do: he hath been a murderer from the beginning, and abode not in the truth, because there is no truth in him. When he speaketh a lie, then speaketh he of his own: for he is a liar, and the father thereof."

4 *Aristotle ... fled* In the *Nichomachean Ethics* 4.7, Aristotle writes, "Falsehood is in itself base and reprehensible, and truth noble and praiseworthy," a passage cited by Thomas Aquinas in *Summa Theologica*.

5 *Actus ... materiam* Latin: An act whose matter is undue. See Thomas Aquinas, *Summa Theologica* 2.2.110.3.

woman; or a mean[1] person to take upon him the title of a prince with counterfeit port, and train, is by outward signs to show themselves otherwise than they are, and so within the compass of a lie, which by *Aristotle's* judgment is naught of itself and to be fled. ...

If [the play] should be played, one must learn to trip it[2] like a lady in the finest fashion, another must have time to whet his mind unto tyranny that he may give life to the picture he presenteth, whereby they learn to counterfeit, and so to sin.

2. from anonymous, *The Life of Long Meg of Westminster, containing the mad merry pranks she played in her lifetime, not only in performing sundry quarrels with diverse ruffians about London: but also how valiantly she behaved herself in wars of Boulogne* (1620, revised 1635)

Long Meg of Westminster was a popular folk heroine in the 1590s and well into the seventeenth century. Similar to Moll Cutpurse, she was something of a roaring girl; a tough, quick-talking, quick-thinking Amazon with a reputation as a merry prankster. There may have been a real Meg, but no known documentation confirms her identity. Her legend states that she was born in Lancashire and uncommonly tall (hence, "Long Meg") and supposedly served in the Battle of Boulogne for Henry VIII. Her first appearance in print was probably a ballad, "Long Meg of Westminster," recorded in the Stationers' Register in 1590, but around that time her legend circulated in many other forms, including a lost play and a lost biography titled *The Life of Long Meg of Westminster* (1590). The 1620 publication of *The Life of Long Meg of Westminster*—possibly a reprint of the 1590 text—presented Meg's story in the form of a jestbook, with eighteen chapters of amusing stories of her adventures in London after arriving from Lancashire, including her time in Henry's army, as a married woman, and as a protector of those in need. Meg's stories feature famous patrons of the Eagle Tavern in Westminster and members of Henry VIII's court: the poet laureate John Skelton (c. 1460–1529); political figure, Lord Chancellor, and writer

---

1   *mean* Lowly.
2   *trip it* Perform the role.

Sir Thomas More (1478–1535); and the court fool and comedian Will Summers (d. 1559). The following extract, taken from the 1635 version of *The Life of Long Meg*, records an incident similar to the encounter of Moll and Laxton in 3.1 of *The Roaring Girl*.

Chap. IV.
Containing the merry skirmish that was between her and Sir James of Castile, a Spanish knight, and what was the end of their combat.

There was a great suitor to Meg's mistress,[1] called Sir James of Castile, to win her love; but her affection was set on Doctor Skelton, so that Sir James could get no grant of any favour. Whereupon he swore, if he knew who were her paramour, he would run him through with his rapier. The mistress (who had great delight to be pleasant) made a match between her and Long Meg, that she should go drest in gentlemen's apparel, and with her sword and buckler go and meet Sir James in Saint George's Fields.[2] If she beat him, she should for her labour have a new petticoat. "Let me alone!" quoth Meg, "The devil take me if I lose a petticoat." And with that her mistress delivered her a suit of white satin, that was one of the guard's that lay at her house. Meg put it on, and took her whinyard[3] by her side, and away she went into Saint George's Fields to meet Sir James. Presently after came Sir James, and found his mistress very melancholy, as women have faces that are fit for all fancies. "What ail you sweetheart," quoth he, "Tell me? Hath any man wronged you? If he hath, be he the proudest champion in London, I'll have him by the ears, and teach him to know, Sir James of Castile can chastise whom he list."[4]

"Now," quoth she, "Shall I know if you love me? A squaring[5] long knave in a white satin doublet hath this day monstrously misused me in words, and I have nobody to revenge it. And in a bravery went out of doors, and bade the proudest champion I had come into Saint George's Fields, and quit my wrong if they durst. Now Sir James, if

---

1 *Meg's mistress* The woman who ran the Eagle Tavern.
2 *Saint George's Fields* Open area in Southwark that was property of the City of London in Meg's time.
3 *whinyard* Short sword, hanger.
4 *whom he list* Whoever he wants.
5 *squaring* Contentious; quarrelsome.

ever you loved me, learn the knave to know how he hath wronged me, and I will grant whatsoever you will request at my hands."

"Marry, that I will," quoth he, "and for that you may see how I will use the knave, go with me, you and Master Doctor Skelton, and be eyewitnesses of my manhood."

To this they agreed, and all three went into Saint George's Fields, where Long Meg was walking by the windmills.

"Yonder," quoth she, "walks the villain that abused me."

"Follow me hostess," quoth Sir James, "I'll go to him." As soon as he drew nigh,[1] Meg, began to settle herself, and so did Sir James: but Meg passed on as though she would have gone by. "Nay sirrah, stay," quoth Sir James, "You and I part not so, we must have a bout 'ere we pass, for I am this gentlewoman's champion, and flatly for her sake will have you by the ears." Meg replied not a word: but only out with her sword, and to it they went. At the first bout Meg hit him on the hand, and hurt him a little, but endangered him diverse[2] times, and made him give ground, following so hotly, that she struck Sir James's weapon out of his hand; then when she saw him disarmed, she stept within him, and drawing her poniard,[3] swore all the world should not save him.

"Oh, save me sir," quoth he, "I am a knight, and 'tis but for a woman's matter. Spill not my blood!"

"Wert[4] thou twenty knights," quoth Meg, "and were the king himself here, he should not save thy life, unless thou grant me one thing."

"Whatsoever it be," quoth Sir James.

"Marry," quoth she, "That is, that this night thou wait on my trencher[5] at supper at this woman's house, and when supper is done, then confess me to be thy better at weapon in any ground in England."

"I will do it, sir," quoth he, "as I am a true knight." With this they departed, and Sir James went home with his hostess sorrowful

---

1 *nigh* Near.
2 *diverse* Several, various.
3 *stept within him* Came in close to his body; *poniard* Small dagger.
4 *Wert* Were.
5 *wait on my trencher* Act as a waiter for me.

and ashamed, swearing that his adversary was the stoutest man in England.

Well, supper was provided, and Sir Thomas More and diverse other gentlemen bidden thither by Skelton's means, to make up the jest: which when Sir James saw invited, he put a good face on the matter and thought to make a slight matter of it, and therefore beforehand told Sir Thomas More what had befallen him: how entering in a quarrel of his hostess, he fought with a desperate gentleman of the court, who had foiled him, and given him in charge to wait on his trencher that night. Sir Thomas More answered Sir James, that is was no dishonour to be foiled by a gentleman, sith[1] Caesar himself was beaten back by their valour.

As thus they were descanting[2] of the valour of Englishmen, in came Meg marching in her man's attire. Even as she entered in at the door, "This, Sir Thomas More," quoth Sir James, "is that English gentleman, whose prowess I so highly commend, and to whom in all valour I account myself so inferior."

"And sir," quoth she, pulling off her hat, and her hair falling about her ears, "he that so hurt him today, is none other but Long Meg of Westminster, and so you are welcome." At this all the company fell in a great laughing, and Sir James was amazed, that a woman should so wap[3] him in a whinyard: well, he as the rest was fain[4] to laugh at the matter, and all that suppertime to wait on her trencher, who had leave of her mistress, that she might be master of the feast: wherewith[5] a good laughter they made good cheer, Sir James playing the proper page, and Meg sitting in her majesty.[6] Thus was Sir James disgraced for his love, and Meg counted for a proper woman.

---

1   *sith*   Since.
2   *descanting*   Remarking on a topic.
3   *wap*   Blow, knock.
4   *fain*   Glad under the circumstances.
5   *wherewith*   Whereat or thereupon.
6   *in her majesty*   In her dignity, assuming a kind of greatness or grandeur.

3. from anonymous, *Hic Mulier: or, The Man-Woman: Being a Medicine to Cure the Coltish Disease of the Staggers in the Masculine-Feminines of our Time* (1620)

The pamphlet *Hic Mulier* offers insight into Jacobean attitudes about cross-dressing and gender identity. The title of the tract, *Hic Mulier*, makes evident the text's main concern over gender ambiguity; although the Latin phrase literally means "This Woman," the article "hic" is the masculine form of "this," so the title might more accurately be translated as "This Masculine Woman." The anonymous author takes the position that women who wear men's clothing or adopt men's accessories or styles are acting against nature and making themselves unnecessarily ugly. The author also associates the disruptive behavior of the man-woman with despicable licentiousness, insisting that only proper female attire signals bashfulness and appropriate modesty.

As critic Sandra Clark relates, *Hic Mulier* marks the zenith of a pamphlet debate over feminine apparel that was at its most intense in 1619–20. By 1615, the phrase "Hic Mulier" was being used disparagingly; it appears in Puritan Thomas Adams's *Mysticall Bedlam, or The World of Mad-Men*, a pamphlet based on his sermons. By 1620, King James had instructed preachers to speak against the insolence of women dressing in masculine attire. Other ballads and poems of 1619–20 also take women to task for cutting their hair short or behaving like "Ganymedes." Within two years of the pamphlet flurry, poets such as John Taylor and Richard Burton were offhandedly still mentioning *Hic Mulier*, but in a way that suggests that the shock and novelty of the debate had worn off.

Hic Mulier. How now? Break Priscian's head[1] at the first encounter? But two words, and they false Latin? Pardon me, good Signor Construction, for I will not answer thee as the Pope did, that I will do it in despite of the grammar. But I will maintain, if it be not the truest Latin in our kingdom, yet it is the commonest. For since the days of Adam women were never so masculine: masculine in their genders and whole generations, from the mother to the youngest daughter;

---

1   *Break Priscian's head*   Break grammatical rules of Latin. Prisican was a Latin grammarian (fl. c. 500 CE) who wrote the *Institutiones Grammaticae*, which became the standard text for teaching Latin in medieval Europe.

masculine in number, from one to multitudes; masculine in case,[1] even from the head to the foot; masculine in mood, from bold speech to impudent action; and masculine in tense, for (without redress) they were, are, and will be still most masculine, most mankind, and most monstrous. Are all women then turned masculine? No, God forbid, there are a world full of holy thoughts, modest carriage, and severe chastity. To these let me fall on my knees and say, "You, O, you women, you good women, you that are in the fullness of perfection, you that are the crowns of nature's work, the complements of men's excellences, and the seminaries[2] of propagation; you that maintain the world, support mankind, and give life to society; you that, armed with the infinite power of virtue, are castles impregnable, rivers unsailable, seas immovable, infinite treasures, and invincible armies; that are helpers most trusty, sentinels most careful, signs deceitless, plain ways failless, true guides dangerless, balms that instantly cure, and honours that never perish. O, do not look to find your names in this declamation, but with all honour and reverence do I speak to you. You are Seneca's Graces,[3] women, good women, modest women, true women—ever young because ever virtuous, ever chaste, ever glorious. When I write of you, I will write with a golden pen, on leaves of golden paper; now I write with a rough quill and black ink on iron sheets the iron deeds of an iron generation.

Come then, you masculine-women, for you are my subject, you that have made admiration an ass, and fooled him with deformity never before dreamed of, that have made yourselves stranger things that ever Noah's Ark unladed, or Nile engendered;[4] whom to name, he that named all things, might study an age to give you a right attribute, whose life are not found in any antiquary's study, in any seaman's travel, nor in any painter's cunning; you that are stranger

---

1 *case* A pun: "case" meant "set of clothes," but is also a grammatical term referring to the inflected forms words take based on their relation to other words in a phrase or sentence. This forms part of a series of grammatical puns on "gender," "number," "mood," and "tense."

2 *seminaries* Places of origin, in this case, women as wombs.

3 *Graces* Three goddesses of Greek mythology, also called the Charites, who were thought to be the essence of beauty, grace, and charm. Seneca discusses the three graces in his *Essays*, particularly "On Benefits."

4 *Nile engendered* See *The Metamorphoses*, Book 1, in which Ovid describes marvelous creatures arising from the fertile mud of the Nile River as the spring sun heats it. The reference was popular in the early modern period.

than strangeness itself, whom wisemen wonder at; boys shout at; and goblins themselves start at; you that are gilt dirt, which embroiders playhouses, the painted statues which adorn carriages, and the perfumed carrion that bad men feed on in brothels: 'tis of you, I entreat, and of your monstrous deformity; you that have made your bodies like antique boscage, or crotesco work,[1] not half-man, half-woman; half fish, half flesh; half beast, half monster: but all odious, all devil, that have cast off the ornaments of your sexes, to put on the garments of shame; that have laid by the bashfulness of your natures, to gather the impudence of harlots; that have buried silence, to revive slander; that are all things but[2] that which you should be, and nothing less than friends to virtue and goodness; that have made the foundation of your highest detested work, from the lowest despised creatures that record can give testimony of; the one cut from the commonwealth at the gallows; the other is well known.[3] From the first you got the false armoury of yellow starch[4] (for to wear yellow on white, or white upon yellow, is by the rules of heraldry baseness, bastardy, and indignity) the folly of imitation, the deceitfulness of flattery, and the grossest baseness of all baseness, to do whatsoever a greater power will command you. From the other, you have taken the monstrousness of your deformity in apparel, exchanging the modest attire of the comely hood, cowl, coif,[5] handsome dress or kerchief, to the cloudy, ruffianly broad-brimmed hat and wanton feather; the modest upper parts of a concealing straight gown, to the loose, lascivious civil embracement

---

1 *antique* Grotesque or bizarre; *boscage* Ornamentation that imitates branches and foliage; *crotesco work* Grotesque painting or sculpture, frequently involving strange distortion or exaggerations in form, and often including foliage and flowers interwoven in the representation of humans or animals.

2 *but* Except.

3 *the one ... known* Refers to Anne Turner and Lady Frances Howard, who both confessed to murdering Sir Thomas Overbury over his objection to Lady Frances' affair with Robert Carr, Earl of Somerset (their marriage followed Howard's annulment of her marriage to Lord Essex). Both women were found guilty, but only Turner—who was also accused of witchcraft—died at the gallows; Howard was saved from her sentence by King James.

4 *yellow starch* It was a fashionable trend to dye cuffs and ruffs yellow using a saffron-based starch, invented supposedly by Anne Turner, who was a dressmaker. The starch gained a reputation as a dangerous affectation, and supposedly Turner was ordered to wear the yellow at her execution, as did her executioner. The trend became associated with vanity, adultery, and witchcraft as a result.

5 *coif* Close-fitting cap that covered the top and sides of the head and was tied under the chin.

of a French doublet,[1] being all unbuttoned to entice, all of one shape to hide deformity, and extreme short-waisted to give a most easy way to every luxurious action; the glory of a fair large hair, to the shame of most ruffianly short locks; the side, thick-gathered, and close guarding safeguards to the short, weak, thin, loose, and every hand-entertaining short bases;[2] for needles, swords; for prayer books, bawdy legs; for modest gestures, giant-like behaviours; and for women's modesty, all mimic and apish incivility: these are your founders, from these you took your copies, and (without amendment) with these you shall come to perdition.

Sophocles being asked, why he presented no women in his tragedies but good ones, and Euripides[3] none but bad ones, answered: he presented women as they should be, but Euripides women as they were. So I present these masculine women in the deformities as they are, that I may call them back to the modest comeliness in which they were. ...

What can be more barbarous than with the gloss of mumming[4] art to disguise the beauty of their creations? To mould their bodies to every deformed fashion, their tongues to vile and horrible profanations, and their hands to ruffianly and uncivil actions? To have their gestures as piebald, and as motley-various[5] as their disguises; their souls fuller of infirmities than a horse or prostitute; and their minds languishing in those infirmities? If this be not barbarous, make

---

1 *straight gown* Garment close-fitting above the waist but with flowing skirts; *French doublet* Typically a short-waisted men's jacket, with or without sleeves, and often padded and worn over a shirt.

2 *safeguards* Outer skirts or petticoat worn by women to protect their skirts, especially while riding; *short bases* Pleated, short skirts attached to a doublet.

3 *Sophocles* Celebrated ancient Greek tragedian of Athens (c. 496–406 BCE), best known as writer of the Theban plays *Oedipus the King*, *Antigone* (whose titular heroine sacrifices herself for her brothers' honor), and *Oedipus at Colonus*; *Euripides* Like Sophocles, a respected Greek tragedian (c. 485–406 BCE) whose most famous play, *Medea*, features a woman who murders her children to exact revenge on her adulterous husband Jason. The author riffs here on Aristotle, who states in his *Poetics* that Sophocles claimed he portrayed *men* as they ought to be, while Euripides portrayed them as they are.

4 *mumming* Wearing a disguise or acting to appear as something else.

5 *piebald* Having mixed or incongruous parts, or especially having contrasting light and dark colors; *motley-various* Mixed or parti-colored, or bringing together diverse elements.

the rude Scythian, the untamed Moor, the naked Indian, or the wild Irish,[1] lords and rulers of well-governed cities.

But rests this deformity then only in the baser? In none but such as are the beggary of desert?[2] That have in them nothing but skittishness, & peevishness? That are living graves, unwholesome sinks?[3] Quartan fevers for intolerable cumber,[4] and the extreme injury and wrong nature? Are these, and none else, guilty of this high treason to God, and nature?

O yes, a world of other, many known great, thought good, wisht happy, much loved, and most admired, are so foully branded with this infamy of disguise, and the marks stick so deep on their naked faces, and more naked bodies, that not all the painting in Rome or Fauna[5] can conceal them, but every eye discovers them almost as low as their middles.

It is an infection that emulates the plague, and throws itself amongst women of all degrees, all deserts, and all ages; from the capitol to the cottage, are some spots or swellings of this disease. Yet evermore the greater the person is, the greater is the rage of this sickness, and the more they have to support the eminence of their fortunes, the more they bestow in the augmentation of their deformities. Not only such as will not work to get bread, will find time to weave herself points[6] to truss her loose breeches. And she that hath pawned her credit to get a hat, will sell her smock to buy a feather; she that hath given kisses to have her hair shorn, will give her honesty to have her upper parts put into a French doublet. To conclude, she that will give her body to have her body deformed, will not stick to give her soul to have her mind satisfied.

---

1   *Scythian*   Nomadic people renowned as warriors; their native Scythia extended over much of Eastern Europe and Central Asia;   *Moor*   Originally a term for people from Mauretania in Northern Africa, and later used to indicate Muslim people, especially those with dark skin, of Arab and Berber descent in Northern Africa;   *Indian*   Native of the Americas or new world;   *Irish*   Like the other groups on this list, Irish natives were seen as brutal, uncivilized, and barbarous.

2   *beggary of desert*   Those impoverished of merit.

3   *sinks*   Cesspits or ground sewers for waste.

4   *Quartan fevers*   Fevers that recur every fourth day;   *cumber*   Burden, trouble, or hindrance.

5   *painting*   Makeup;   *Rome*   According to the pamphlet, Rome is where the best makeup is sold;   *Fauna*   Generally, nature.

6   *points*   Ribbons, cords, or laces.

But such as are able to buy all at their own charges, they swim in the excess of these vanities and will be manlike not only from the head to the waist, but to the very foot & in every condition: man in body by attire, man in behaviour by rude complement, man in nature by aptness to anger, man in action by pursuing revenge, man in wearing weapons, man in using weapons: and, in brief, so much man in all things that they are neither men, nor women, but just good for nothing. ...

Remember how your maker made for our first parents coats, not one coat, but a coat for the man, and a coat for the woman?[1] Coats of several[2] fashions, several forms, and for several uses: the man's coat fit for his labour, the woman's fit for her modesty. And will you lose the model left by this great workmaster of heaven?

The long hair of a woman is the ornament of her sex, and bashful shamefastness her chief honour; the long hair of a man, the vizard[3] for a thievish or murderous disposition. And will you cut off that beauty to wear the other's villainy? The vestals in Rome wore comely garments of one piece from the neck to the heel, and the swordplayers,[4] motley doublets with gaudy points. The first begot reverence; the latter, laughter. And will you lose that honour for the other's scorn? The weapon of a virtuous woman was her tears, which every good man pitied and every valiant man honoured. The weapon of a cruel man is his sword, which neither law allows, nor reason defends. And will you leave the excellent shield of innocence for this deformed instrument of disgrace? Even for goodness' sake (that can ever pay her own with her own merits) look to your reputations, which are undermined with your own follies, and do not become the idle sisters of foolish Don Quixote, to believe every vain fable which you read, or to think you may be attired like Bradamant,[5] who was often

---

1   *Remember ... woman*   See Genesis 3.21: "Unto Adam also and to his wife did the Lord God make coats of skins, and clothed them."

2   *several*   Separate.

3   *vizard*   Mask.

4   *vestals*   Virgin priestesses who tended the scared fire in Rome's Temple of Vesta;   *swordplayers*   Roman gladiators.

5   *Don Quixote*   Eponymous hero of Miguel de Cervantes' parodic romance (1605, 1615) who comes to believe he is a great heroic knight after losing his sanity because he has read too many chivalric romances;   *Bradamant*   Bradamante, Heroine of Ludovico Arisoto's romance *Orlando Furioso* (1516, 1532). She is a great female knight who falls in love with the Muslim warrior Ruggerio and marries him after he converts to Christianity.

taken for Ricardetto, her brother; that you may fight like Marfisa, and win husbands with conquest; or ride astride like Claridiana,[1] and make giants fall at your stirrups. The morals will give you better meanings, which if you shun and take the gross imitations, the first will deprive you of all good society, the second, of noble affections; and the third, of all beloved modesty. You shall lose all the charms of women's natural perfections, have no presence to win respect, no beauty to enchant men's hearts, nor no bashfulness to excuse the vilest imputations.

The fairest face covered with a foul vizard, begets nothing but affright or scorn, and thus noblest person, in an ignoble disguise, attains to nothing but reproach, and scandal. Away then with these disguises and foul vizards; these unnatural paintings and immodest discoveries; keep those parts concealed from the eyes that may not be toucht with the hands. Let not a wandering and lascivious thought read, in an enticing index, the contents of an unchaste volume. Imitate nature: and as she hath placed on the surface and superficies of the Earth, all things needful for man's sustenance, and necessary use; as herbs, plants, fruits, corn and such like, but lockt up close in the hidden caverns of the Earth, all things which appertain to his delight and pleasure: as gold, silver, rich minerals, and precious stones. So do you discover unto men all things that are fit for them to understand from you: as bashfulness in your cheeks, chastity in your eyes, wisdom in your words, sweetness in your convention, pity in your hearts, and a general and severe modesty in the whole structure or seam of your universal composition. But for those things which belong to this wanton and lascivious delight and pleasure—as eyes wandering, lips billing,[2] tongue enticing, bared breasts seducing, and naked arms embracing—O, hide them, for shame hide them in the closest prisons of your strictest government. Shield them with modest and comely garments, such as are warm and wholesome, having every window closed with a strong casement, and every loophole furnished

---

1   *Ricardetto*   Bradamante's brother; they are male and female twins who look alike; *Marfisa* Another heroine of *Orlando Furioso*, a pagan warrior who fights against the French and falls in love with Ruggerio, who turns out to be her long-lost brother; *Claridiana* Heroine featured in *The Mirror of Knighthood*, a Spanish romance popular in the sixteenth century and a featured title in Don Quixote's library.

2   *billing*   Kissing.

with such strong ordinance, that no unchaste eye may come near to assail them, no lascivious tongue woo a forbidden passage, nor no profane hand touch relics so pure and religious. Guard them about with counterscarps[1] of innocence, trenches of human reason, and impregnable walls of sacred divinity. ...

Remember that God in your first creation did not form you of slime and earth, like man, but of a more pure and refined metal;[2] a substance much more worthy: you in whom are all the harmonies of life, the perfection of symmetry, the true and curious consent of the most fairest colours and the wealthy gardens which fill the world with living plants. Do but you receive virtuous inmates (as what palaces are more rich to receive heavenly messengers?) and you shall draw men's souls unto you with that severe, devout, and holy adoration, that you shall never want praise, never love, never reverence. ...

Nay, the very art of painting (which to the last age shall ever be held in detestation) they have so cunningly stolen and hidden amongst their husbands hordes of treasure, that the decayed stock of prostitution (having little other revenues) are hourly in bringing their action of detinue[3] against them. Hence (being thus troubled with these popinjays, & loth still to march in one rank with fools and zanies[4]) have proceeded these disguised deformities, not to offend the eyes of goodness, but to tire with ridiculous contempt the never-to-be-satisfied appetites of these gross and unmannerly intruders. Nay, look if this very last edition of disguise, this which is so full of faults, corruptions and false quotations, this bait which the devil hath laid to catch the souls of wanton women, be not as frequent in the demi-palaces of burghers and citizens, as it is either at masque, triumph, tiltyard,[5] or playhouse. Call but to account the tailors that are

---

1 *counterscarps* Fortifications, specifically the outer walls of a ditch that support a covered way.

2 *God ... metal* In Genesis 2.6–7, God forms the first man (Adam) from the earth after having watered the ground. In 2.21–23, God forms the first woman (Eve) from Adam's rib; *metal* Clay or other material, here referring to the rib.

3 *action of detinue* Action at law to recover personal chattel or payment that has been detained.

4 *popinjays* Literally, parrots; the term is often applied to vain people; *zanies* Buffoons, especially ones who imitate others.

5 *masque* Courtly dramatic entertainment involving music, dancing, elaborate costumes, and sometimes stage mechanics; *triumph* Public celebration in the form of a pageant or tournament, often celebrating a victory; *tiltyard* Yard for jousting tournaments.

contained within the circumference of the walls of the City, and let but their hells and their hard reckonings be justly summed together, and it will be found they have raised more new foundations of this new disguise, and metamorphosed more modest old garments, to this new manner of short base and French doublet (only for the use of freemen's wives and their children) in one month, than hath been worn in court, suburbs, or country, since the unfortunate beginning of the first devilish invention.

Let therefore the powerful Statute of Apparel[1] but lift up his battle-axe, and crush the offenders in pieces, so as everyone may be known by the true badge of their blood, or fortune. ...

But when they thrust virtue out of doors, and give a shameless liberty to every loose passion, that either their weak thoughts engenders, or the discourse of wicked tongues can charm into their yielding bosoms (much too apt to be opened with any pick-lock of flattering and deceitful insinuation) then they turn masquers, mummers, nay monsters in their disguises, and so they may catch the bridle[2] in their teeth, and run away with their rulers, they care not into what dangers they plunge either their fortunes or reputations, the disgrace of the whole sex, or the blot and obloquy of their private families. According to the saying of the poets:

Such is the cruelty of womenkind,
When they have shaken off the shamefaced band
With which wise nature did them strongly bind,
T'obey the hests[3] of man's well-ruling hand;
That then all rule and reason they withstand
To purchase a licentious liberty;
But virtuous women wisely understand,

---

1   *Statute of Apparel*   Body of sumptuary regulations to standardize the materials, clothing, and accessories that could legally be worn according to gender and status. Under King James I (r. 1603–25), many of the Elizabethan and earlier regulations on apparel were repealed.

2   *masquers*   Participants in a masque;   *mummers*   Imitators, or more specifically, costumed participants in a mummer's play—a traditional play of folklore or history performed at private houses by traveling companies;   *bridle*   Head-gear for a horse or other beast of burden, by which the animal is controlled.

3   *hests*   Behests, commands.

That they were born to mild humility,
Unless the heavens them lift to lawful sovereignty.[1]

To you therefore that are fathers, husbands, or sustainers of these
new hermaphrodites,[2] belongs the cure of this impostume;[3] it is you
that give fuel to the flames of their wild indiscretion. You add the oil
which makes their stinking lamps defile the whole house with filthy
smoke, and your purses purchase these deformities at rates both dear
and unreasonable. Do you but hold close your liberal hands or take
strict account of the employment of the treasure you give to their
necessary maintenance, and these excesses will either cease, or else die
smothered in prison in the tailor's trunks for want of redemption. ...
And therefore to knit up this imperfect declamation, let every
female-masculine that by her ill example is guilty of lust, or imitation,
cast off her deformities and clothe herself in the rich garments which
the poet bestows upon her in these verses following:

Those virtues that in women merit praise
Are sober shows without, chaste thoughts within.
True faith and due obedience to their mate,
And of their children honest care to take.[4]

FINIS

4. anonymous, *Haec-Vir:*[5] *or, The Womanish-Man* (1620)

Shortly after *Hic Mulier* argued against the monstrosity of cross-dressing, and especially of "women turned masculine," another anonymous
pamphlet, *Haec-Vir, or the Womanish-Man,* answered it directly. *Haec-
Vir* offers a dialogue between "Haec-Vir" and "Hic-Mulier," allowing
the man-woman an opportunity to defend herself and to expose the
flawed opinions of the so-called womanish man.

---

1   *Such is ... lawful sovereignty*   The lines are taken with slight alterations from Edmund Spen-
    ser's *Faerie Queene* 5.5.25 (1596).
2   [Anonymous marginal note] A warning to husbands and fathers.
3   *impostume*   Festering sore or swelling, here used figuratively to imply a moral corruption.
4   *Those virtues ... to take*   From Ludovico Ariosto, *Orlando Furioso* 7.63 (translation by John
    Harington, 1591).
5   *Haec-Vir*   Literally "This Man," but "haec" is the feminine version of "this," so the phrase
    means "this womanish man."

The Speakers

HAEC-VIR: The Womanish-Man
HIC-MULIER: The Man-Woman

HAEC-VIR. Most redoubted and worthy sir, (for less than a knight I cannot take you) you are most happily given unto mine embrace.

HIC-MULIER. Is she mad? Or doth she mock me? Most rare and excellent lady, I am the servant of your virtues and desire to be employed in your service.

HAEC-VIR. Pity of patience, what doth he behold in me, to take me for a woman? Valiant and magnanimous Sir, I shall desire to build the tower of my fortune upon no stronger foundation than the benefit of your grace and favour.

HIC-MULIER. Oh! Proud ever to be your servant.

HAEC-VIR. No, the servant of your servant.

HIC-MULIER. The tithe[1] of your friendship, good lady, is above my merit.

HAEC-VIR. You make me rich beyond expression. But, fair knight, the truth is I am a man, and desire but the obligation of your friendship.

HIC-MULIER. It is ready to be sealed and delivered to your use. Yet I would have you understand, I am a woman.

HAEC-VIR. Are you a woman?

HIC-MULIER. Are you a man? O Juno Lucina,[2] help me!

HAEC-VIR. Yes, I am.

HIC-MULIER. Your name, most tender piece of masculine?

HAEC-VIR. *Haec-Vir*. No stranger either in court, city, or country. But what is yours, most courageous counterfeit of Heracles and his distaff?[3]

---

1 *tithe* Tenth or small portion given.

2 *Juno* Roman goddess and figure of stately beauty, a daughter of Saturn and wife of Jupiter; *Lucina* As an epithet for Juno, this means "she who brings children into the light."

3 *Heracles* Greek name for Hercules, the extremely strong hero of classical mythology; *distaff* Three-foot staff used for spinning fibers by hand. While undergoing penance as a slave to the Queen of Lydia, Omphale, Heracles had to trade his club for a distaff to spin wool.

HIC-MULIER. Near a kin to your goodness and compounded of fully as false Latin. The world calls me *Hic-Mulier*.

HAEC-VIR. What, Hic-Mulier, the Man-Woman? She that like a larum bell[1] at midnight hath raised the whole kingdom in armies against her? Good, stand, and let me take a full survey, both of thee and all thy dependents.

HIC-MULIER. Do freely. And when thou hast daubed me over, with the worst colours[2] thy malice can grind, then give me leave to answer for myself, and I will say thou art an accuser just and indifferent. Which done, I must entreat you to sit as many minutes, that I may likewise take your picture and then refer to censure, whether[3] of our deformities is most injurious to Nature, or most effeminine to good men, in the notoriousness of the example.

HAEC-VIR. With like condition of freedom to answer. The articles are agreed on: therefore stand forth, half Birchenlane, half St. Thomas Apostles:[4] the first lent thee a doublet, the latter a nether-skirt; half Bridewell, half Blackfriars: the one for a scurvy block, the other for a most profane feather;[5] half Mulled Sack the Chimney-sweeper, half Garret the Fool at a tilting: the one for a yellow ruff, the other for a scarf able to put a soldier out of countenance;[6] half Bedlam, half Birmingham: the one for a base

---

1 *larum bell* Alarm bell, or a warning bell sounded to indicate danger.

2 *colours* Pigments ground into powders for making dyes, paints, and cosmetics.

3 *sit* Pose; *take your picture* Draw your figure; *whether* Which.

4 *Birchenlane* Street in central London, near the Royal Exchange and the Merchant Taylor's Hall, a place for buying apparel; *St. Thomas Apostles* Parish church near Bow Lane (once called Hosier Lane), in a neighborhood known for hosiery shops.

5 *Bridewell* Neighborhood of Bridewell, a prison, hospital, and workhouse; *Blackfriars* Neighborhood in London named for the monastery that had been on the site but had become a theater, associated with fashionable Londoners and wealth; *block* Puns on the idea of the "block" as the place for beheading prisoners and as a tool for making hats; *profane feather* The feather in the hat is an emblem of frivolity associated with wealth and gallants (like Jack Dapper in *The Roaring Girl*).

6 *Mulled Sack* Warmed, spiced sack, a sweet white wine from Spain; also a pun on the punishment of being drowned in a sack, or given "the sack"; *Garret* Name for the fool, but also the Spanish punishment of the "garrotte," the practice of strangulation using a cord twisted about the neck by means of a garrotte, or stick; *a tilting* A joust; *yellow ruff* See *Hic Mulier* above, footnote 4, page 172; *scarf* Sash, or broad band of material, indicative of rank in a military context if worn across the body or around the waist. The image may also refer back to the punishment of the garrotte, indicating the possible use of the scarf as a weapon; *out of countenance* Make disconcerted or overcome.

sale boot, the other for a beastly, leaden-gilt spur;[1] and to conclude, all Hell, all Damnation: for a shorn, powdered, borrowed hair;[2] a naked, lascivious, bawdy bosom; a Leadenhall dagger;[3] a highway pistol; and a mind and behaviour suitable or exceeding every repeated deformity. To be brief, I can but in those few lines delineate your proportion, for the paraphrase or compartment, to set out your ugliness to the greatest extent of wonder. I can but refer you to your God-child that carries your own name (I mean the book of *Hic-Mulier*). There you shall see your character and feel your shame, with that palpable plainness that no Egyptian darkness[4] can be more gross and terrible.

HIC-MULIER. My most tender piece of man's flesh, leave this lightning and thunder and come roundly to the matter; draw mine accusation into heads,[5] and then let me answer.

HAEC-VIR. Then thus: in that book,[6] you are arraigned and found guilty, first of baseness, in making yourself a slave to novelty, and the poor invention of every weak brain that hath but an embroidered outside. Next, of unnaturalness, to forsake the creation of God and customs of the kingdom; to be pieced and patched up by a French tailor, an Italian baby-maker, and a Dutch soldier[7] (beat from the army for the ill example of ruffianly behaviour); then of shamelessness, in casting off all modest softness and civility to run through every desert and wilderness of men's opinions, like careless untamed heifers or wild savages. Lastly, of foolishness,

---

1   *Bedlam*   Asylum for the mad in North London;   *Birmingham*   English town associated with counterfeiting;   *base sale boot*   Low-quality boot;   *leaden-gilt spur*   Spur that appears golden but is actually made out of lead, referring to the association of Birmingham with counterfeit coins and plated or lacquered goods.

2   *shorn ... hair*   Short-haired wig that has been treated with white powder.

3   *Leadenhall dagger*   The right to make daggers was contested; Leadenhall was the only place in London after 1619 where foreign (non-London) cutlers could sell their wares.

4   *Egyptian darkness*   The intense darkness experienced by the Egyptians in Exodus 10.22: "Then Moses stretched forth his hand toward heaven, and there was a black darkness in all the land of Egypt three days." Generally, "Egyptian" was also used as an adjective to describe darkness of skin.

5   *draw ... heads*   Come to a point in your accusations (so that they may be addressed).

6   *that book*   *Hic Mulier.*

7   *French tailor*   Tailors were associated with lasciviousness and effeminacy, and "French" suggests sexual adventurousness or excess or can imply sexual disease, especially syphilis;   *baby-maker*   Maker of dolls;   *Dutch soldier*   Soldier of the lowlands or Germany, places associated with mercenaries.

in having no moderation or temper either in passions or affections, but turning all into perturbations and sicknesses of the soul, laugh away the preciousness of your time and, at last, die with the flattering sweet malice of an incurable consumption.[1] Thus baseness, unnaturalness, shamelessness, foolishness, are the main hatchments, or coat-armours,[2] which you have taken as rich spoils to adorn you in the deformity of your apparel: which, if you can excuse, I can pity and thank Proserpina[3] for thy wit, though no good man can allow of the reasons.

HIC-MULIER. Well, then, to the purpose: first, you say I am base in being a slave to novelty. What slavery can there be in freedom of election, or what baseness to crown my delights with those pleasures which are most suitable to mine affections? Bondage, or slavery, is a restraint from those actions which the mind (of its own accord) doth most willingly desire: to perform the intents and purposes of another's disposition, and that not but by mansuetude[4] or sweetness of entreaty, but by the force of authority and strength of compulsion. Now for me to follow change, according to the limitation of mine own will and pleasure, there cannot be a greater freedom. Nor do I in my delight of change, otherwise than as the whole world doth, or as become a daughter of the world to do. For what is the world, but a very shop or warehouse of change? Sometimes winter, sometimes summer. Day and night. They hold sometimes riches, sometimes poverty; sometimes health, sometimes sickness; now pleasure, presently anguish; now honour, then contempt. And to conclude, there is nothing but change, which doth surround and mix withal our fortunes. And will you have poor woman such

---

1   *incurable consumption*   Untreatable disease, usually leading to wasting or decaying. Later, consumption would be synonymous with tuberculosis.

2   *hatchments*   Armorial devices granted in recognition of service;   *coat-armours*   Coats of arms. The image suggests that Hic-Mulier wears the abstract qualities of foolishness, baseness, etc. as if they were heraldic symbols.

3   *Proserpina*   Roman goddess whose abduction by the king of the underworld, Pluto, caused her mother, the goddess Ceres, to halt the growing season. Proserpina was compelled to spend half of each year on the surface and half the year in the underworld, giving rise to seasons of growth and fallowness on earth.

4   *mansuetude*   Meekness, gentleness.

a fixed star,[1] that she shall not so much as move or twinkle in her own sphere? That were true slavery indeed, and a baseness beyond the chains of the worst servitude. Nature, to everything she hath created, hath given a singular delight in change: as to herbs, plants and trees a time to wither and shed their leaves, a time to bud and bring forth their leaves, and a time for their fruits and flowers; to worms and creeping things a time to hide themselves in the pores and hollows of the earth, and a time to come abroad and suck the dew; to beasts, liberty to choose their food, liberty to delight in their food, and liberty to feed and grow fat with their food. The birds have the air to fly in, the waters to bathe in, and the earth to feed on. But to man, both these and all things else, to alter, frame and fashion, according as his will and delight shall rule him. Again, who will rob the eye of the variety of objects, the ear of the delight of sounds, the nose of smells, the tongue tastes, & the hand of feeling? & shall only woman, excellent woman—so much better in that she is something purer—be only deprived of this benefit? Shall she be the bondslave of time, the handmaid of opinion, or the strict observer of every frosty or cold benumbed imagination? It were a cruelty beyond the rack or strappado.[2]

But you will say it is not change? What novelty is? But novelty, from which you deter us—a thing that doth evert[3] the good, and erect the evil; prefer the faithless, and confound desert; that with the change of opinions breeds the change of states; and with continual alterations thrusts headlong forward both ruin and subversion. Alas, soft sir, what can you christen by that new imagined title, when the words of a wise man are: "That what was done, is but done again. All things do change, & under the cope of Heaven there is no new thing."[4] So that whatsoever we do or imitate, it is neither slavish, base, nor a breeder of novelty.

---

1   *fixed star*   I.e., star. In early modern astronomy, stars were considered to be "fixed" on a "celestial sphere" that rotated as a single unit, while planets were referred to as "wandering stars" as their movement across the sky was less predictable.

2   *rack*   Torture device made of a frame on which an individual, whose hands and feet were attached to rollers, was stretched;   *strappado*   Form of torture in which a prisoner's hands were tied behind the back and secured to a pulley, which hoisted the prisoner off the ground, only to drop the victim and then stop the descent with a painful jerk.

3   *evert*   Overthrow; turn over.

4   *That ... thing*   Ecclesiastes 1.9.

Next, not unnatural. You condemn me of unnaturalness, in for-saking my creation, and contemning[1] custom. How do I forsake my creation, that do all the rights and offices due to my creation? I was created free, born free, and live free: what lets me then so to spin out my time, that I may die free? ...
Cato Junior[2] held it for a custom never to eat meat but sit-ting on the ground. The Venetians kiss one another ever at the first meeting, and even at this day it is a general received custom amongst our English that when we meet or overtake any man in our travel or journeying, to examine him whither he rides, how far, to what purpose, and where he lodges. Nay, and with that unmannerly boldness of inquisition, that it is a certain ground of a most insufficient quarrel not to receive a full satisfaction of those demands which go far astray from good manners, or comely civility; and will you have us to marry ourselves to these mimic and most fantastic customs? ... To ride on side-saddles at first was counted here abominable pride, &c. I might instance in a thou-sand things that only custom and not reason hath approved. To conclude: custom is an idiot, and whosoever dependeth wholly upon him, without the discourse of reason, will take from him his pied-coat,[3] and become a slave indeed to contempt and censure.

But you say we are barbarous and shameless, and cast off all softness, to run wild through a wilderness of opinions. In this you express more cruelty than in all the rest, because I stand not with my hands on my belly like a baby at Bartholomew Fair,[4] that move not my whole body when I should but only stir my head like Jack of the Clockhouse,[5] which hath no joints, that am not dumb when wantons court me, as if ass-like I were ready for all burdens, or

---

1   *contemning*   Treating with contempt.

2   *Cato Junior*   Cato the Younger, Marcus Porcius Cato (c. 95–46 BCE), a politician with a reputation for upstanding morality. He opposed Julius Caesar (100–44 BCE) and supported the Roman Republic.

3   *pied-coat*   Black and white coat, or coat colored with dabs of color. The coat indicates the status of a beggar or a motley fool.

4   *baby*   Doll; *Bartholomew Fair*   Fair held annually at West Smithfield (London) the week of St. Bartholomew's day (24 August).

5   *Jack of the Clockhouse*   Mechanical figure that strikes the bell on a large public clock. Such a figure might have a movable head but not movable limbs.

because I weep not when injury gripes me, like a worried[1] deer in the fangs of many curs. Am I therefore barbarous or shameless? He is much injurious that so baptized us: we are as free-born as men, have as free election, and as free spirits, we are compounded of like parts, and may with like liberty make benefit of our creations. My countenance shall smile on the worthy, and frown on the ignoble; I will hear the wise, and be deaf to idiots; give counsel to my friend, but be dumb to flatterers; I have hands that shall be liberal to reward defeat, feet that shall move swiftly to do good offices, and thoughts that shall ever accompany freedom and severity. If this be barbarous, let me leave the city and live with creatures of like simplicity.

To conclude, you say we are all guilty of most infinite folly and indiscretion. I confess, that discretion is the true salt which seasoneth every excellency, either in man or woman, and without it nothing is well, nothing is worthy: that want[2] disgraceth our actions, staineth our virtues, and indeed makes us most profane and irreligious. Yet, it is ever found in excess, as in too much, or too little. And of which of these are we guilty; do we wear too many clothes or too few? If too many, we should oppress nature; if too few, we should bring sickness to nature. But neither of these we do, for what we do wear is warm, thrifty, and wholesome; then no excess and, so, no indiscretion. Where is then the error? Only in the fashion, only in the custom. Oh, for mercy sake, bind us not to so hateful a companion, but remember what one of our famous English poets says:

Round-headed custom th'apoplexy is
Of bedrid nature, and lives led amiss,
And takes away all feeling of offence.[3] ...

And will you be so tyrannous, then, to compel poor woman to be a mistress to so unfaithful a servant? Believe it, then we must call up our champions against you, which are beauty and frailty,

---

1   *worried*   Mangled or killed by biting.
2   *that want*   I.e., the lack of discretion.
3   *Round-headed ... offence*   The lines, by George Chapman, are featured in *England's Parnassus, or the Choysest Flowers of Our English Poets* (1600), a miscellany.

and what the one cannot compel you to forgive, the other shall enforce you to pity or excuse. And thus, myself imagining myself free of these four imputations, I rest to be confuted by some better and graver judgment.

HAEC-VIR. You have wrested out some wit to wrangle forth no reason, since everything you would make for excuse approve your guilt still more ugly. What baser bondage or what more servile baseness than for the flattering and soothing of an unbridled appetite, or delight, to take a willful liberty to do evil, and to give evil example? This is to be Hell's prentice, not Heaven's free-woman.[1] It is disputable amongst our divines, whether upon any occasion a woman may put on man's attire, or no: all conclude it unfit, and the most indifferent will allow it, but only to escape persecution. Now you will not only put it on, but wear it continually; and not wear it, but take pride in it; not for persecution, but wanton pleasure; not to escape danger, but to run into damnation; not to help others, but to confound the whole sex by the evilness of so lewd an example. ...

Now, who knows not that to yield to baseness must needs be folly? (For what wisdom will be guilty of its own injury?) To be foolishly base, how can there be an action more barbarous? And to be base, foolish, and barbarous, how can there appear any spark, twinkle, or but ember of discretion or judgment? So that notwithstanding your elaborate plea for freedom, your severe condemnation of custom, your fair promise of civil actions, and your temperate avoiding of excess—whereby you would seem to hug and embrace discretion; yet till you wear hats to defend the sun, not to cover shorn locks; cauls to adorn the head, not Gregorians[2] to warm idle brains; till you wear innocent white ruffs, not jealous yellow jaundiced bands; well shaped, comely, and close gowns, not light skirts and French doublets; for poniards, samplers;[3] for pistols, prayer-books; and for ruffled boots and spurs, neat shoes, and clean-gartered stockings, you shall never lose the title of baseness, unnaturalness, shamelessness, and foolishness, you shall feed

---

1 *free-woman* Contrasted to "prentice," (i.e., apprentice) the phrase is a modification of "freeman," the title conferred on those who become full members of a trade guild and gain the freedom to practice their craft in the City of London.
2 *cauls* Women's close-fitting caps; *Gregorians* Fashionable men's wigs.
3 *poniards* daggers; *samplers* Simple exercises in embroidery.

ballads,[1] make rich shops, arm contempt, and only starve and make poor yourselves and your reputations. To conclude, if you will walk without difference, you shall live without reverence: if you will contemn order, you must endure the shame of disorder; and if you will have no rulers but your wills, you must have no reward but disdain and disgrace. ...

HIC-MULIER. Sir, I confess you have raised mine eyelids up, but you have not clean taken away the film that covers the sight: I feel—I confess—cause of belief, and would willingly bend my heart to entertain belief, but when the accuser is guilty of as much or more than that he accuseth, or that I see you refuse the potion, and are as grievously infected, blame me not then a little to stagger, and till you will be pleased to be cleansed of that leprosy which I see apparent in you, give me leave to doubt whether mine infection be so contagious, as your blind severity would make it.

Therefore to take your proportion in a few lines, (my dear feminine masculine) tell me what charter, prescription, or right of claim you have to those things you make our absolute inheritance? Why do you curl, frizzle, and powder your hairs, bestowing more hours and time in dividing lock from lock, and hair from hair, in giving every thread his posture, and every curl his true sense and circumference than ever Caesar did in marshalling his army, either at Pharsalia, in Spain, or Britain? Why do you rob us of our ruffs, of our earrings, carkanets, and mamillions, of our fans and feathers, our busks and French bodies, nay, of our masks, hoods, shadows, and shapinas?[2] Not so much as the very art of painting,[3] but you have so greedily engrossed it, that were it not for that little fantastical sharp-pointed dagger that hangs at your chins, & the cross hilt[4] which guards your upper lip, hardly would there be any difference between the fair mistress & the foolish servant. But is this theft the uttermost of our spoil? Fie, you have gone a

---

1 *feed ballads* I.e., inspire satirical ballad makers with your appearance.

2 *carkanets* Gold or bejeweled ornamental collars, necklaces, or headpieces; *mamillions* Coverings for the chest; *busks* Headdresses; *bodies* Women's close fitting garments for the upper body, tight fitting and fastened at the crotch; *shadows* Coverings that protect the face from sun; *shapinas* Headdresses.

3 *painting* Application of cosmetics.

4 *sharp-pointed dagger ... cross hilt* Reference to sharply manicured beards and mustaches.

world further, and even ravished from us our speech, our actions, sports, and recreations. Goodness leave me, if I have not heard a man court his mistress with the same words that Venus did Adonis,[1] or as near as the book could instruct him; where are the tilts and tournies, and lofty galliards[2] that were danced in the days of old, when men capered in the air like wanton kids on the tops of mountains, and turned above ground as if they had been compact of fire or a purer element? Tut, all's forsaken, all's vanished, those motions showed more strength than art, and more courage than courtship. ... For this you have demolished the noble schools of horsemanship—of which many were in this City—hung up your arms to rust, glued up those swords in their scabbards that would shake all Christendom with the brandish, and entertained into your minds such softness, dullness and effeminate niceness, that it would even make Heraclitus himself laugh against his nature to see how pulingly[3] you languish in this weak entertained sin of womanish softness: to see one of your gender either show himself—in the midst of his pride or riches—at a playhouse, or public assembly how, (before he dare enter) with the Jacob's Staff[4] of his own eyes and his page's, he takes a full survey of himself, from the highest sprig in his feather, to the lowest spangle[5] that shines in his shoestring. How he prunes and picks himself like a hawk set a-weathering,[6] calls every several garment to auricular confession, making them utter both their mortal great stains, and their venial

---

1 *Venus ... Adonis* Venus and Adonis were lovers in Greek myth, as featured in Ovid's *Metamorphoses* (c. 10 CE), but the book more likely here referenced is Shakespeare's minor epic *Venus and Adonis* (1593), based on Ovid. In Shakespeare's text, the smitten Venus pursues a resistant Adonis unrelentingly; the poem opens with Venus chasing the man she calls "Thrice fairer than myself."

2 *galliards* Dances in triple time.

3 *niceness* Wantonness, foolishness; *Heraclitus* Fifth-century Greek known as the "weeping philosopher" for his melancholy (such that laughter would be against his nature). He asserted that the universe operates in a state of flux and that opposites unify, and so the unification of masculine and feminine should confirm his beliefs. However, here the author suggests that unification is so ridiculous that even Heraclitus would laugh at it; *pulingly* In a weak or whining manner.

4 *Jacob's Staff* Instrument used for surveying, especially to measure distances and heights.

5 *spangle* Shining metal rings used in decorating fabrics.

6 *hawk ... a-weathering* To weather a hawk is to allow it to sit on an outdoor perch.

and less blemishes, though the mote be much less than an atom![1] Then to see him pluck and tug everything into the form of the newest received fashion; and by Durer's[2] rules make his leg answerable to his neck; his thigh proportionable with his middle, his foot with his hand, and a world of such idle disdained foppery; to see him thus patched up with symmetry, make himself complete and even as a circle, and lastly, cast himself amongst the eyes of the people (as an object of wonder) with more niceness than a virgin goes to the sheets of her first lover, would make patience herself mad with anger and cry with the poet:

O hominum mores, O gens, O tempora dura,
Quantus in urbe dolor; quantus in orbe dolus![3]

Now since according to your own inference, even by the laws of nature, by the rules of religion, and the customs of all civil nations, it is necessary there be a distinct and special difference between man and woman, both in their habit and behaviours. What could we poor weak women do less (being far too weak by force to fetch back those spoils you have unjustly taken from us) than to gather up those garments you have proudly cast away, and therewith to clothe both our bodies and our minds—since no other means was left us to continue our names—and to support a difference? ... Hence we have preserved (though to our own shames) those manly things which you have forsaken, which, would you again accept, and restore to us the blushes we laid by, when first we put on your masculine garments doubt not but chaste thoughts and bashfulness will again dwell in us, and our palaces being newly gilt,

---

1   *mote*   Stain, though "mote" was also used as a synonym for "atom";   *atom*   According to some early modern thinkers, atoms were the smallest particles of matter.

2   *Durer*   German printmaker, painter, and draftsman Albrecht Dürer (1471–1528), best known for his woodcuts and illustrations. Dürer's 1525 treatise on geometry made him the first Northern Renaissance artist to explain the practice of perspective in art. He was also the author of *Four Books of Human Proportion* (1528), referenced in the line following.

3   *O hominum ... dolus*   Latin: O, men's customs, O, nation, O, the time immeasurable, / How great the sadness of the city; how great the sadness of the world! The poet is unknown, but the line references the famous quotation "*O tempora o mores*" (Latin: "Oh the times, oh the customs"); see Cicero's *Against Verres* 2.4 (70 BCE).

trimmed, and re-edified, draw to us all the graces, all the muses;[1] which that you may more willingly do, and (as we of yours) grow into detestation of that deformity you have purloined, to the utter loss of your honours and reputations? ... Cast, then, from you our ornaments and put on your own armours: be men in shape, men in show, men in words, men in actions, men in counsel, men in example. Then will we love and serve you; then will we hear and obey you; then will we like rich jewels hang at your ears to take our instructions, like true friends follow you through all dangers, and like careful leeches[2] pour oil into your wounds. Then shall you find delight in our words, pleasure in our faces, faith in our hearts, chastity in our thoughts, and sweetness both in our inward & outward inclinations. Comeliness shall be then our study, fear our armour, and modesty our practice. Then shall we be all your most excellentest thoughts can desire and have nothing in us less than impudence and deformity.

HAEC-VIR. Enough: You have both raised mine eyelids, cleared my sight, and made my heart entertain both shame and delight at an instant: shame in my follies past; delight in our noble and worthy conversion. Away, then, from me these light vanities, the only ensigns of a weak and soft nature, and come you grave and solid pieces,[3] which arm a man with fortitude and resolution: you are too rough and stubborn for a woman's wearing. We will here change our attires, as we have changed our minds, and with our attires, our names. I will no more be Haec-Vir, but Hic Vir, nor you Hic-Mulier, but Haec Mulier.[4] From henceforth, deformity shall pack to Hell: and if at any time he hide himself upon the earth, yet it shall be with contempt and disgrace. He shall have

---

1 *graces* In Greek mythology, the three sisters who were the attendants of Aphrodite and who bestowed beauty and charm; *muses* Also from Greek mythology, nine daughters of Zeus and Mnemosyne (Memory) who presided over the arts.

2 *leeches* Doctors.

3 *vanities* Light entertainments, worthless things, empty tales; *grave and solid pieces* Things of seriousness and substance, with wordplay referencing multiple meanings of "piece": firearm, piece of armor, and piece of clothing.

4 *Hic Vir* This formulation replaces the "haec," the feminine form of "this," with the masculine "hic"; the resulting phrase, meaning "this man," follows the rules of Latin grammar; *Haec Mulier* This formulation replaces the masculine "hic" with the feminine "haec" to produce a grammatically correct Latin phrase meaning "this woman."

no friend but poverty, no favorer but folly, nor no reward but shame. Henceforth we will live nobly like ourselves, ever sober, ever discreet, ever worthy; true men, and true women. We will be henceforth like well-coupled doves, full of industry, full of love: I mean, not of sensual and carnal love, but heavenly and divine love, which proceeds from God; whose unexpressable nature none is able to deliver in words, since it is like his dwelling, high and beyond the reach of human apprehension, according to the saying of the poet, in these verses following:

Of love's perfection perfectly to speak,
Or of his nature rightly to define,
Indeed doth far surpass our reason's reach,
And needs his priest t'express his power divine,
For long before the world he was ybore,[1]
And bred above i'th'highest celestial sphere,
For by his power the world was made of yore,
And all that therein wondrous doth appear.[2]

FINIS

---

1 *ybore* Born.
2 *Of love's perfection ... doth appear* The quoted lines are from Edmund Spenser's "Colin Clout's Come Home Again" (1595).

C. On Criminals

1. from Thomas Harman, *A Caveat for Common Cursitors, Vulgarly Called Vagabonds* (1566, revised 1567/68)

Thomas Harman's *A Caveat or Warning for Common Cursitors, Vulgarly Called Vagabonds*, first printed in 1566, figured itself as a guidebook to the criminal underworld. Two editions followed shortly after (1567/8) and a fourth (1573) was published with additional material. The text was also used liberally by other authors, including Thomas Dekker, and parts of *A Caveat* were reproduced in other works until the nineteenth century. Little is known about the author, Thomas Harman, esquire, a gentleman of Kent whose grandfather had served in the government of Henry VII. While Harman appears to have researched his subject in detail, *A Caveat* should not be assumed to be accurate. It was, however, often cited by early modern authors and helped to shape popular ideas of a social underworld.

In the sixteenth century, views such as Harman's were consistent with the treatment of vagrants as criminals who posed a danger to the rest of society. Laws throughout the early modern period often attempted to use force to address the social ills of poverty and unemployment. The 1572 "Act for the Punishment of Vagabonds, and for Relief of the Poor and Impotent," for example, required parishioners to contribute money for the upkeep of the poor, mandated that Justices of the Peace survey and register the poor and infirm in their parishes (which allowed them to distribute collected money), and allowed justices to license select vagrants to beg in a given parish. However, harsh corporal punishment could be exacted against any vagabonds who were not registered or were caught begging without a license. Able-bodied vagrants could be sent to workhouses or otherwise punished if found idle.

The first of the following excerpts describes one of the female rogue types, a Doxy. Notably, female rogues in *A Caveat* are often defined in terms of their sexual purity or lack thereof, showing that women were often treated as criminals or aligned with criminals for perceived immorality, even if crimes had been committed against them.

A Doxy.

These Doxies be broken and spoiled of their maidenhead, by the upright men,[1] and then they have their name of Doxies, and not afore. And afterward she is common and indifferent for any that will use her as *homo* is a common name to all men. Such as be fair and somewhat handsome, keep company with the walking Mortes,[2] and are ready always for the upright men, and are chiefly maintained by them, for others shall be spoiled for their sakes. The other inferior sort will resort to noblemen's places and gentlemen's houses, standing at the gate, either lurking on the backside about back-houses[3] either in hedge rows or some other thicket, expecting their prey, which is for the uncomely company of some courteous guest of whom they be refreshed with meat and some money, where exchange is made ware for ware. This bread and meat they use to carry in their great hosen,[4] so that these beastly bribering breeches[5] serve many times for bawdy purposes. I chanced not long sithens[6] familiarly to common with a Doxy that came to my gate, and surely a pleasant harlot,[7] and not so pleasant as witty, and not so witty as void of all grace and goodness. I found by her talk that she had passed her time lewdly eighteen years in walking about. I thought this a necessary instrument to attain some knowledge by, and before I would grope her mind I made her both to eat and drink well, that done I made her faithful promise to give her some money if she would open and discover to me such questions as I would demand of her, and never to bewray her[8] neither to disclose her name. "And you should," sayeth she, "I were undone."

"Fear not, that" quoth I, "but I pray thee" quoth I, "say nothing but truth."

---

1   *upright men*   Strong, sturdy men who are, according to Harman, the second highest ranking in the vagabond social structure. Harman describes them as men who choose to wander and compel charity—perhaps by claiming to be injured soldiers or other unfortunates—by guile or force rather than to practice the trades or skills in which they have been educated.

2   *walking Mortes*   According to Harman, older and unmarried vagabond women, many of whom have or had children, and who beg for a living.

3   *back-houses*   Subsidiary buildings or out-buildings, located behind a larger, main house.

4   *hosen*   Hose, stockings.

5   *bribering*   Thieving;   *breeches*   Garment covering the upper legs, generally reaching to the knees.

6   *sithens*   Subsequently.

7   *harlot*   Unchaste woman.

8   *bewray her*   Disgrace her by revealing her secrets.

"I will not," sayeth she.

"Then first tell me," quoth I, "how many upright men and rogues dost thou know or hast thou known and been conversant with, and what their names be."

She paused a while and said "Why do you ask me, or wherefore?"

"For nothing else as I said, but that I would know them when they came to my gate."

"Now by my troth," quoth she, "then are ye never the nearer, for all mine acquaintance for the most part are dead."

"Dead," quoth I, "how died they, for want of cherishing,[1] or of painful diseases?"

Then she sighed, and said "they were hanged."

"What, all?" quoth I, "and so many walk abroad, as I daily see?"

"By my troth," quoth she, "I know not past six or seven by their names, and named the same to me."

"When were they hanged?" quoth I.

"Some seven years agone, some three years, and some within this fortnight," [she said] and declared the place where they were executed, which I knew well to be true, by the report of others.

"Why," quoth I, "did not this sorrowful and fearful sight much grieve thee, and for thy time long and evil spent?"

"I was sorry," quoth she, "by the mass, for some of them were good loving men. For I lackt not when they had it, and they wanted not when I had it, and diverse of them I never did forsake, until the gallows departed us."

"O, merciful God," quoth I, and began to bless me.

"Why bless ye?" quoth she, "Alas, good gentleman, everyone must have a living." Other matters I talked of, but this now may suffice to show the reader as it were in a glass,[2] the bold beastly life of these Doxies. For such as hath gone any time abroad, will never forsake their trade, to die therefore. I have had good proof thereof. There is one a notorious harlot of this affinity called Besse Bottome-lye, she hath but one hand, and she hath murdered two children at the least. ...

---

1 *cherishing* Care or tenderness and comfort.
2 *glass* Mirror.

[Following the sketches of the various rogue types in the text, Harman provides supplementary materials, including a list of known criminals and a selection of stories about rogues. Perhaps the most often reproduced part of *A Caveat* was Harman's canting glossary, a guide to the supposed secret language of the rogues, as shown below.]

Here I set before thee good reader, the lewd lousy language of these loitering lusks and lazy lorels,[1] wherewith they buy and sell the common people as they pass through the country, which language they term peddlers' French, an unknown tongue only, but to these bold beastly bawdy beggars, and vain vagabonds, being half-mingled with English, when it is familiarly talked, and first placing things by their proper names, as an introduction to this peevish speech.

- *Nab.* A head.
- *Nabchet.* A hat or cap.
- *Glazers.* Eyes.
- *A smelling chete.* A nose.
- *Gan.* A mouth.
- *A prattling chete.* A tongue.
- *Crashing chetes.* Teeth.
- *Hearing chetes.* Ears.
- *Fambles.* Hands.
- *A famblinge chete.* A ring on thy hand.
- *Quaromes.* A body.
- *Prat.* A buttock.
- *Stampes.* Legs.
- *A caster.* A cloak.
- *A togeman.* A coat.
- *A commission.* A shirt.
- *Drawers.* Hosen.
- *Stampers.* Shoes.
- *A muffling chete.* A napkin.
- *A belly chete.* An apron.
- *Dudes.* Clothes.

---

1   *loitering* Engaging in vagrancy;   *lusks* Idlers;   *lorels* Rogues, degenerates.

- *A lag of dudes.*   A buck of clothes.
- *A slate or slats.*   A sheet or sheets.
- *Lybbege.*   A bed.
- *Bunge.*   A purse.
- *Lowre.*   Money.
- *Mynt.*   Gold.
- *A borde.*   A shilling.
- *Halfe a borde.*   Six pence.
- *Flagg.*   A groat.
- *A wyn.*   A penny.
- *A make.*   A halfpenny.
- *Bowse.*   Drink.
- *Bene.*   Good.
- *Benshyp.*   Very good.
- *Quiet.*   Nought.
- *A gage.*   A quart pot.
- *A skew.*   A cup.
- *Pannam.*   Bread.
- *Cassan.*   Cheese.
- *Varum.*   Milk.
- *Lap.*   Butter, milk, or whey.
- *Pek.*   Meat.
- *Poppelars.*   Porridge.
- *Ruff pek.*   Bacon.
- *A grunting chete or a patrico's kinchin.*[1]   A pig.
- *A cackling chete.*   A cock or capon.
- *A margery-prater.*   A hen.
- *A Roger or Tib of the buttery.*   A goose.
- *A quacking chet or a red shanke.*   A drake or duck.
- *Grannam.*   Corn.
- *A lowing chet.*   A cow.
- *A bleating chet.*   A calf or sheep.
- *A prance.*   A horse.
- *Antem.*   A church.
- *Salomon.*   An altar or mass.
- *Patrico.*   A priest.

---

1   *patrico's kinchin* Literally this would mean a priest's (especially a vagabond priest's) child.

- *Nosegent.* A nun.
- *A gybe.* A writing.
- *A Jark.* A seal.
- *A ken.* A house.
- *A stalling ken.* A house that will receive stolen ware.
- *A bousing ken.* An ale house.
- *A lypken.* A house to lie in.
- *A lybbege.* A bed.
- *Glymmar.* Fire.
- *Rome bouse.* Wine.
- *Lage.* Water.
- *A skyppar.* A barn.
- *Strommell.* Straw.
- *A gentry cofe's kenne.* A noble or gentle man's house.
- *A gygger.* A door.
- *Bufe.* A dog.
- *The lightmans.* The day.
- *The darkmans.* The night.
- *Rome vyle.* London.
- *Dewse a vile.* The country.
- *Rome morte.* The Queen.
- *A gentrye cofe.* A noble or gentleman.
- *A gentrye mort.* A noble or gentlewoman.
- *The quyer cuffyn.* The justice of the peace.
- *The harman-beck.* The constable.
- *The harmanes.* The stocks.
- *Quyerken.* A prison house.
- *Quyer cramprings.* Bolts or fetters.
- *Trinynge.* Hanging.
- *Chattes.* The gallows.
- *The hygh pad.* The highway.
- *The ruffmanes.* The woods or bushes.
- *A smelling chete.* A garden or orchard.
- *Crassinge chetes.* Apples, pears or any other fruit.
- *To fyltche.* To beat.
- *To strike.* To rob.
- *To nyp a bong.* To cut a purse.
- *To scour the cramprings.* To wear bolts or fetters.

- *To heave abough.* To rob or rifle a booth.
- *To cly the gerke.* To be whipped.
- *To cutte bevie.* To speak gently.
- *To cutte bene whyddes.* To speak or give good words.
- *To cutte quyre whyddes.* To give evil words or evil language.
- *To cutte.* To say.
- *To towre.* To see.
- *To bowese.* To drink.
- *To maunde.* To ask or require.
- *To stall.* To make or ordain.
- *To cante.* To speak.
- *To wyll a ken.* To rob a house.
- *To pryggs.* To ride.
- *To dup the giger.* To open the door.
- *To couch a hogshead.* To lie down, sleep.
- *To niggle.* To have to do with a woman carnally.
- *Stow you.* Hold your peace.
- *Bynge a waste.* Go you hence.
- *To the ruffian.* To the devil.
- *The ruffian cly thee.* The devil take thee.

2. from Thomas Dekker, *The Bellman of London Bringing to Light the Most Notorious Villainies That Are Now Practised in the Kingdom* (1608)

Thomas Dekker's *The Bellman of London*, one of his popular pamphlets about London life, offers the reader a glimpse of the criminal underworld and its practices. It often draws material from other pamphlets and stories, particularly borrowing from Thomas Harman's *A Caveat for Common Cursitors.*

The excerpt begins as the Bellman is walking in the city. He spies a strange puff of smoke, which leads him to a secret feast and gathering of all the city's rogues. The ensuing description includes an explanation of different kinds of villainous tricks, or criminal "laws," such as "The Prigging Law" (horse thievery); "The Sacking Law" (prostitution and bawdry); and "The Figging Law" (the ways of cutpurses and pickpockets), from which the excerpt below is drawn. The segments on the laws explain the workings of each criminal trade, touching on the special cant language of the practice, the practitioners' techniques, their haunts, and their self-governance and hierarchy.

THE FIGGING LAW.

The parliament of these hell-hounds,[1] it seems will soon break up, for they stand now only upon the least law; which they call *Figging Law*: in making of which law two persons have the chiefest voices, that is to say the *Cutpurse* and the *Pickpocket*, and all the branches of this law reach to none but them and such as are made free denizens of their incorporation. This *Figging Law* (like the body of some monstrous and terrible beast) stands upon ten feet, or rather lifts up proudly ten Dragon-like heads: the names of which heads are these, *viz.*:

He that cuts the purse is called the *Nip*.
He that is half with him is the Snap, or the *Cloyer*.
The knife is called a *Cuttle-bung*.
He that picks the pocket is called a *Foist*.
He that faceth the man is the *Stale*.
The taking of the purse is called *Drawing*.
The spying of this villainy is called *Smoking* or *Boyling*.
The purse is the *Bung*.
The money the *Shels*.
The act doing is called *Striking*.

This *Figging Law* hath more quirks and quiddities in it than any of the former; it is as dangerous to meddle with as the *High-Law*:[2] in pleading whose cases, men are at daggers drawing. The scholars of this art are cunning sophisters,[3] and had need to have more eyes than two in one head, because the arguments they hold, and their bold villainies which they practice, are argued upon and justified to his teeth, with whom they contend. The *Foist* and the *Nip* (that is to say the pocket-picker and the cutpurse) are pewfellows together and of one religion, but differ in some points. A purse well-lined is the wet

---

1 *parliament ... hell-hounds* The gathering of rogues.
2 *High-Law* Highway robbery.
3 *sophisters* Debaters who use fallacious arguments and specious reasoning to confound an opponent.

eel they both bob for, but they strive to catch it by the tail after several fashions. For the *nip* works with his knife, the *Foist* with his hand: the *nip* cuts the purse, the *foist* draws the pocket. Both their occupations are taught them by the devil, yet they both brag of the excellency of them and are ready sometimes to stab one another about defending which is best, for the *foist* counts himself the better man, and therefore is called (by the livery of his company)[1] a gentleman *foist* and so much scorns the title of a cutpurse, that he wears not a knife about him to cut his own meat, lest he be held in suspicion to be a *nip*, which he esteems the basest office in the whole Army of Cheaters.

These scholars of the *Figging Law* are infinite in number, their College is great, their orders many, and their degrees (which are given to them by the seniors of the house) very ancient but very abominable.

The language which they speak is none of those which came in at the confusion of tongues,[2] for neither infidel nor Christian (that is honest) understands it, but the dialect is such and so crabbed that seven years study is little enough to reach to the bottom of it, and to make it run off glib from the tongue. By means of this gibberish, they know their own nation when they meet, albeit they never saw one another before; and so conformable are they to the ordinances of the brotherhood,[3] that whatsoever wicked elders amongst them shall prescribe, *actum est*,[4] tis a law, and they will not break it, yea not the proudest of them dare be so bold as to exercise his art in any other place but in those that are appointed to him, nor once presume to set his foot into another's walk, but by license of the *Signiorie*.[5]

For that purpose therefore, (as if a whole kingdom were theirs) they allot such countries to this band of *foists*, such towns to those, and such a city to so many *nips*: whereupon some of these boot-halers

---

1 *livery of his company* Representative garb or sign of one's guild or company—i.e., of the pickpockets—that means *not* wearing a knife in this case.

2 *language ... speak* Dekker refers to the rogues' secret language of cant, for which he provides a partial glossary (largely taken from Harman's *Caveat*) in his pamphlet; *confusion of tongues* According to Genesis 11, all people spoke the same language before the construction of the Tower of Babel, an incredibly high tower intended to reach Heaven. God stopped the tower's construction and caused people to speak different languages.

3 *brotherhood* Secret society of thieves and criminals.

4 *actum est* Latin: is done.

5 *Signiorie* The Grand Signiorie presides over the rogue assembly and inducts new members.

are called termers, and they ply Westminster Hall: Michaelmas Term[1] is their harvest and they sweat in it harder than reapers or haymakers do at their works in the heat of summer, no counselor, attorney, pettifogger nor solicitor[2] is up earlier than they: nor at the hall sooner than they. When clients begin to come crowding in, watermen ply not their fares more nimbly than the *nips*, & *foists* bestir themselves to pick up their *shells*; the hall and the old palace are their hives and they work in them like bees: the Exchequer Chamber, Star Chamber, Kings Bench, and Common Pleas and Chancery[3] are the beds of flowers, to which they fly humming to and fro continually to suck the honey of gold and silver. If a poor client do but stand by his lawyer, whilst he is pleading, and draws out his purse to pay his fees for counsel, or to the court for dispatch of his business, these furies[4] are sure to be at his elbow, watching (with hawk's eyes) on which side he puts up his purse, to that side they fly, and if their talents can but touch it, it is their own. Others of them have all the flesh and fish markets allowed them for their walks, as Cheapside, Eastcheap, the shambles, both Fishstreets, the Stocks, and the Borough in Southwark,[5] in which places these faithful stewards of Lucifer's household, cheapen[6] all commodities, only to note what money wives or servants that come to buy have in their purses, and where they put it up, which being well observed, the *stall* plies his market, and follows him or her (whose silver is condemned) till they come to a press of people: then does the *stall* keep a thrusting and a justling, whilst in the mean time the *foist* is either in their pocket, or the *nip* hath the purse fast by the strings. Others haunt ale-houses only, & the bear-garden;[7] some have their precinct lying in the walks of Paul's, their hours of meeting

---

1 *boot-halers* Marauders; *termers* Those in London for the new term of law; *Michaelmas Term* The first law term after the long summer vacation, and typically the busiest season for the courts and for London.

2 *counselor ... solicitor* This list names members of the legal profession, largely those who would handle the paperwork of a case and give advice or handle lesser, petty cases but would not argue before a judge.

3 *Exchequer ... Chancery* The law courts in Westminster Hall.

4 *furies* Allusion to avenging deities in classical mythology. Furies pursue their victims relentlessly.

5 *Cheapside* Widest street in London and a major market; *Cheapside ... Southwark* Main goods, meat, fish, and food markets in London.

6 *cheapen* Bargain over, haggle.

7 *bear-garden* Place for bear-baiting matches and other blood sports.

there being between 10 and 11, the strokes they strike being sometimes in the middle aisle,[1] if it be in term-time, when the walks are full, but most commonly at the doors of the church, which they will choke, and strive for passage, whilst another does the feat. At running at tilt, the Lord Mayor's day, any great shooting, any fray, any solemn arraignment, or execution, is better to these Hell-hounds, than a quarter day is to a landlord, or than five sessions[2] are to the hangman. Yea so fearless are these devils to be thrown headlong and quick into the pit of damnation, that even in God's own house and the sacred temple do they desperately commit their villainies, standing most devoutly with eyes elevated up to heaven before the preacher, where the press of people is thickest, whilst their hands are nibbling in honest men's pockets for their purses, who are careless of such worldly matters there, as not mistrusting that any so bad-minded dare enter into so holy a place. These *nips* and *foists* go oftentimes cleanly away with the shells which they get, but oftentimes are they dogged by certain fellows (called *cloyers*) who hang upon them like burrs, and are more troublesome than wasps: for no sooner is a *bung* drawn, but the *cloyer* steps in for his tenth, which he calls *snappage*, if the *nip* deny *snappage*, the *cloyer* forthwith *boyles* him, that is, bewrays him or seizes on his cloak.

You must understand likewise, that both of *nips* and *foists* there are two sorts, for there be city *nips* and country *nips* whose office is to haunt nothing but fairs: these country *nips* never come into London to do any piece of service, but at *Bartholmewtide*[3] only. Between these two sects is mortal enmity, for if the city *foist* spy one of the country *foists* in London, he forthwith labours and lays wait to smoke or boil him, the like does the country *nip* or *foist* by him of the city. There are also women *foists* and *nips* as well as men, but far more dangerous than men: All the troops of both sexes being subject to the discipline of the *grand nips* & *foists*, and from whom, the better to receive dir-

---

1   *middle aisle*   Nave of St. Paul's.
2   *quarter day*   When rents are collected; *sessions*   Meetings of the criminal court. On quarter days and on sessions days, the landlord and the hangman, respectively, can expect to be paid well.
3   *Bartholmewtide*   August 24, the time of year for celebrating the martyrdom of St. Bartholomew, which was accompanied in London by Bartholomew Fair, a great cloth and pleasure fair held in Smithfield. Its crowds and festival atmosphere were so great as to attract the country nips.

ections both what to do, and what quarters to keep (for they shift their walks according to the pleasure of the chief rangers). They have a certain house, sometimes at one end of the town, sometimes at another, which is their hall; at this hall the whole company do meet very orderly: by which means whensoever any notable or workman-like stroke is stricken, though it were as far as the north-borders, yet can the rest of the *fig-boys*[1] here resident in London, tell by whom this worthy act was played.

At this solemn meeting in their hall, they choose wardens and steward. The warden's office is to establish wholesome laws to keep life in their rotten commonwealth, and to assign out to every man his stations. The treasurer's office is very truly (though he be an arrant thief) to render an account of such monies as are put into his hands upon trust: for of every purse (that is cleanly conveyed and hath good store of shells in it) a ratable portion is delivered (in bank as it were) to the treasurer, to the intent that when any of them is taken and cast into prison, a flag of truce may presently be hung out, and composition offered to the wronged party, thereby to save a brother of the society from riding westward.[2] This had wont to be an order amongst them: but now the under-keepers of Newgate,[3] (if complaint be made to them for the loss of any purse) have a trick to get a warrant, into which warrant they put the names of nine or ten of the most notorious *foists* and *nips* that are free of their jail (which they call Whittington College) and those *nips* or *foists* do the jailors nip, till the money (perhaps double) restored, albeit not one of them that are specified in the warrant were guilty of the fact. This trick doth greatly impoverish the tradesmen of this mystery,[4] and may in time utterly overthrow the students of the *Figging Law*.

---

1 *fig-boys* Pickpockets.
2 *riding westward* Being hanged, or riding west to the gallows at Tyburn.
3 *under-keepers* Lower custodians or wardens; *Newgate* Prison.
4 *mystery* Trade; in this case, the term is used ironically to indicate pickpocketing.

D. On Tobacco

1. from anonymous, "A Merry Progress to London to see Fashions, by a young Country Gallant, that had more Money than Wit" (1615)

Broadside ballads were a popular form of entertainment. Printed on large single sheets called broadsides, they were typically marketed as new lyrics to tunes that consumers would have already known. For example, "A Merry Progress to London" was set to the existing tune of "Riding to Rumford." Like many ballads of the early seventeenth century, "A Merry Progress" is written in two parts and features woodcut illustrations.

The poem details the journey of a country gallant into London and through the city. The first part of the progress tells the story of the gallant's prodigal practices, as he squanders the ten pounds left to him by his mother; sells his plow, cart, horses, and land; and finally finds himself left with almost nothing. He rides to London to enjoy plays, prostitutes, and tobacco after selling off the cattle remaining from his inheritance. In the second part of the progress, the gallant moves through the city, encountering different neighborhoods and distractions (primary among them women, smoking, and drinking).

THE SECOND PART OF THE MERRY PROGRESS TO LONDON.
(TO THE SAME TUNE.)

Then tracing the gallant streets of London City,
A damsel me kindly greets,
    courteous and witty:
She like a singing lark,
Led me into the dark,
Where I soon paid a mark[1]   5
    for a pipe of tobacco.

To Smithfield[2] then gallantly
    took I my journey,

---

1   *mark* Two thirds of a pound.
2   *Smithfield* Major meat and cattle market in east London.

10 Where I left soon behind
  part of my money:
There I found out a punk,[1]
With whom I was so drunk,
That my purse bottom shrunk
15 away with tobacco.

Pickt-hatch and Clerkenwell,[2]
  made me so merry,
Until my purse at last;
  began to grow weary:
20 Yellow-starcht[3] bonny Kate,
 with her fine nimble pate,
Cozened me of my plate,[4]
 with a pipe of tobacco.

Then for good-fellowship,
25 to garden-alley,
I hied° me to search for   *moved with haste*
  daughters of folly:
There I found roaring boys,
With their fair female joys,
30 And the devil making toys[5]
 to take tobacco.

After, to Shoreditch[6] then,
  stood I beholding:
Where I found sinner's store,
35 of the devil's moulding:

---

1 *punk* Prostitute.
2 *Pickt-hatch* District of London known for its brothels; *Clerkenwell* Northern area of
  Finsbury, just beyond the city wall, a place of resort in the early seventeenth century.
3 *Yellow-starcht* Yellow starch was associated with unseemliness; see *Hic Mulier*, footnote 4,
  page 172 above.
4 *Cozened me of* Tricked me out of; *plate* Coin or other gold or silver valuables.
5 *devil ... toys* Someone making trifles—like pipes—for smoking or imbibing tobacco. The
  "devil" appears a few times in these stanzas as an allegorical figure.
6 *Shoreditch* Suburban area north of London along the road that ran north from Bish-
  opsgate out of the city; it was the home of James Burbage's Curtain Theatre (opened 1577).

I speak for no slander,
The punk and her pander,
Like a goose and her gander,
    took whiffs of tobacco.

To Saint Katharine's[1] passed I next,   40
    not without trouble:
Where my purse lashed out,
    drinking beer double:
A tester for each toast,
Paid I there to my host,   45
And the sauce to my cost,
    was a crown for tobacco.

To Ratcliff and Wapping[2] then,
    went I for shipping;
Where as a lass lovingly   50
    gave me a whipping:
There was a bonny wench,
Stroke a nail would not clench,
That taught me finely French,[3]
    taking tobacco.   55

Then straight to Westminster[4]
    made I adventure,

---

1 *Saint Katharine's*   East End London neighborhood on the Thames that was well known for
its taverns and bawdy houses.
2 *Ratcliff*   Near Limehouse and Shadwell, Ratcliff or Radcliffe was in 1611 a growing suburban location on the outskirts of the London. It was characterized by Stow in *A Survey of
London* (1603) as the haunt of ruffians and thieves but also as a place with a free school and
large almshouse;   *Wapping*   Suburban area down the Thames from St. Katharine's in the
East End. It was associated with executions, especially of pirates and sea criminals.
3 *Stroke ... French*   The young man has a dalliance with the wench, and she apparently gives
him venereal disease; his learning French means getting syphilis, also called the French
Pox. The innuendo depends on the method of clinching nails (in which one hammers the
nail through two pieces of wood, and then bends the end back through again), which was
especially used in shipbuilding.
4 *Westminster*   Home of Parliament, Whitehall, and other important English political insti-
tutions. It sits at the opposite end of the Thames compared to Wapping, Ratcliff, and St.
Katharine's, but is easy to reach via water.

To find good fellows (who)
    willed me to enter,
60 Where I felt such a smoke,
    As might the devil choke,
    There went away my cloak,
        with the smoke of tobacco.

Backward to Barbican[1]
65   quickly I hasted:
    There met I honest John,
        my money being wasted:
    A pipe and a pot (quoth he)
    My friend I'll bestow on thee;
70 Then lets[2] to nobody,
        there's the best tobacco.

Now farewell good fellowship,
    London I leave thee:
Never more whilst I live,
75   shall they deceive me.
Every street, every lane,
Holds me in disdain,
London hath wrought my bane,
    so, farewell tobacco.

2. from King James I, *A Counterblast to Tobacco* (1604)

The importation of tobacco from the new world prompted a new fashion for smoking, as "A Merry Progress" and *The Roaring Girl* show.
However, while gallants enjoyed a new affectation, and some insisted
that tobacco was a useful medical cure, others argued that it was a
harmful and dirty habit.

---

1 *Barbican* Watchtower or line of fortifications; the original barbican of the city was sup-
    posed to have been located near Cripplegate. The name "Barbican" was retained by a street
    near St. Giles, and here implies that the speaker has gone to the poor suburbs at the edge of
    the city.
2 *lets* Let's go.

James I (r. 1603–25) was one of tobacco's more vocal detractors. In *A Counterblast to Tobacco,* the king offers a long disquisition on the evils of the new herb and debunks the claims then being made that tobacco was a miracle drug. James's arguments also take aim at the vicissitudes of fashion and the allure of tobacco's exoticism.

That the manifold abuses of this vile custom of tobacco-taking, may the better be espied, it is fit, that first you enter into consideration both of the first original thereof, and likewise of the reasons of the first entry thereof into this country.[1] For certainly as such customs that have their first institution, either from a godly, necessary, or honourable ground, and are first brought in by the means of some worthy, virtuous, and great personage; are ever, and most justly holden[2] in great and reverent estimation and account by all wise, virtuous and temperate spirits. So should it, by the contrary, justly bring a great disgrace into that sort of customs, which having their original from base corruption and barbarity, do, in like sort, make their first entry into a country, by an inconsiderate and childish affectation of novelty, as is the true case of the first invention of tobacco-taking, and of the first entry thereof among us. For tobacco being a common herb, which (though under diverse names) grows almost everywhere, was first found out by some of the barbarous Indians to be a preservative, or antidote, against the pox,[3] a filthy disease, whereunto these barbarous people are (as all men know) very much subject, what through the uncleanly and adust[4] constitution of their bodies, and what through the intemperate heat of their climate: so that as from them was first brought into Christendom, that most detestable disease: so from them likewise was brought this use of tobacco, as a stinking and unsavory antidote for so corrupted and execrable a malady; the stinking suffumigation whereof they

---

1   *country* England.
2   *holden* Held.
3   *pox* Common euphemism for syphilis.
4   *adust* Term used to describe an overconcentration of any of the body's four humors—blood, phlegm, choler (yellow bile), and melancholy (black bile)—that were thought to determine an individual's physical and mental health.

yet use against that disease, making so one canker[1] or venom to eat out another.

And now, good countrymen, let us (I pray you) consider what honour or policy can move us to imitate the barbarous and beastly manners of the wild, godless and slavish Indians, especially in so vile and stinking a custom. Shall we that disdain to imitate the manners of our neighbour France, (having the style[2] of the first Christian kingdom) and that cannot endure the spirit of the Spaniards (their king being now comparable in largeness of dominions to the great Emperor of Turkey); shall we, I say, that have been so long civil and wealthy in peace, famous and invincible in war, fortunate in both; we, that have been ever able to aid any of our neighbours (but never deafed any of their ears with any of our supplications for assistance); shall we, I say, without blushing, abase ourselves so far as to imitate these beastly Indians, slaves to the Spaniards, refuse to the world, and as yet aliens from the holy covenant of God? Why do we not as well imitate them in walking naked, as they do, in preferring glasses, feathers, and such toys, to gold and precious stones, as they do? Yea, why do we not deny God, and adore the devil, as they do? …

[James addresses four claims arguing for smoking: two from the category of "reason" and two from the category of "experience." Below are his counters to the claims from "experience."]

Do we not daily see that a man can no sooner bring over from beyond the seas any new form of apparel, but that he cannot be thought a man of spirit, that would not presently imitate the same; and so from hand to hand it spreads, till it be practiced by all; not for any commodity that is in it, but only because it is come to be the fashion. For such is the force of that natural self-love in every one of us, and such is the corruption of envy bred in the breast of everyone, as we cannot be content, unless we imitate everything that our fellows do, and so prove ourselves capable of everything whereof they are capable, like

---

1   *suffumigation* Fumigation as from below, usually by means of burning herbs or incense
    to create fumes or vapors to rise up and penetrate the body;   *canker* Worm or caterpillar
    that infects plants or leaves, or more generally, a corrupting and malignant influence that is
    difficult to expel.
2   *style* Title, or demeanor.

apes, counterfeiting[1] the manners of others to our own destruction. For let one or two of the greatest masters of mathematics in any of the two famous universities but constantly affirm any clear day that they see some strange apparition[2] in the skies; they will, I warrant you, be seconded by the greatest part of the students in that profession; so loathe will they be, to be thought inferior to their fellows either in depth of knowledge or sharpness of sight. And, therefore, the general good liking, and embracing of this foolish custom,[3] doth but only proceed from that affectation of novelty and popular error, whereof I have already spoken.

And the other argument drawn from a mistaken experience, is but the more particular probation of this general, because it is alleged to be found true by proof, that by the taking of tobacco, diverse, and very many, do find themselves cured of diverse diseases, as on the other part, no man ever received harm thereby. In this argument, there is first a great mistaking, and next a monstrous absurdity. For is it not a very great mistaking, to take *non causam pro causa*,[4] as they say in the logics; because peradventure when a sick man hath had his disease at the height, he hath at that instant taken tobacco, and afterward his disease taking the natural course of declining, and consequently the patient of recovering his health, O, then the tobacco, forsooth, was the worker of that miracle! Beside that, it is a thing well known to all physicians that the apprehension and conceit of the patient hath, by wakening and uniting the vital spirits, and so strengthening nature, a great power and virtue to cure diverse diseases. ... And all these toys do only proceed from the mistaking *non causam pro causa*, as I have already said; and so if a man chance to recover one of any disease after he hath taken tobacco, that must have the thanks of all. But by the contrary, if a man smoke himself to death with it (as many have done), O, then some other disease must bear the blame for that fault. ...

---

1   *counterfeiting*   Mimicking, with the connotation of doing so to deceive.
2   *apparition*   Something that becomes visible, likely a star, planet, or other celestial body.
3   *foolish custom*   Smoking.
4   *non causam pro causa*   Logical fallacy in which one, through an error in reasoning, falsely identifies something (here, the smoking of tobacco) as the cause of something else (here, recovery from a disease).

And what greater absurdity can there be than to say, that one cure shall serve for diverse, nay contrarious sorts of diseases. ... For one cure must not ever be used for the self-same disease, but according to the varying of any of the aforesaid circumstances, that sort of remedy must be used which is fittest for the same: whereby the contrary in this case, such is the miraculous omnipotency of our strong-tasted tobacco, as it cures all sorts of diseases (which never any drug could do before) in all persons, and at all times. ... Here in England it is refined, and will not deign to cure here any other than cleanly and gentlemanly diseases. O, omnipotent power of tobacco! And if it could by the smoke thereof chase out devils, as the smoke of Tobias's fish[1] did (which, I am sure, could smell no stronglier) it would serve for a precious relic, both for the superstitious priests, and the insolent puritans, to cast out devils withal.[2] ...

Thus having, as I trust, sufficiently answered the most principal arguments that are used in defense of this vile custom, it rests only to inform you what sins and vanities you commit in the filthy abuse thereof. First, are you not guilty of sinful and shameful lust, (for lust may be as well in any of the senses as in feeling) that although you be troubled with no disease, but in perfect health, yet can you neither be merry at an ordinary, nor lascivious in the stews, if you lack tobacco to provoke your appetite to any of those sorts of recreation, lusting after it as the children of Israel did in the wilderness after quails.[3] Secondly, it is as you use, or rather abuse it, a branch of the sin of drunkenness, which is the root of all sins. For, as the only delight that drunkards take in wine is in the strength of the taste, & the force of the fume thereof that mounts up to the brain; for no drunkards love any weak or sweet drink; so are not those (I mean the strong heat and fume) the only qualities that make tobacco so delectable to all the lovers of it? And as no man likes strong heady drink the first day (because *nemo repente fit turpissimus*)[4] but by custom is piece and piece allured,

---

1   *Tobias's fish* In Tobit 6–8, Tobias marries a woman named Sarah, who is afflicted by a demon. On their first night together, he burns the organs of a fish with incense, thus creating a smoke that flushes out the demon.

2   *withal* Likewise.

3   *ordinary* Usual meal; *the children ... quails* In Numbers 11, the Israelites complain of a desire for meat, and the Lord gives them a bounty of quails, but punishes them for their "lust."

4   *nemo ... turpissimus* Latin: No one ever became totally evil all of a sudden. See Juvenal (c. first–second century CE), *Satire* 2.83.

while, in the end, a drunkard will have as great a thirst to be drunk, as a sober man to quench his thirst with a drought, when he hath need of it. … Thirdly, is it not the greatest sin of all, that you, the people of all sorts of this kingdom, who are created and ordained by God to bestow both your persons and goods for the maintenance both of the honour and safety of your king and commonwealth, should disable yourselves in both? In your persons having by this continual vile custom brought yourselves to this shameful imbecility, that you are not able to ride or walk the journey of a Jew's sabbath, but you must have a reeky[1] coal brought you from the next poor house to kindle your tobacco with? Whereas he cannot be thought able for any service in the wars, that cannot endure oftentimes the want of meat, drink and sleep, much more then must he endure the want of tobacco. …

Now how you are by this custom disabled in your goods, let the gentry of this land bear witness, some of them bestowing three, some four hundred pounds a year upon this precious stink, which, I am sure, might be bestowed upon many far better uses. I read indeed of a knavish courtier, who for abusing the favour of the Emperor Alexander Severus, his master, by taking bribes to intercede for sundry persons in his master's ear (for whom he never once opened his mouth) was justly choked with smoke, with this doom:[2] *Fumo pereat qui fumum vendidit.*[3] But of so many smoke-buyers as are at this present in this kingdom, I never read nor heard.

And for the vanities committed in this filthy custom, is it not both great vanity and uncleanness, that at the table, a place of respect, of cleanliness, of modesty, men should not be ashamed to sit tossing off tobacco-pipes, and puffing of the smoke of tobacco one to another,

---

1 *journey of a Jew's sabbath* The distance from home that a Jewish person would be allowed to travel during the Sabbath (from Friday evening until Saturday morning) without breaking the law; *reeky* Smoking.
2 *Alexander Severus* Roman emperor (r. 222–35 CE) who was just thirteen when he became emperor and whose mother and grandmother largely held power. Alexander was seen as weak and his army was undisciplined. His empire was threatened by the Germanic Alemanni tribe, to whom he attempted to pay tribute rather than fight. As a result, his soldiers murdered him; *knavish … doom* The story of Vetronius Turinus, who in "selling smoke" was offering empty promises. He was executed by smoke inhalation, being forced to stand over a pile of burning green wood that emitted thick smoke but did not burn the man to death.
3 *Fumo … vendidit* Latin: He that sold smoke is punished by smoke.

making the filthy smoke and stink thereof to exhale athwart[1] the dishes, and infect the air, when very often men that abhor it are at their repast? ... No, it is become in place of a cure, a point of good fellowship; and he that will refuse to take a pipe of tobacco among his fellows (though by his own election he would rather smell the savour of a sink)[2] is accounted peevish, and no good company; even as they do with tippling[3] in the cold eastern countries. ...

Moreover, which is a great iniquity, and against all humanity, the husband shall not be ashamed to reduce thereby his delicate, wholesome, and clean-complexioned wife to that extremity, that either she must also corrupt her sweet breath therewith, or else resolve to live in a perpetual stinking torment.

Have you not reason then to be ashamed, and to forbear this filthy novelty, so basely grounded, so foolishly received, and so grossly mistaken in the right use thereof? In your abuse thereof sinning against God, harming yourselves both in persons and goods, and raking also thereby the marks and notes of vanity upon you: by the custom thereof, making yourselves to be wondered at by all foreign civil nations, and by all strangers that come among you, to be scorned and condemned. A custom loathsome to the eye, hateful to the nose, harmful to the brain, dangerous to the lungs, and in the black stinking fume thereof, nearest resembling the horrible Stygian[4] smoke of the pit that is bottomless.

---

1   *tossing off*   I.e., casually smoking;   *athwart*   All over.
2   *sink*   Sewer, cesspit.
3   *tippling*   Drinking alcohol.
4   *Stygian*   Hellish; a reference to the underworld River Styx.

Further Reading

Modern Editions of *The Roaring Girl*:

Kahn, Coppélia, editor. *The Roaring Girl* in *Thomas Middleton: The Collected Works*. General editors Gary Taylor and John Lavagnino. Oxford: Clarendon Press, 2007. 721–78.

Mulholland, Paul A., editor. *The Roaring Girl*, by Thomas Middleton and Thomas Dekker. The Revels Plays, Manchester: Manchester University Press, 1987, reprinted 1999.

Panek, Jennifer, editor. *The Roaring Girl*, by Thomas Middleton and Thomas Dekker. Norton Critical Editions, New York: W.W. Norton and Company, 2011.

Other Works:

Anonymous, *The life and death of Mrs. Mary Frith commonly called Mal Cutpurse exactly collected and now published for the delight and recreation of all merry disposed persons*. London: W. Gilbertson, 1662.

Baston, Jane. "Rehabilitating Moll's Subversion in *The Roaring Girl*." *SEL: Studies in English Literature, 1500–1900* 37.2 (1997): 317–35.

Dawson, Anthony B. "Mistris Hic and Haec: Representations of Moll Frith." *SEL: Studies in English Literature, 1500–1900* 33.2 (1993): 385–404.

Dekker, Thomas. *Thomas Dekker*, ed. E.D. Pendry. Stratford-Upon-Avon Library 4. Cambridge: Harvard University Press, 1968.

Howard, Jean E. "Crossdressing, The Theatre, and Gender Struggle in Early Modern England." *Shakespeare Quarterly* 39.4 (1988): 418–40.

Korda, Natasha. "The Case of Moll Frith: Women's Work and the 'All-Male Stage.'" *Women Players in England, 1500–1650: Beyond the All-Male Stage*. Eds. Pamela Allen Brown and Peter Parolin. Burlington, Vt: Ashgate, 2005. pp. 71–87.

Middleton, Thomas. *Thomas Middleton: The Collected Works.* General editors Gary Taylor and John Lavagnino. Oxford: Clarendon Press, 2007.

Mulholland, P.A. "The Date of *The Roaring Girl.*" *The Review of English Studies,* new ser., 28.109 (1977): 18–31.

"Officium Domini Contra Mariam Frith." *Consistory Court of London Correction Book* (ref. DL/C/310 fols. 19–20, January 27, 1611/12. (London Consistory Court Office Act Book: Whole Diocese, Nov 1611–Oct 1613.) Also transcribed in Mulholland, pp. 262–63; Panek, pp. 147–48.

Rose, Mary Beth. "Women in Men's Clothing: Apparel and Social Stability in *The Roaring Girl.*" *English Literary Renaissance* 14.3 (1984): 367–91.

Rustici, Craig. "The Smoking Girl: Tobacco and the Representation of Mary Frith." *Studies in Philology* 96.2 (1999): 159–79.

Taylor, Gary. "Middleton, Thomas (*bap.* 1580, *d.* 1627)," *Oxford Dictionary of National Biography,* Oxford University Press, 2004; online ed, May 2008.

---. "Thomas Middleton: Lives and Afterlives," in *Thomas Middleton: The Collected Works.* General Editors Gary Tayor and John Lavagnino. Oxford: Oxford University Press. pp. 25–58.

Twyning, John. "Dekker, Thomas (*c.* 1572–1632)," *Oxford Dictionary of National Biography,* Oxford University Press, 2004; online ed, Jan. 2008.

Ungerer, Gustav. "Mary Frith, Alias Moll Cutpurse, in Life and Literature." *Shakespeare Studies* 28 (2000): 42–84.

"Will of Mary Markham alias Frith, Widow of Saint Bride Fleet Street, City of London." 24 July 1660. National Archives, KEW. PROB 11/299/618. Also transcribed in Panek, pp. 150–51.

From the Publisher

A name never says it all, but the word "Broadview" expresses a good deal of the philosophy behind our company. We are open to a broad range of academic approaches and political viewpoints. We pay attention to the broad impact book publishing and book printing has in the wider world; for some years now we have used 100% recycled paper for most titles. Our publishing program is internationally oriented and broad-ranging. Our individual titles often appeal to a broad readership too; many are of interest as much to general readers as to academics and students.

Founded in 1985, Broadview remains a fully independent company owned by its shareholders—not an imprint or subsidiary of a larger multinational.

For the most accurate information on our books (including information on pricing, editions, and formats) please visit our website at www.broadviewpress.com. Our print books and ebooks are also available for sale on our site.

broadview press
www.broadviewpress.com

This book is made of paper from well-managed FSC® - certified
forests, recycled materials, and other controlled sources.

MIX
Paper from
responsible sources
FSC® C103567

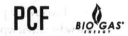

PERMANENT